A HISTORY OF EVANGELICALISM
PEOPLE, MOVEMENTS AND IDEAS IN THE ENGLISH-SPEAKING WORLD

VOLUME 2

THE EXPANSION OF EVANGELICALISM

The Age of Wilberforce, More, Chalmers and Finney

JOHN WOLFFE

InterVarsity Press
Downers Grove, Illinois

InterVarsity Press
P.O. Box 1400, Downers Grove, IL 60515-1426
World Wide Web: www.ivpress.com
E-mail: email@ivpress.com

Cover design: Cindy Kiple
Cover image: HIP/Art Resource, NY

ISBN 978-0-8308-2582-0

Printed in Canada ∞

Library of Congress Cataloging-in-Publication Data

Wolffe, John.
  The expansion of evangelicalism: the age of Wilberforce, More,
  Chalmers, and Finney/John Wolffe
      p. cm.—(A history of evangelicalism series)
  Includes bibliographical references and index.
  ISBN: 978-0-8308-2582-0 (cloth: alk. paper)
  1. Evangelicalism—Great Britain—History—18th century. 2.
  Evangelicalism—United States—History—18th century. 3.
  Evangelicalism—Great Britain—History—19th century. 4.
  Evangelicalism—United States—History—19th century. I. Title.
    BR1642.G7W65 2007
    274.1'081—dc22
                                             2006101778

P	16	15	14	13	12	11	10	9	8	7	6	5	4	3	2	1
Y	19	18	17	16	15	14	13	12	11	10	09	08	07			

CONTENTS

ACKNOWLEDGMENTS

The idea for this book, and the series of which it is a part, originally took shape at the conference "Evangelicalism in Trans-Atlantic Perspective" held at Wheaton College, Wheaton, Illinois, in April 1992. During the intervening years I have incurred many intellectual and personal debts to members of the international network of historians of evangelicalism that the gathering in Wheaton did so much to foster, in the context particularly of the subsequent Evangelicalism and Globalization and Currents in World Christianity projects. No list can be comprehensive, but I would like to mention especially Stewart J. Brown, David Hempton, Bruce Hindmarsh, J. W. ("Hoffie") Hofmeyr, Mark Hutchinson, Donald Lewis, Peter Lineham, Dick Pierard, Mark Smith, John Reynolds, Brian Stanley and John Walsh. Above all, the series editors, David Bebbington and Mark Noll, have been unfailing sources of encouragement, bibliographical suggestions and penetrating but constructive criticism.

I am also grateful to those whose invitations and hospitality have made it possible for me to visit many of the countries and regions discussed in this book. Research was carried out in numerous libraries on four continents, where I have received much valuable assistance. I have drawn particularly on the rich resources of the British Library, and would like to pay tribute to the consistent efficiency and courtesy of the many staff members who have facilitated my access to the collections. Philip Duce of IVP has been the most patient of editors.

Others have helped in less direct but equally vital ways. My colleagues in the Faculty of Arts at the Open University have been generous in assuming extra responsibilities to facilitate my study leave in 2005, and in tolerating my preoccupation with the task of completing this book. I also owe a great deal to my family: my mother has continued to provide the historical as well as parental inspiration that she and my late father gave me in the earlier stages of my career; my son David has rejoiced in reminding me that there are other things in life than dead evangelicals. The dedication is a feeble expression of my indebtedness to my wife, who was unwise enough four years ago to take on a husband with an unredeemed book contract.

ABBREVIATIONS

SBDEB   Donald M. Lewis, ed., *The Blackwell Dictionary of Evangelical Biography, 1730-1860*, 2 vols. (Oxford: Blackwell, 1995).

CMS   Church Missionary Society

DSCHT   Nigel M. de S. Cameron, ed., *Dictionary of Scottish Church History and Theology* (Edinburgh: T & T Clark, 1993).

1

LANDSCAPES AND PERSONALITIES

During years of rapid growth between the 1790s and the 1840s English-speaking evangelicalism was a turbulent sea pulled by powerful tides of spiritual impulse and social change, generating many lesser currents and eddies. These flows were transforming religious life in the evangelical heartland of the British Isles and North America, and were beginning to touch the shores of every other continent. Evangelical conviction molded the lives of countless individuals in enormously diverse situations, from the very rich to the very poor; men, women and children; black and white, slaves and free. It had profound implications for gender roles and family life, for the fabric of society and for political endeavor. Before turning to systematic analysis, it is helpful to begin this book with a few specific initial illustrations of the variety and scope of the movement. These will also introduce the four individuals named in the title of this book, along with others, both famous and obscure, who all contributed to the expansion of evangelicalism.

PERSONALITIES

At the beginning of the nineteenth century the village of Clapham in Surrey, now long since swallowed up by metropolitan London, still enjoyed a sense of distance from the bustle of the city. On the western side of Clapham Common was a large house, Battersea Rise, the home of the wealthy banker Henry Thornton (1760-1815), with a handsome library and extensive secluded gardens which were the main meeting place for the group of evangelicals that was in later years to be known as the Clapham Sect. Their gatherings were recalled by James Stephen (1789-1859), "a youth who listened, while he seemed to read the book spread out before him."[1] His father, also James (1758-1832), was an active member of the group and a shrewd lawyer who gave crucial advice to William Wilberforce (1759-1833) in his long campaign against the slave trade. Along with Wilberforce himself, whom Stephen described as "the very sun of the Claphamite system," and the "affectionate, but passionless" Thornton, other leading members included Zachary Macaulay (1768-1838), "animated by one master passion" of delivering the world from slavery, Charles Grant (1746-1823), director of the East India Company, regarded "as the real ruler of the rulers of the east," and Lord Teignmouth (1751-1834), the founding president of the Bible Society.[2] "Such were they," Stephen wrote, "whom the second generation of the Evangelical party acknowledged as their secular chiefs."[3] Their efforts secured significant changes in national policy, their greatest achievement coming in 1807 with the abolition of the British slave trade. Moreover, they played a central role in an extensive network of evangelical inspiration and influence: their gatherings at Clapham drew together "a knot of legislators, rehearsing, in sport or earnestly, some approaching debate; or travellers from distant lands; or circumnavigators of the worlds of literature and science."[4]

The scene at Battersea Rise was not, however, one of unrelieved earnestness. On a sunny summer evening the calm of the garden, shaded by elms and firs, was broken by the play of the numerous Thornton, Wilberforce and Macaulay children. They were encouraged by the adults, especially William Wilberforce, who joined them in giving vent to the lighthearted and spontaneous side of his character. Women also had an important role in the party, not merely as wives and mothers, but actively joining in the conversations. Foremost among them was Hannah More (1745-1833), a close friend of the Wilberforce and Thornton families, who lived in Somerset but was a frequent visitor to Clapham. More was a prolific writer of tracts directed to the poor and substantial works of advice on morality, conduct and spirituality directed to the more well-to-do,

---

[1] James Stephen, "The Clapham Sect," *The Edinburgh Review* 80 (1844): 252.
[2] Ibid., pp. 256, 258, 271, 275, 289; John Campbell Colquhoun, *William Wilberforce: His Friends and His Times* (London: Longman, Green, Reader & Dyer, 1866), p. 188.
[3] Stephen, "Clapham Sect," p. 260.
[4] Ibid., p. 251.

who played a strategic role in popularizing evangelicalism and extending its influence. The Clapham Sect were not only a group of spiritual and moral reformers, but also sought to live out among themselves an ideal of evangelical family and community life, in which Christianity was deep-seated but not austere.[5] In their public lives, while faithfully adhering to their convictions, they lacked the "blunt and uncompromising tone of their immediate predecessors" and gained in influence through their ability to understand and respect their opponents.[6]

Evangelicalism, however, also took root in much harsher social and geographical landscapes than that peaceful Surrey garden, and saw much more rough-edged expressions of Christian conviction than the comfortable urbanity of the upper-middle-class Clapham Sect. In the bleak industrial valleys of northern England, in the mining and fishing villages of Cornwall and on the expanding American frontier, the very years of the Clapham Sect's heyday were a time of considerable hardship and uncertainty for working people. Such environments saw intense revivalism leading to the rapid expansion of Methodism and other forms of popular evangelicalism. It shaped a spirituality that emphasized the transience of this world and the reality of the Christian's true security in heaven. A hymn used by a group of women revivalists in Yorkshire, led by Ann Carr (1783-1841), put it this way:

> Tell us, O Women! We would know
> Wither so fast ye move?
> We, call'd to leave the world below,
> Are seeking one above.
>
> Whence come ye, say—and what the place
> That ye are trav'ling from?
> From tribulation, we thro' grace,
> Are now returning home.[7]

---

[5]Colquhoun, *Wilberforce*, pp. 306-7.

[6]Stephen, "Clapham Sect," pp. 259-60. The "immediate predecessors" Stephen had in mind presumably included Henry Thornton's father, John (1720-1790), and John Venn's father, Henry (1724-1797).

[7]Quoted in Deborah M. Valenze, *Prophetic Sons and Daughters: Female Preaching and Popular Religion in Industrial England* (Princeton, N.J.: Princeton University Press, 1985), p. 198.

For others a sense of spiritual journey translated into physical travel to the furthest parts of the globe. The Clapham circle was linked to the Eclectic Society, a gathering of London clergy around John Newton (1725-1807), the patriarch of Anglican Evangelicalism. When in 1786 the British government decided to establish a convict colony in New South Wales, the Eclectics lobbied through Wilberforce to secure the appointment as chaplain of one of their number, the Yorkshire-born Richard Johnson (1755-1827). On February 3, 1788, Johnson celebrated the first Anglican service in Australia in the place that was to become Sydney. He found his subsequent ministry an uphill struggle: although some convicts were receptive, others were contemptuous, and the authorities were unsupportive.[8] In 1792, frustrated by the small size of his congregations, he circulated a printed address in which he summed up his understanding of the Christian message:

> That you are sinners, that Jesus Christ is an all-sufficient and willing Saviour, and that the word of God both warrants and commands you to look to him for salvation. This looking unto Jesus, is what we particularly mean by faith or believing.[9]

Johnson went on to advise the colonists on their way of life in this world. They should read and study the Scriptures, "our only sure and infallible guide," observe and reverence the Sabbath, come regularly to public worship, and be constant and diligent in prayer. They should avoid swearing and adultery, a sin equally odious in the sight of God in Australia and England, as well as theft and all kinds of dishonesty. They must be wary of idleness, being "diligent and industrious in your lawful callings," and pay all due respect to their superiors. They must set an example to the neighboring Aborigines, lest bad conduct by white men lead them to become prejudiced "against that pure and holy religion which we profess." Above all, they must live in constant expectation of the "awful day of judgement."[10] The address probably only had a minimal impact on

---

[8] Neil K. Macintosh, *Richard Johnson: Chaplain to the Colony of New South Wales: His Life and Times 1755-1827* (Sydney: Library of Australian History, 1978), pp. 24-30, 49-59; Allan M. Grocott, *Convicts, Clergymen and Churches: Attitudes of convicts and ex-convicts 39 the churches and clergy in New South Wales from 1788-1851* (Sydney: Sydney University Press, 1980), pp. 58-65.

[9] Richard Johnson, *An Address to the Inhabitants of the Colonies Established in New South Wales and Norfolk Island* (London, 1792), p. 33.

[10] Ibid., pp. 37-72.

the people of the colony, but it was a revealing statement of evangelical spiritual and moral priorities in a challenging social environment.

Johnson continued to find it hard to get the seed of the gospel to take any root in Australian soil. He soldiered on until 1800, when he returned to England in order to recover his health. In the meantime, in 1794, Samuel Marsden (1765-1838) had arrived in New South Wales as assistant chaplain, and became senior chaplain after Johnson's resignation. Marsden was another Yorkshireman, also associated with the Eclectic Society and a close friend of Charles Simeon (1759-1836), the Evangelical vicar of Holy Trinity, Cambridge, who inspired generations of university students. Marsden and his family made a permanent home in New South Wales, where he enjoyed considerable success as a farmer, playing a pioneering role in the introduction of sheep to Australia, and became a very wealthy man. His social distance from his parishioners and his reputation as a harsh magistrate meant that he was much less successful pastorally. Nevertheless, in his later years Marsden played an important role, in association with the Church Missionary Society (CMS), in launching missions to New Zealand, which he visited seven times between 1814 and 1837. Geographically isolated as he was, Marsden remained very conscious of the importance of wider evangelical networks: he named his son Charles Simeon, and in 1804 he wrote of his yearning to return to England and "enjoy the society of God's people again." At the end of his life, in 1837, on a ship off the coast of New Zealand, he still vividly recalled the evangelical friendships of his youth, with those who had now preceded him to the "eternal world."[11]

Just as Marsden's zeal to spread the gospel led him to cross and recross the Tasman Sea, others felt led to traverse the still broader, if better traveled, waters of the Atlantic. In October 1799 Lorenzo Dow (1777-1834), a young American Methodist who had already ministered for several years as an itinerant preacher in his native New England and in Canada, set sail for Ireland from

---

[11]A. T. Yarwood, *Samuel Marsden: The Great Survivor* (Carlton: Melbourne University Press, 1977), pp. 15-16, 132-36, 226-27, 278-79; Grocott, *Convicts, Clergymen and Churches*, pp. 232-36; George Mackarness, ed., *Some Private Correspondence of the Rev. Samuel Marsden and Family 1794-1824* (Sydney: D. S. Ford, 1942), p. 34; John R. Elder, ed., *The Letters and Journals of Samuel Marsden* (Dunedin, New Zealand: Otago University Council, 1932), pp. 529-30; cf. Stuart Piggin, *Evangelical Christianity in Australia: Spirit, Word and World* (Melbourne: Oxford University Press, 1996), pp. 1-20.

Quebec. Amidst a storm off Newfoundland he reflected, "My body may sink to the bottom; but my soul will fly to the paradise of God."[12] Eventually, in late November, he landed safely at Larne, and spent the next sixteen months in Ireland, living in poverty, criss-crossing the island to stir the fires of revival and surviving a serious attack of smallpox. In April 1801 he returned to America, but continued to itinerate relentlessly. In 1802 he traveled not only to Georgia and South Carolina, but also to Upper Canada; in 1803 he traversed the South, going as far west as the Mississippi; in 1804 his wanderings extended from Massachusetts to Florida. In November 1805, now accompanied by his new wife Peggy, he again set sail across the Atlantic, arriving in Liverpool the following month. For some months he was occupied with preaching tours of Lancashire and Cheshire, and then in May and June 1806 he revisited Ireland. In July he came back to the north of England, only to return to Dublin in August. While there, he reflected on his labors of the last seven years, believing that he had been appointed "to lay a foundation for the enlargement of Zion's borders."[13] Convinced that John Wesley himself had appeared to him in a dream to tell him God had called him to preach the gospel, and that his own experiences were powerful testimony to the dealings of God with humankind, Dow was to continue this restless peripatetic existence for the rest of his life.[14] He returned to America in 1807, but made a third visit to Britain in 1818-1819. He was the first in a long succession of American revivalists to visit Britain. Notable such travelers later in the period included James Caughey (c. 1810-1891), also a Methodist, and Charles Finney (1792-1875), a Presbyterian minister and the greatest revivalist of the age. By the time he first came to Britain in 1849, Finney had already had a major impact in his native United States, stirring mass conversions in upstate New York, preaching at the Broadway Tabernacle in New York City and helping to establish evangelical higher education in frontier Ohio.

---

[12]Lorenzo Dow, *The Dealings of God, Man and the Devil; as Exemplified in the Life, Experience and Travels of Lorenzo Dow* (New York: Cornish Lamport, 1850), p. 37.

[13]Ibid., pp. 39-55, 114-29, 162-63.

[14]Ibid., p. 17 and passim. See also *BDEB*, pp. 320-21; Richard Carwardine, *Transatlantic Revivalism: Popular Evangelicalism in Britain and America 1790-1865* (Westport, Conn.: Greenwood Press, 1978), pp. 104-7. Dow's role in revivals is discussed further below, pp. 65-66.

For every such famous traveler, though, there were many hundreds of obscure evangelical ministers and committed laypeople who moved westward as well as eastward across the Atlantic and beyond, driven both by a longing to make Christ known and by the practical necessity of securing a livelihood. Part of the life of one such man, George William Emanuel Metzger, can be reconstructed from the letters he sent to the secretary of the CMS in London. Metzger was born in southern Germany, probably around 1800. At this early period in its history the CMS recruited missionaries in Germany as well as Britain, and in 1822 the society sent him to Sierra Leone, the colony established by Henry Thornton and others thirty years before as a refuge for freed slaves and a base for legitimate commerce in West Africa. While there, Metzger's first wife died and he married Mary Hickson, a black woman.[15] In 1833 difficulties in the Sierra Leone mission forced his return to Europe, and in the summer of 1834 he traveled with his family to the United States. His initial impressions were of a religiously lukewarm country where his wife was immediately exposed to distressing racial prejudice. Eventually he found a position as minister of a German congregation at Liverpool, Ohio.[16] Conditions were diffcult: Metzger, his wife and six children lived for the next decade in a single-room log house twenty-two feet by twenty. Her color meant that the family could not easily integrate into the local community and they faced difficulties in educating their mixed-raced children.[17] For Metzger, like Johnson and Marsden in Australia, ministry often seemed discouraging. He initially complained that most of his congregation were "as yet converted rather to the Church than to the Lord Jesus Christ." Even when he noticed that some showed "an outward reformation in their lives and conversation," he worried that this did not necessarily mean any internal spiritual change.[18] There was a split in his church, apparently because some, "who are of the worst moral characters," did not like the stringency of Metzger's teaching. Nevertheless, he labored on, and in 1843 formed with other ministers "the Evangelical Lutheran Synod in Michigan and the adjacent states," which ordained a missionary to work among the Chippeway In-

---

[15]*BDEB*, pp. 767-68.
[16]University of Birmingham Library, Special Collections: CMS, G/AC/15/111/1, 4, 5 (September 6, 1833; August 26, 1834; February 5, 1835).
[17]Ibid., G/AC/15/111/12, 26 (July 15, 1838; July 29, 1845).
[18]Ibid., G/AC/15/111/5, 6 (February 5, 1835; August 1, 1835).

dians. In 1845 he was considering building a larger house.[19] Sadly, though, the correspondence closed on a note of personal tragedy: Mary Metzger's health was in decline, and in February 1847 she died. He described this bereavement, with characteristic evangelical resignation, as "her happy departure from this world in which she had large shares of troubles and annoyances especially in these United States." He recalled how hymns had comforted her in her illness, especially Charles Wesley's "Jesu lover of my soul" and John Newton's "Be gone unbelief, my Saviour is near." Metzger concluded:

> I humbly hope in the Lord that He will grant unto me and unto all my children His Grace to put our trust in Him and that He will gather us all in due time in His heavenly home where my dear wife is now singing the praises of the Lamb that was slain for us.[20]

In the same month of July 1847 in which Metzger wrote to the CMS with news of his wife's death, Americans heard of the sudden death in Edinburgh some weeks before of Thomas Chalmers (b. 1780), not only the dominant personality in Scottish church life in the early nineteenth century, but a central figure in the wider English-speaking world. In Glasgow from 1815 to 1823 Chalmers had pioneered a new approach to urban ministry, in the 1820s he had published major Christian contributions to social and economic thought, in the 1830s he had led efforts to secure expanded pastoral provision by the Church of Scotland, and in the 1840s he played a central role in the Disruption leading to the formation of the Free Church of Scotland. Writing to his widow from Albany, New York, William Buell Sprague (1795-1876), a Presbyterian minister and writer, paid tribute to Chalmers's international significance and noted that his death had aroused deep emotions "on this side [of] the water." Here was further testimony to the evangelical movement's sense of coherence across a wide geographical span during its age of expansion.[21]

These introductory cameos immediately reveal evangelicalism as an enormously diverse movement, developing in widely spread geographical locations,

---

[19]Ibid., G/AC/15/111/14, 25, 26 (July 27, 1839; February 4, 1843; July 29, 1845).
[20]Ibid., G/AC/15/111/29 (July 29, 1847).
[21]Stewart J. Brown, *Thomas Chalmers and the Godly Commonwealth in Scotland* (Oxford: Oxford University Press, 1982); New College, Edinburgh: Chalmers Papers, CHA 2.5.97, Sprague to Grace Chalmers (July 18, 1847).

among all social classes and a range of Protestant denominations. Alongside the expectation of revival and substantial actual numerical growth were specific pastoral situations in which the predominant experience was of continual conflict and very limited success. In tension with a sense of common evangelical identity was a recurrent internal divisiveness, apparent both at the level of individual churches and at the wider denominational and political level. Evangelicals showed a deep and often moving spirituality, particularly in their sense of the presence of Jesus and their ability to see personal stresses and tragedies in the perspective of eternity, but they could sometimes appear insensitive and hypocritical in their dealings with fellow human beings. Women were seen as possessing real spiritual worth and some, such as Hannah More, exercised an important influence, but they were liable to be constrained or even exploited by a predominant patriarchalism. Some communities were transformed by evangelicalism, whereas in others its impact was marginal.

SCOPE AND DEFINITIONS

These issues will be explored in more depth in subsequent chapters of this book, the second in the History of Evangelicalism series.[22] The series is distinctive in developing an international perspective on a movement more generally studied in national or local context. Such geographically focused accounts are essential in understanding the history of evangelicalism, but it is the underlying premise of this book and its companions that there is also great value in a broader comparative approach. By viewing the English-speaking world as a whole, parallels and contrasts are illuminated and due attention is paid to international connections and networks such as those described in the preceding paragraphs. The aspiration is to provide an overall framework for understanding evangelicalism in this way; systematic coverage of all the regions under examination would obviously require a very much longer book.

In common with the other volumes in the series, this book takes as its starting point David Bebbington's definition of evangelicalism in terms of four "special marks":

- *conversionism*, the belief that lives need to be changed;

---

[22]For the overall approach of the series see also Mark A. Noll, *The Rise of Evangelicalism: The Age of Edwards, Whitefield and the Wesleys* (Leicester, U.K.: Inter-Varsity Press, 2004), pp. 18-20.

- *activism,* the expression of the gospel in effort;

- *biblicism,* a particular regard for the Bible;

- *crucicentrism,* a stress on the sacrifice of Christ on the cross.[23]

Note how these "special marks" were apparent in the lives of the individuals and groups described above. Ministering on the boundaries of the evangelical world, both Richard Johnson and George Metzger were convinced of the need for people to experience a radical change of inner life, rather than merely to conform outwardly to the church. Activism was expressed not only in the endless energetic traveling to preach the gospel by men such as Dow, Finney and Marsden but also in the "unrelenting activity"[24] in support of philanthropic and religious concerns that characterized Hannah More and her Clapham Sect associates. Johnson's conviction that the Bible was "our only sure and infallible guide" in the rough society of early Sydney was shared by Lord Teignmouth and his associates in faraway London as they launched the Bible Society to promote its wider publication and distribution throughout the world. Crucicentrism undergirded Johnson's description of Jesus as "an all-sufficient and willing Saviour" and it was also implicit in Charles Wesley's hymn "Jesu lover of my soul," which comforted the dying Mary Metzger:

> Just and holy is Thy name,
> I am all unrighteousness;
> False and full of sin I am,
> Thou art full of truth and grace.
>
> Plenteous grace with Thee is found,
> Grace to cover all my sin;
> Let the healing streams abound;
> Make and keep me pure within.[25]

Bebbington's definition relates to a very fluid movement that, although fertile in forming and reshaping institutions and structures, can never be understood solely in institutional terms. Thus this book is not a history of particular de-

---

[23]David W. Bebbington, *Evangelicalism in Modern Britain: A History from the 1730s to the 1980s* (London: Unwin Hyman, 1989), pp. 2-3.

[24]Anne Stott, *Hannah More: The First Victorian* (Oxford: Oxford University Press, 2003), p. 153.

[25]*The Church Hymnary* (Edinburgh: Henry Frowde, 1898), no. 193.

nominations or organizations as such, although these bodies formed crucial mechanisms for the expansion of evangelicalism. Indeed Bebbington's model, identifying evangelicals by their convictions and attitudes rather than their affiliations, is particularly helpful in facilitating an awareness of how evangelical impulses transcended and sometimes subverted the efforts of those who sought to direct them into closely defined channels. It is acknowledged that some of these "special marks" were manifested by nonevangelicals. For example, activism is a widespread chararacteristic of committed adherents to any cause, religious or secular; biblicism was also a feature of the pre-evangelical Puritan tradition which was still a significant influence in Baptist, Congregationalist and Presbyterian churches in the late eighteenth century; and, of course, almost all Christians of every sort honor the cross of Christ in some way. Bebbington's point, though, is that a genuine evangelical needs in some way to manifest all four characteristics, although one or more may well be less prominent than the others in particular individuals or historical contexts. This framework moreover facilitates an understanding of the wider affinities of evangelicals, for instance in their readiness to associate with nonevangelical activists in the campaign against the slave trade, or to join with other Protestants in upholding the preeminent religious and cultural authority of the Bible.

The definition is a tool for identifying evangelicals, and does not characterize them in a comprehensive way. In particular it is worth also highlighting at the outset the individualism of evangelicals, which followed from an emphasis on personal conversion and a conviction of the importance and duty of everyone to study and apply the Bible for him- or herself. Individualism was in an intriguing tension, sometimes creative and sometimes destructive, with the parallel impulse of evangelicals to find support in the community of believers, in the local church, in communication with wider networks through correspondence, publications and travel, and in a sense of overarching identity as part of a dynamic global movement fulfilling the purposes of God for fallen humanity.

The use of the term "English-speaking world" also requires definition and clarification. In the context of this book it is used to denote those countries or territories in which English was, or was to become, the culturally and politically dominant language, especially Great Britain, Ireland, the United States, Canada, the West Indies, southern Africa, Australia and New Zealand. There are, however, significant ambiguities relating to this definition. There were also other

countries and regions, above all India, where English had an influential but still
minority presence, and which formed part of the British Empire. The "English-
speaking world" included substantial populations who spoke other tongues,
including Welsh, Gaelic (in Ireland and Scotland), French (in Canada), Dutch
(in North America and southern Africa), German (in North America), Maori
(in New Zealand), and a wide variety of African, Native American and Aboriginal languages. It is important to acknowledge the presence of such groups, but
it will obviously be impossible to consider such non-English cultures in any detail. In particular, discussion of missions to non-European societies will be limited to their context in the English-speaking evangelical world, and no attempt
will be made to assess their impact on other cultures. This book gives more attention to society and politics and less to theology and culture than the preceding and succeeding volumes in the series.[26] This emphasis is appropriate for a
period in which evangelical social engagement was particularly profound and far
reaching. Theologically, on the other hand, although the early nineteenth century
saw significant developments, notably from the impact of revivalism and premil-
lennialism, it was an age of relative stability in comparison both to the formative
years of the eighteenth century and to the intellectual turbulence of the later
nineteenth century.[27]

SOCIAL AND ECONOMIC LANDSCAPES

In the remainder of this chapter the scene will be set more fully through a survey of the social, political and religious landscapes of the English-speaking
world in the decades between 1790 and 1850. A fundamentally important
socioeconomic reality was very rapid population growth. The figures for some
of the major English-speaking countries are given in table 1. In England and
Wales the population more than doubled between 1790 and 1851; in the
United States it increased nearly sixfold and in British North America more
than tenfold, albeit from a much smaller initial base. Despite the tiny extent of
European settlement in Australia at the beginning of the period, by 1850 there

---

[26]Noll, *Rise of Evangelicalism*; David W. Bebbington, *The Dominance of Evangelicalism: The Age of
Spurgeon and Moody* (Leicester, U.K.: Inter-Varsity Press, 2005).

[27]For discussion of theological and cultural trends that had their origins in this period, but
were only fully developed later in the century, see Bebbington, *Dominance of Evangelicalism*,
chaps. 4-6.

were more white people there than there had been in British North America in 1790. Relative population strengths also changed. In 1790 probably three quarters of the English-speaking population of the world lived in Great Britain or Ireland; by 1850 that proportion was down to around a half. The population of the United States surpassed that of England and Wales during the 1830s, and that of the whole of Great Britain during the 1840s. Only in Ireland, with the demographic disaster of the Great Famine of 1846-1847, did the seemingly inexorable multiplication of human souls come to a shuddering halt.

Table I: Population 1790-1851 (thousands)[a]

	England and Wales	Scotland	Ireland	Unied States	British North America	Australia
1790/I	8,500 (estimate)		4,753	3,929	233	2
1800/I	8,893	1,608		5,308	362	5
1810/II	10,164	1,806		7,240	517	12
1820/I	12,000	2,092	6,802	9,638	750	34
1830/I	13,897	2,364	7,767	12,866	1,085	70
1840/I	15,914	2,620	8,175	17,069	1,654	190
1850/I	17,028	2,889	6.552	23,192	2,436	438

[a]Figures for the United States, British North America and Australia do not include the Native American or Aboriginal populations. Sources: B. R. Mitchell, *Abstract of British Historical Statistics* (Cambridge: Cambridge University Press, 1962); B. R. Mitchell, *International Historical Statistics: The Americas 1750-2000* (Basingstoke: Palgrave Macmillan, 2003); B. R. Mitchell, *International Historical Statistics: Africa, Asia and Oceania 1750-2000* (Basingstoke: Palgrave Macmillan, 2003).

Systematic figures for other parts of the English-speaking world are not available, but the following counts in thousands (sometimes estimates) can be offered:

Newfoundland (then separate from Canada) 1836: 75; 1845: 97
New Zealand (Europeans only) 1851: 27
Southern Africa:
    Cape Colony (all ethnic groups) 1798: 62; 1822: 120; 1854: 225
    Natal (Europeans only) 1854: 8
West Indies (all ethnic groups):
    Barbados 1786: 79; 1815: 94; 1851: 136
    British Guyana (Demerara): 1815: 111; 1841: 98; 1851: 128

Jamaica 1791: 290; 1815: 403; 1844: 377
Trinidad 1815: 36; (with Tobago) 1851: 83
Smaller islands and territories (totals) c. 1815: 233; c. 1850: 237
Total British West Indies c. 1815: 877; c. 1850: 961

Estimates of indigenous populations include 200,000 for British North America in 1815, 500,000 for Australia in 1815, and 70-90,000 for New Zealand in 1840.[28] The rapid rise of evangelicalism during this period was both fueled and challenged by this general growth in population.

Also highly significant was the mobility of the population. The difference in growth rates between Britain and Ireland on the one hand and the United States, British North America and Australia on the other is, of course, attributable in large part to migration from the former to the latter. There were nearly 2.5 million immigrants into the United States between 1820 and 1850.[29] Migrants, moreover, were disproportionately young adults and children whose own families then added substantially to population growth in their countries of settlement. As we have already seen, young evangelical clergy such as Samuel Marsden and George Metzger were themselves part of this movement of peoples. Although a large proportion of migrants came from Britain and, increasingly, Ireland, settlers in the United States also included significant groups from continental European countries, especially Germany, the Netherlands and Scandinavia. On the other hand, the ending of the Atlantic slave trade in 1807 meant that the large-scale enforced migration of Africans to the Americas came to an end, although some clandestine imports continued into the American south, where there was also an active internal slave trade. In the West Indies, following the ending of the slave trade, population numbers declined or were stagnant as the existing slave populations did not reproduce themselves. For people on the move, or uprooted from their homelands,

---

[28]Mitchell, *The Americas*, pp. 3-8; Mitchell, *Africa, Asia and Oceania*, pp. 5, 11; P. J. Marshall, ed., *The Oxford History of the British Empire: Volume II: The Eighteenth Century* (Oxford: Oxford University Press, 1998), p. 433; Andrew Porter, ed., *The Oxford History of the British Empire: Volume III: The Nineteenth Century* (Oxford: Oxford University Press, 1999), pp. 533, 548, 581.

[29]Maldwyn A. Jones, *The Limits of Liberty: American History 1607-1992* (Oxford: Oxford University Press, 1995), p. 694.

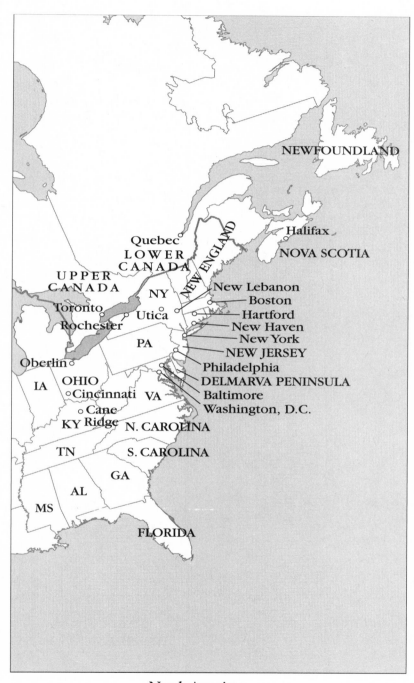

North America

Britain and Ireland

evangelical faith could be a powerful source of identity, encouragement and inspiration.

This period also saw a substantial increase in the proportion of the population living in large towns. London's preeminence as the largest city in the English-speaking world was still unchallenged in the middle of the nineteenth century. However, whereas in 1800 Dublin was the only other city with a population of more than 100,000, by 1850 that figure was also surpassed by numerous other towns. Table 2 provides figures for some illustrative examples, showing that cities on both sides of the Atlantic grew at an even faster rate than the population as a whole. To the west of the Appalachians, where there had been nothing but scattered settlements at the end of the eighteenth century, substantial towns, such as Cincinnati, developed by 1850. Although in 1850 there were still no cities with more than 100,000 people outside the British Isles and the United States, significant towns were already emerging elsewhere. In 1850 Sydney had 44,000 people; in 1851 Toronto had 31,000, and in 1856 Cape Town had 35,000.[30] Across the English-speaking world evangelicals had to learn how to respond to the new challenges of urban mission and ministry.

Table 2: Growth of Major Towns 1800-1851 (populations in thousands)[a]

	London	Manchester	Glasgow	Dublin	New York	Philadelphia	Cincinnati
1800/1	1,117	75	77	165	60	69	
1820/1	1,600	135	147		131	119	10
1850/1	2,685	329	363	272	696	340	115

[a]Mitchell, *British Historical Statistics*, pp. 19, 24-27; Mitchell, *Americas*, pp. 46-49; Mitchell, *International Historical Statistics: Europe 1750-2000* (Basingstoke: Palgrave Macmillan, 2003), p. 74.

The period was also one of spectacular economic growth in Britain, where it is characterized as one of "industrial revolution." For example, coal output increased from 11 million tons in 1800 to 49.4 million in 1850; cotton imports, which came increasingly from the United States, from 28.6 million pounds (weight) in the 1790s to 550 million in the 1840s. The proportion of the labor force working in manufacturing, mining and industry increased from 29.7 percent in 1801 to 42.9 percent in 1851, while the group employed in

---

[30]Mitchell, *Americas*, p. 49; Mitchell, *Africa, Asia and Oceania*, pp. 38, 44, 46.

agriculture, forestry and fishing declined from 35.9 percent to 21.7 percent.[31]
By contrast, the United States remained in this period a predominantly agricul-
tural economy. Although small-scale industrial enterprises proliferated in New
England and the Middle Atlantic states, there was a lack of the heavy industry
and concentration in large factories that drove the British industrial revolution
forward. Elsewhere in the English-speaking world, economic life continued to
be largely limited to agriculture and trade. Evangelicalism had to adapt to very
diverse and fluid economic conditions.

There were also important developments in transport. Britain's canal network, which had developed in the later eighteenth century, provided essential
infrastructure for the industrial revolution, although as late as 1816 there were
only 100 miles of canals in America. At that time, though, the invention of
commercially viable steamboats enabled the Americans to exploit the potential
of their major navigable rivers, especially the Hudson and the Mississippi and
its tributaries, where nearly 200 boats were already in operation by 1830.
Moreover, the Erie Canal, built between 1817 and 1825, linked the Hudson at
Albany to Lake Erie at Buffalo, thus creating a continuous route all the way
from New York to the Great Lakes, giving an important economic stimulus and
reducing travel time dramatically. The Erie Canal was also to facilitate evangelistic outreach in upper New York State, most notably in Charles Finney's revivals of the late 1820s and early 1830s.[32] In 1834 the Metzger family, like many
others, journeyed by boat from New York to Buffalo on the way to their new
home in Ohio.[33] By this time, too, the railway age was already dawning: Britain's
first steam line, the Stockton and Darlington, was opened in 1825, and across
the Atlantic the first section of the Baltimore and Ohio railroad followed in
1830. Expansion was very rapid during the next decade, with the United States,
where distances were of course much greater, rapidly outstripping Britain. By
1840 there were 3,328 miles of track in the United States and in 1845 there
were 2,441 in Britain. While in 1850 the full impact of this development re-

---

[31]Peter Mathias, *The First Industrial Nation: An Economic History of Britain 1700-1914* (London:
    Methuen, 1969), pp. 481, 486; N. L. Tranter, "The Labour Supply 1780-1860," in *The
    Economic History of Britain Since 1700: Volume 1: 1780-1860*, ed. Roderick Floud and Donald
    McCloskey (Cambridge: Cambridge University Press, 1981), p. 206.
[32]See below, pp. 71-79.
[33]CMS, G/AC/15/111/4 (August 26, 1834).

mained in the future, there was a firm trend during the period to faster communication and easier travel, a trend which facilitated the expansion of evangelicalism and the development and maintenance of organizational structures and
networks across long distances.[34]

Nevertheless, it is important also to bear in mind the continuing obstacles
to long-distance communication. Although Samuel F. B. Morse, himself an
evangelical, patented the electric telegraph in 1837, his invention was not to be
extensively implemented until the second half of the century. Hence, throughout our period, news could not normally travel faster than people and accordingly there could be no reliable knowledge of what was taking place at a distance. Also, although internal travel in both Britain and North America was
becoming easier and quicker, intercontinental journeys continued to be lengthy
and hazardous. Transatlantic voyages took several weeks, and ships to Australia
took many months, if they arrived at all. Hence a letter might not receive a reply
for a year or more. Such circumstances are important to bear in mind in understanding the flow of people, information, books and ideas in the early
nineteenth-century evangelical world.

POLITICAL LANDSCAPES

A few days during the northern spring of 1789 saw three symbolically momentous turning points in world history.[35] On April 30, in New York City,
George Washington took the oath of office as the first President of the
United States; on May 4, the gathering of the Estates-General at Versailles
near Paris began the train of events that was to lead rapidly to the French Revolution and two decades of European and worldwide warfare; on May 12, in
the House of Commons at Westminster, William Wilberforce rose to pro-
pose the abolition of the slave trade. The ramifications of these two weeks
were in different ways profoundly to shape the context in which evangelical-

---

[34]Jones, *Limits of Liberty*, pp. 113-16, 126-29; Mathias, *First Industrial Nation*, p. 488.

[35]This section draws on a range of standard works, which should be consulted for further
detail. In particular see Ian R. Christie, *Wars and Revolutions: Britain 1760-1815* (London:
Edward Arnold, 1982); Norman Gash, *Aristocracy and People: Britain 1815-1865* (London:
Edward Arnold, 1979); Jones, *Limits of Liberty*; T. O. Lloyd, *The British Empire 1558-1995*
(Oxford: Oxford University Press, 1996), and volumes 2 and 3 of the *Oxford History of the
British Empire*.

ism developed during the period surveyed in this book.

In 1790 the American War of Independence of 1775-1783 was still a very recent memory, and the United States still a very new nation. The Constitution had only been drawn up in 1787, and Rhode Island, the last of the original thirteen states to ratify it, did not do so until May 1790. In the 1790s it was by no means clear where in the long term the balance of power and identity would lie between the federal government and the individual states, and even whether the new federal government would survive at all. Essential institutions such as Congress, the Supreme Court and the presidency itself were still untested. There was still little settlement west of the Appalachians and major parts of what was to become the United States were under nominal Spanish rule. However, following the development of the midwest in the three decades after 1790, the Louisiana Purchase of 1803, the accession of Texas in 1845 and the cession by Mexico in 1848 of further vast territories in the southwest, by mid-century the United States stretched from the Atlantic to the Pacific. This development was symbolized by the accession of California, the thirty-first state, in September 1850. In parallel with territorial expansion there was a gradual development and maturing of the central institutions of nationhood, and the widening of the electoral franchise. Americans forged a stronger sense of common national identity both by confronting their former colonial masters in the War of 1812 with Britain and subsequently, in 1818, by defining the northern border with Canada. In 1828 the election as president of Andrew Jackson, a war hero who was perceived as a man of the people, marked a transition from the elitism of the founding fathers to a genuine democracy. Although, as the Civil War of the 1860s was to demonstrate, very significant unresolved tensions remained, a major new nation had been created.

To most English-speaking observers the French Revolution initially seemed a welcome constitutional adjustment and evolution, bringing France into line with developments that had already taken place elsewhere. In the early 1790s, however, events began to take a much more radical turn: working-class unrest in France inspired emulation in Britain, while conservatives were further alarmed by the execution of King Louis XVI in January 1793, by the hostility of the revolutionaries toward religion, and by the subsequent atrocities of the Terror against perceived opponents of the regime. Meanwhile, in February 1793, war broke out between France and Britain, a conflict that was to continue until the final defeat of Napoleon at the Battle of Waterloo in 1815, apart from short intervals between 1802 and 1804 and in 1814-1815. The war involved all the major European powers, and was fought on an unprecedented scale and with extensive worldwide ramifications. Unrest in Ireland erupted in rebellion in 1798, followed by the Union of 1800 in which the Dublin Parliament was abolished and Ireland brought under direct rule from Westminster. Although the United States was not directly involved in the wider Revolutionary and Napoleonic Wars, the War of 1812 with Britain arose because of resentment at British interference with American trade and shipping, which the British government believed to be necessary to maintain strategic interests against France.

The Congress of Vienna in 1815 brought peace to Europe, but only fragile stability. In Britain economic depression following the war contributed to further radical unrest. This was firmly repressed by the authorities, notably in the notorious Peterloo Massacre of 1819, in which troops fired on a peaceful demonstration in Manchester and killed eleven people. There was another revolution in France in 1830, ending the reactionary rule of Louis XVI's younger brother Charles X, and replacing him with a more liberal constitutional monarchy under Louis-Philippe. At the same time, Britain was going through substantial constitutional shifts, albeit without any change of regime such as that which occurred in France. In 1828, the repeal of the Test and Corporation Acts gave Protestant Nonconformists the right to hold public office without the need for demeaning annual exemptions from a requirement for formal conformity to the Church of England. In 1829 an upsurge in Roman Catholic agitation in Ireland led to the passing of Catholic Emancipation, which gave Roman Catholics the right to sit in parliament, to the horror of conservatives who perceived exclusive Protestantism to be an essential feature of the British constitution. Then in 1832 the "Great" Reform Act modernized the distribution of parliamentary seats and extended the franchise, strengthening the presence of the middle class in the political system. The 1830s saw further substantial reforms, notably the abolition of colonial slavery (in Africa as well as the West Indies) in 1833 and the New Poor Law of 1834. There was also continuing extraparliamentary agitation in the 1830s and 1840s, especially by the Anti-Corn Law League, which advocated free trade in the interests of industry rather than agriculture, and the Chartists, who pressed for further parliamentary reform to extend the franchise to working-class men. In 1846 the Corn Laws were repealed in response to the Irish famine, but no significant concessions were made to the Chartists. At the end of the period, in 1848, a wave of revolutions swept Europe, leading to significant political change in France, Germany, Austria and Italy. The English-speaking countries were not directly affected, but the 1840s ended as the 1790s had begun, in an atmosphere of political insecurity and international instability.

William Wilberforce's launching of the parliamentary campaign for the abolition of the slave trade was a less immediately momentous event than the collapse of an old political order in France and the creation of a new one in America. Nevertheless, it is highlighted here, not only because of its immediate relevance to the history of evangelicalism, but also because it symbolizes an important developing shift in attitudes to non-European territories and people. Alongside their political activities Wilberforce and his associates founded the colony of Sierra Leone on the west coast of Africa, as a basis for civilizing and Christianizing its native peoples, rather than uprooting and brutalizing them. The abolition of the slave trade in 1807 was a major watershed in Britain's relations with Africa. The eventual ending of slavery itself in British dominions in 1833 had profound implications for society and politics in the West Indies, although local assemblies in the islands continued to be dominated by whites, who raised property qualifications for the franchise in order to deny the vote to ex-slaves. Meanwhile, in the United States slavery continued to be a crucial and divisive political issue. On a wider front the campaign against slavery reflected a growing feeling, inspired not only by Christianity but also by the currents of secular thought stemming from the Enlightenment, that the non-European world should be civilized rather than merely exploited. Older attitudes were slow to die: for example, the continuing transportation of convicts to Australia in the early nineteenth century implied that the southern continent was useful primarily as a dumping ground for Britain's social and moral problems. Nevertheless, a different approach was evident in, for example, the establishment in the 1820s of racial equality under the law in Cape Colony, and the negotiation in 1840 of the Treaty of Waitangi with the Maori, which, despite its limitations, ensured that the subsequent white settlement of New Zealand would be carried out with rather greater respect for the rights of the indigenous population than had been the case in North America or Australia.

In British colonies, as in the United States, this was a period of significant territorial expansion and institutional development. The population of British North America had been swelled by 40,000 refugees from the south who wished to remain British in the aftermath of the American War of Independence, and who settled both in the Maritimes to the east and in the region around Lake Ontario to the west. An Act of 1791 gave elected assemblies to Lower Canada, the predominantly Catholic and French-speaking region along the St. Lawrence, and Upper Canada, Protestant and largely English-speaking, with its capital at York, later Toronto. The Maritimes—New Brunswick, Newfoundland, Nova Scotia and Prince Edward Island—remained separate colonies and had little contact with the rest of British North America. Upper Canada was in subsequent decades to become a popular destination for emigrants from Britain, especially Scotland, who wished to remain under British rule. Further constitutional change came after a small-scale rebellion in 1837. In 1840 the two Canadas were merged, with a single legislature, and the late 1840s saw the establishment of the principle that ministers were responsible to this local assembly rather than mere agents of the imperial government in London. A similar growth of responsible government took place in the Maritimes around the middle of the century, but a Confederation linking them to Canada was not set up until 1867.

In Australia, a second convict colony was established in 1804 in Van Diemen's Land (Tasmania), while nonconvict colonies developed in Western Australia from 1829; Victoria, initially part of New South Wales, from 1835; and South Australia from 1836. The colonies remained institutionally separate, with overland communication between them continuing to be difficult. There was a gradual transition from the military government of the early years to genuinely representative institutions introduced under the Australian Colonies Government Act of 1850, but federation was not achieved until 1901. Until formal annexation in 1840 permanent European settlement in New Zealand had been limited, but thereafter the white population increased very rapidly and self-government was to be introduced in 1852.

British rule in southern Africa had begun with the capture of Cape Town from the Dutch in 1795, and initially the territory was retained not so much for its own sake but because of its strategic importance in relation to the route to India. After 1815, however, more British settlement was encouraged by the government, if only as a counterweight to the Afrikaner descendants of the original Dutch settlers, whose confrontational attitude toward indigenous Africans was already giving cause for concern. Between 1834 and 1840, in the so-called Great Trek, some 15,000 Afrikaners moved north from the eastern Cape to escape British rule and in due course to establish autonomous republics in the Transvaal and Orange Free State. In the meantime the British annexed Natal in 1844. Continuing difficult relations with neighbors, both African and Afrikaner, were a factor causing the government in London to maintain closer direct control in southern Africa than in other English-speaking colonies.

Thus the history of evangelicalism in this period needs to be viewed against a background of substantial political turmoil and tension, as well as, between 1793 and around 1820, the economic and social dislocations associated with war and its aftermath. The expansion of evangelicalism was also part and parcel of the geographical expansion and institutional development of the English-speaking peoples themselves.

THE RELIGIOUS LANDSCAPE OF THE 1790S

The above brief survey of social, economic and political changes has extended over the whole period in order to provide some background for understanding the expansion of evangelicalism itself. In turning finally to consider the religious environment, it is appropriate initially to focus our attention largely on the 1790s. Evangelicalism itself was to be the most dynamic religious force in the English-speaking world during the following decades, and later developments will be better discussed in subsequent chapters as its impact is evaluated.

In the 1790s, and throughout the period, Anglicanism was the official state religion in England, Wales and Ireland. The union of the Dublin and Westminster parliaments in 1800 brought the Church of England and the Church of Ireland into closer association. Constitutional privilege did not, however, mean numerical monopoly: in particular the Church of Ireland existed in the face of a population that was approximately three-quarters Roman Catholic. Even within the Protestant minority Anglicans barely had a majority over Presbyterians, although the concentration of Presbyterians in the northeast meant that Anglicanism was the predominant Protestant tradition in other parts of Ireland. In England and Wales the ostensible numerical position of the Church of England was much stronger, with the nominal identification of the majority of the population, but commitment and practice were often limited. In Scotland Episcopalianism was a minority creed, which had in the past been subject to persecution.

Evangelical and secular critics have tended to portray late eighteenth-century Anglicanism as spiritually somnolent and pastorally ineffective. This stereotype contains more than a grain of truth, but still should not be accepted without qualification. The most recent scholarship has indicated that, while examples to support the stereotype can readily be found, the situation was a very diverse one.[36] Theologically, although latitudinarian (liberal) views were influential during much of the eighteenth century, in its closing decades they were somewhat in retreat. In any case, by this date an earlier tendency for latitudinarianism to slide into deism had been checked, and there were serious attempts to develop a Christian response to the Enlightenment that was not mere surrender to the scepticism of Hume and Voltaire. There was also continuity in committed High Churchmanship, which, if anything, was growing in ideological vigor at the end of the eighteenth century. In the parishes there was certainly much anecdotal evidence of neglect and the situation was not helped by the besetting sins of the eighteenth-century church, pluralism (the holding of more than one office by the same clergyman) and nonresidence of incumbents in their parishes. Nevertheless, it should be noted that the impact of these failings on the ground was mitigated in the numerous cases where pluralism or nonresidence was merely technical, with the incumbent living nearby albeit not actually in the parish, or where curates (assistant ministers) deputized effectively for an absentee vicar. While the overall pattern up to around 1800 appears to have been of somewhat declining religious practice, there were still some districts that showed a reverse trend. For example, in part of northeast Norfolk in the later eighteenth century both frequency of celebrations of holy Communion and attendance at them rose, and in the Oldham and Saddleworth area (northwest England) an extensive program of Anglican church-building in the years before 1800 reflected genuine popu-

---

[36]See in particular John Walsh, Colin Haydon and Stephen Taylor, eds., *The Church of England c. 1689–c. 1833 From Toleration to Tractarianism* (Cambridge: Cambridge University Press, 1993); Jeremy Gregory and Jeffrey Chamberlain, eds., *The National Church in Local Perspective* (Woodbridge: Boydell Press, 2003).

lar demand for more provision for public worship.[37] Elsewhere, however, the Church of England was already showing itself unable to develop and reorganize its pastoral structures sufficiently to keep up with the increase in the population, and in particular with the development of substantial settlements remote from existing parish churches. These therefore were left unchurched or became fertile soil for Methodism.

By 1790, Evangelicals[38] themselves, although still a small minority, were beginning to leaven the lump of Anglicanism. The earliest pioneers of Anglican Evangelicalism were now dead or superannuated, but John Newton, who had been appointed to the London living of St. Mary Woolnoth in 1780, remained active and very influential. Other strategic ministries, such as those of William Richardson at St.-Michael-le-Belfrey, York, from 1771, Charles Simeon at Holy Trinity, Cambridge, from 1783, and Thomas Scott at the Lock Hospital chapel in London from 1785, were already well under way. Joseph Milner (1744-1797) as headmaster of Hull Grammar School was busy educating a generation of boys who were grounded in Evangelical convictions that they were to promote in later life, in both clerical and lay roles. Clerical societies such as the Eclectic Society in London and the Elland Society in Yorkshire were providing stimulus and encouragement for isolated Evangelical clergy and support for new recruits to the ministry. Prominent laymen, above all those who came to be associated with the Clapham Sect, were exercising a significant influence on public life.

North of the border, the established Church of Scotland was Presbyterian. Like the Church of England, it had considerable internal diversity, in respect both of theological commitments and of pastoral effectiveness. Evangelicals were already in 1790 a substantial party in the church, with a particular strength in the major towns. Key figures included John Erskine (1720-1803), minister of Old Greyfriars, Edinburgh, from 1767, Sir Henry Wellwood Moncrieff (1750-1827), minister of St. Cuthbert's, Ed-

---

[37]W. M. Jacob, "Church and Society in Norfolk, 1700-1800," in *The National Church in Local Perspective*, ed. Jeremy Gregory and Jeffrey Chamberlain (Woodbridge: Boydell Press, 2003), p. 194; Mark Smith, *Religion and Industrial Society: Oldham and Saddleworth 1740-1865* (Oxford: Clarendon Press, 1994), pp. 34-36.

[38]In this book, as in the other volumes in this series, the convention is followed of using a capital "E" for the Evangelical parties in the Church of England and the Church of Scotland, but the word is otherwise lowercase except in proper names.

inburgh, from 1775, and Stevenson Macgill (1765-1840), who became minister of the Tron Church in Glasgow in 1791. The Church's General Assembly, however, was controlled by the moderates, who in contrast to the Evangelicals stood for a closer assimilation between the church and secular society, and for a greater accommodation to the ideas of the Enlightenment. In what was to become a crucial issue during the course of our period, there were also tensions between moderates and Evangelicals over the issue of the lay patronage, the right of local landowners or town councils to appoint ministers, which reflected the deeper question of whether the church should be fully integrated with civil society or assert its independence under the spiritual headship of Christ. Evangelicals were well represented among the various secessions from the Church of Scotland that had taken place during the eighteenth century, the Associate Synod, the General Associate Synod and the Relief Church, which were a significant presence both in the cities and the rural Lowlands. Presbyterianism was also a major force in the religious life of the north of Ireland, where it had been brought by Scottish settlers in earlier generations. It received some financial support from the state in the form of the so-called *regium donum* (royal gift), which had been paid since the seventeenth century and increased after the rebellion of 1798 to secure Presbyterian loyalty. Although some of the diversity of Scottish Presbyterians was reflected among their Irish cousins, in 1790 evangelicalism had a less developed presence among them and more liberal theological attitudes predominated. In England during the eighteenth century, Presbyterians were a small group who predominantly moved away from mainstream Christian orthodoxy toward Unitarianism and hence were largely untouched by evangelicalism.

The main remaining denominations in Britain making up the so-called Old Dissent, whose seventeenth-century origins predated the evangelical movement, were the Baptists, Independents (Congregationalists) and Society of Friends (Quakers). All three remained quite small groups: total Baptist membership in England—including the minority of (Arminian) General Baptists as well as the (Calvinist) Particular Baptists—in 1790 has been estimated at 20,000, while the Independents (or Congregationalists) numbered around 26,000. Both groups were relatively strong in Wales and had a scattered presence in Scotland. There were 24,000 Quakers in 1800 in the whole of Great

Britain.[39] By 1790, although older more rationalistic traditions persisted, the Old Dissent was coming under significant evangelical influence. The Baptists were the most receptive and the Quakers, with their own highly distinctive spirituality and religious practice, most resistant. George Whitefield had an enormous impact on many men who were to become Baptist or Independent ministers in succeeding decades, while a significant number of evangelical converts at odds with Anglican authority or uncomfortable with Methodist itinerancy also took Dissenting pastorates.[40]

In 1791, the year of John Wesley's death, Methodism, the "New Dissent" and the most conspicuous institutional expression of the wider evangelical movement, was already half a century old, but still in many respects in a process of formation. In that year Wesleyan membership stood at 56,605 in England, 534 in Wales, 1,079 in Scotland and 14,158 in Ireland.[41] There were also smaller "Connexions" founded by George Whitefield and the Countess of Huntingdon (who also died in 1791), and the separate Calvinistic Methodists in Wales, who greatly outnumbered the Wesleyans in the principality. The deaths of two founding figures made 1791 a significant watershed for Methodism. In the ensuing vacuum many of the Countess's chapels became associated with the Independents, a logical movement for them in view of their shared Calvinist outlook. Wesleyan Methodism had to face the reality that its founder was irreplaceable and potential successors such as Thomas Coke and Alexander Mather were unable to impose their authority. There was also a need to clarify the relationship of the Connexion to the Church of England, to which many remained loyal in theory, however much the logic of Methodist development was carrying them into Dissent. The 1790s were therefore years of considerable internal tension, instability and some division. The Plan of Pacification in 1795 established a working compromise by allowing Methodists to celebrate the sacraments in their own chapels, under certain conditions, although others con-

---

[39]Robert Currie, Alan Gilbert and Lee Horsley, *Churches and Churchgoers: Patterns of Church Growth in the British Isles Since 1700* (Oxford: Oxford University Press, 1977), pp. 147, 151, 159.

[40]John Walsh, "Methodism at the end of the eighteenth-century," in *A History of the Methodist Church in Great Britain, Volume I*, ed. Rupert Davies, A. Raymond George and Gordon Rupp (London: Epworth Press, 1965), pp. 293-98. The two succeeding paragraphs are also heavily indebted to Walsh's chapter.

[41]Currie, Gilbert and Horsley, *Churches and Churchgoers*, p. 139.

tinued also to attend their Anglican parish churches. Nevertheless, 5,000 members led by Alexander Kilham seceded in 1797 to form the Methodist New Connection, because they wanted a more emphatic break with the Church of England and a more democratic mode of governance, according real power to the laity as well as the preachers.

The theological controversies of the mid-eighteenth century, which had divided evangelicalism sharply on Arminian-Calvinist lines, were receding by the 1790s. It was true that Methodism itself was institutionally divided between Calvinists and Arminians, and that there was a wider distinction between the Arminian Wesleyan Methodists and Anglican, Baptist and Independent evangelicals, who all inclined toward Calvinism. However, the Calvinism of the Anglicans was usually of a very moderate kind, and that of the Dissenters had already become less pronounced and was susceptible to further softening under Methodist influence. While some Arminian-Calvinist tensions remained, especially within the Baptist and Independent communities, the issue had now lost the divisive potential it had had in the early decades of the evangelical movement.

The most fundamental difference in the religious situation of the United States from that in Britain and Ireland was the emphatic severance of links between church and state that came about in the aftermath of the Revolution, and which was enshrined in the Constitution in the First Amendment of 1791, that "Congress shall make no law respecting an establishment of religion, or prohibiting the free exercise thereof."[42] It was true that this prohibition applied only to the federal government, and forms of religious establishment continued for a few decades in some of the New England states, until 1833, when Massachusetts rescinded the privileged status of Congregationalism. Even without formal establishment, many Congregational churches in New England continued to operate as pillars of the local political and social fabric. Nevertheless, the First Amendment marked a crucial watershed which meant that in the ensuing decades American evangelicals came overwhelmingly to affirm the separation of church and state as a virtual article of faith. In particular, for Episcopalians it reinforced the adverse impact of independence, which had cut them

---

[42]For overviews of American religious history see Robert T. Handy, *A History of the Churches in the United States and Canada* (Oxford: Clarendon Press, 1976), and Mark A. Noll, *A History of Christianity in the United States and Canada* (Grand Rapids: Eerdmans, 1992).

off from links with the Church in England and meant that they lacked bishops until the consecration of Samuel Seabury in 1784. By 1790 the Protestant Episcopal Church in the United States, as it came to be known, was beginning to reorganize itself, but remained a small and vulnerable institution. The number of functioning Episcopal churches had declined from 356 in 1770 to 170 in 1790,[43] with Virginia, where Anglicanism had enjoyed established status before the Revolution, particularly badly affected.

For the United States, while the prospects for evangelical Christianity in 1790 were mixed, it is important not merely to perpetuate an adverse stereotype. Although in the War of Independence and its aftermath religious observance and commitment had been disrupted, no other denomination suffered as badly as the Episcopalians. Congregationalism was experiencing internal theological tensions, there was a movement of some congregations toward Unitarianism, and evangelicalism did not seem to be gaining ground in the denomination. Nevertheless, at an intellectual and educational level, the work of men such as Samuel Hopkins (1721-1803) and Timothy Dwight (1752-1817), who became president of Yale in 1795, was laying a theological foundation for a future in which evangelicalism would show itself responsive to the Enlightenment without merely capitulating to secular thought. Presbyterians were suffering from a leadership vacuum and some strategic uncertainty and division, but still had an activist evangelical presence which showed potential for future growth.[44]

Most significantly, however, during the 1770s and 1780s there had already been dramatic expansion in the two leading evangelical denominations, the Baptists and the Methodists. In 1790 the four largest Protestant denominations had approximately equal numbers of churches: the Congregationalists 750, the Presbyterians 725, the Baptists 858 and the Methodists 712. However, whereas the numbers of Congregationalist and Presbyterian churches had increased fairly modestly since 1770, from 625 and 500 respectively, church provision in the other two denominations had mushroomed: in 1770 there had been only 150 Baptist churches and 20 Methodist ones. Baptist membership in the United States had expanded from 35,101 in 1784 to 65,345 in

---

[43]Mark A. Noll, *America's God From Jonathan Edwards to Abraham Lincoln* (New York: Oxford University Press, 2002), p. 162.
[44]For more detail see Noll, *Rise of Evangelicalism*, pp. 188-89, 199-200.

1792; Methodist numbers from 5,000 in 1776 to 58,000 in 1790. At a local level growth could be even more spectacular; in the Delmarva peninsula to the east of the Chesapeake Bay there had been a mere 253 Methodists in 1775, but in 1792 there were already 9,911.[45]

Behind the rough equality of denominational strengths at a national level, there were major differences in regional distribution: Congregationalism was concentrated in New England and Presbyterianism in the Middle Atlantic states, while the spectacular growth of the Baptists and Methodists was occurring primarily in the south, and in the regions of new settlement to the west. In 1790 half of American Baptists and 87 percent of Methodists lived in the five southern states.[46] These denominations had the flexibility to move quickly both into the vacuum left by the decline of Episcopalianism and into hitherto unchurched territories, while offering a ready appeal to slaves. In Delmarva in the early 1790s over a third of Methodists were black.[47]

In the 1790s evangelical influence on the remaining smaller Protestant groups in the United States was still limited. In relation to the Quakers this was, as in Britain, a consequence of distinctive religious culture; while the Lutherans and the Dutch and German Reformed traditions were insulated by language and by a confessional heritage that anchored them in the continental Reformation. Nevertheless, some of the latter were touched by pietist influences that gave them affnities to English-speaking evangelicals.

Whereas in Ireland fluctuating tensions with the Roman Catholic majority were an inescapable feature of the religious landscape for evangelical Protestants, in the 1790s Britain and the United States were predominantly Protestant countries in which regionally concentrated Catholic minorities were invisible to most people. Nevertheless, the Catholic presence was not insignificant, with communities estimated at 80,000 in England in 1770, at least 30,000 in Scotland in the 1760s and 35,000 in the United States in the 1790s. In Canada there were an estimated 140,000 French-speaking Roman

---

[45]Noll, *America's God*, pp. 162, 169, 181; William Henry Williams, *The Garden of American Methodism: The Delmarva Peninsula 1769-1820* (Dover, Del.: United Methodist Church Peninsula Conference, 1984), pp. 58-59.

[46]Noll, *Rise of Evangelicalism*, p. 202; John H. Wigger, "Taking Heaven by Storm: Enthusiasm and Early American Methodism, 1770-1820s," *Journal of the Early Republic* 14 (1994): 192.

[47]Williams, *Delmarva*, p. 111.,

Catholics in 1791.[48] Sectarian tensions had been apparent in America when disquiet at the recognition of Canadian Catholics given by the Quebec Act of 1774 had been a factor fueling resentment against Britain, and in London in 1780 an attempt to make constitutional concessions to Catholics had led to the violent disturbances of the Gordon Riots. In the 1790s these storms had receded, but in the subsequent decades stresses became greater as natural increase and migration caused Catholic populations to grow rapidly, and spiritual renewal and political liberalization gave greater confidence to their leaders. By the 1840s such pressures were to bring to the surface a potent anti-Catholic strand in evangelicalism.

Elsewhere in the English-speaking world, the small populations of the 1790s were generally under the nominal oversight of scattered Anglican clergy who might be supported by the civil authorities in principle, but seldom in practice. Some such clergy, like Richard Johnson in New South Wales, did their best under difficult circumstances, but others, including two out of the three Anglican ministers in Upper Canada at the end of the eighteenth century, were wholly ineffective.[49] The consequence was, depending on local circumstances, either popular religious indifference or an open door to other denominations. The presence of the Church of England was more developed in the West Indies, but there it was perceived as the planters' church and had little or no impact on black people. Moravian missionaries had been working among the slaves since the 1730s, and in the 1780s evangelical influence diversified and gathered momentum. In 1784 George Liele, a Baptist ex-slave from Georgia, established a church in Kingston, Jamaica, where he claimed during the next seven years to have baptized 400 people. Thomas Coke initiated Methodist activity in the West Indies in 1786, and the movement also grew fast, already having 6,570 members in the islands in February 1793, nearly all of them black.[50] Several thousand miles further north in the

[48] John Bossy, *The English Catholic Community 1570-1850* (London: Darton, Longman & Todd, 1975), p. 298; *DSCHT*, p. 728; Jay P. Dolan, *The American Catholic Experience: A History from Colonial Times to the Present* (Notre Dame, Ind.: University of Notre Dame Press, 1992) p. 111; Terrence Murphy, ed., *A Concise History of Christianity in Canada* (Toronto: Oxford University Press, 1996), p. 83.
[49] G. A. Rawlyk, *The Canada Fire: Radical Evangelicalism in British North America, 1775-1812* (Montreal/Kingston, Ontario: McGill-Queen's University Press, 1994), p. 104.
[50] Arthur Charles Dayfoot, *The Shaping of the West Indian Church 1492-1962* (Gainesville: University Press of Florida, 1998), p. 127; *Arminian Magazine*, 16 (1793): 547.

Maritimes, social conditions were very different, but in the 1780s it was similarly the Baptists and the Methodists who were making the spiritual running in movements of intense revivalism. These were inspired by preachers such as the Baptists Henry Alline and David George (an American former slave), and the Methodists William Black and Freeborn Garretson.[51]

THE EXPANSION OF EVANGELICALISM

The history of evangelicalism in the English-speaking world between the 1790s and the 1840s needs to be seen in the context of rapidly changing societies, experiencing very considerable stresses due to major population growth, migration, industrialization and radical political change. Against this background the religious world too was in a state of flux, adapting to the challenges and opportunities brought by the formal ending of established churches in the United States, the inability of the established churches to meet all the spiritual needs of the people of Britain, and the failure to export convincingly the Anglican establishment to Britain's burgeoning colonies. Neither the state churches of England and Wales, Ireland and Scotland, nor the socially privileged Congregationalism and Presbyterianism of the United States were by any means moribund. They were themselves to become important channels for the expansion of evangelicalism. Nevertheless, such older wineskins were unable to contain more than a small proportion of the new evangelical wine that was about to be poured out across the English-speaking world.

The organization of this book is thematic rather than chronological. In chapters two and three we shall turn to explore the "Second Great Awakening," the movement of revival that, with the antecedents we have already noted, gathered momentum in the 1790s and early 1800s, and continued to reverberate until the 1840s. Subsequent chapters are then conceived as making an outward movement from the individual to the global. Thus in chapter four the relationship of evangelicals to God in their spiritual lives and worship is explored, and chapter five analyzes the role of evangelicalism in forming gender roles, and the relationships of men and women to each other, in the context of the family, the smallest human community. Chapter six then discusses the interaction of evangelicals with the wider nonevangelical community, both in mission and moral

---

[51]Rawlyk, *Canada Fire*; for Canada see also Murphy, *Concise History of Christianity in Canada.*

and social activism. Chapter seven considers the political activities of evangelicals, their role in campaigns against slavery, and their changing relationships to
the state. Chapter eight describes and assesses the evolving sense of global vision and aspirations for unity that achieved both culmination and nemesis in
the founding conference of the Evangelical Alliance in 1846. Back in 1739
John Wesley had written, "I look upon all the world as my parish: thus far I
mean, that, in whatever part of it I am, I judge it meet, right, and my bounden
duty to declare unto all that are willing to hear the glad tidings of salvation."[52]
During the half-century after Wesley's death, the expansion of evangelicalism
was to demonstrate the continuing explosive vitality of this state of mind.

---

[52]Nehemiah Curnock, ed., *The Journal of the Rev. John Wesley, AM,* 8 vols. (London: Robert Cul-
ley and Charles H. Kelly, 1909-1916), 2:218 (June 11, 1739).

2

REVIVALS AND
REVIVALISM, 1790-1820

In the late summer of 1791, William Black, a leading Methodist preacher in Nova Scotia, made a visit to the scattered fishing communities on the Avalon peninsula of southeast Newfoundland. Despite their remoteness, these people, many of whom returned to Britain or Ireland for the winter, were part of wider transatlantic social and religious networks and Black's journal of the visit was published in installments by Methodism's key monthly, *The Arminian Magazine*, the following year. On August 11, Black first came to Carbonear, where there had been a great spiritual stirring some twenty years before, but where he found there was now no organized Methodist society, although a group of women met informally.[1] On August 16, he preached in the village church, and recorded what happened next:

> Under the sermon some began to cry out. I stopped preaching and began to pray. My voice was soon drowned. I left the pulpit and went up and down the church, exhorting those that were wounded and crying for mercy, to look unto Jesus as the only Redeemer. Weeping was on every side. About thirty were under deep distress, if one might so conclude from weeping eyes, heaving breasts, solemn groans, shrill cries, self accusations, and serious reiterated enquiries "What shall I do to be saved?"
>
> In the midst of this general distress, one young woman rose up and declared the loving kindness of the Lord to her soul. She appeared almost carried beyond herself. The happiness she found within, sparkled in her eyes, and gave an uncommon beauty to each feature: so that she looked not like the same person.

---

[1] *The Arminian Magazine* 15 (1792): 120-23.

Black left to preach in the nearby settlement of Harbour Grace, where he found similarly responsive congregations, but on August 20, returned to Carbonear, where he again found much weeping and praying. Three more people professed "converting grace," and by August 24, there were "five or six who have professed redemption in the blood of Christ within these few days. Many backsliders are healed, and not a few under deep convictions for sin."[2] On September 4, Black administered Communion to about 130 people, when he had a sense of "universal shaking" among the people. "The cries of the penitents, together with the songs of those who were converted, drowned my voice, so that it could not be heard." Their faces showed "inward joy and rapture." Black acknowledged that "part of this work may be natural or animal; may arise from sympathy; but it is evident much of it is divine. Nothing but the Spirit of God can awaken and alarm the sleepy guilty conscience of fallen man."[3]

Revivals have been defined as "intense periods of unusual response to gospel preaching linked with unusual efforts at godly living," or, in more theologically loaded nineteenth-century language, as "an outpouring of the Holy Spirit, which has consisted of deep conviction, followed by sound conversion, upon many souls about the same time and under the same religious instructors."[4] Such "unusual response" and "deep conviction" was sometimes, but not necessarily, expressed physically in ways such as the weeping observed by Black, and more extreme and, for some, disturbing reactions including collapse into semiconsciousness and uncontrolled jerking of the body. Revivalism is best understood as the distinctive form of spirituality prevalent in times of revival and also in the ongoing spiritual life of Christian groups particularly orientated toward revival. It implies an openness to the work of the Holy Spirit and prayerful expectation of numerous and intense conversions. Revivalism, particularly as expressed in prayer and preaching, was likely often to precede the outbreak of actual revival, but once revival was underway, revivalistic fervor was likely both to be intensified in the place of initial outbreak and to spread to other locations.

The outbreak of revival in Newfoundland in August 1791 exhibited many

---

[2]Ibid., pp. 176-81.

[3]Ibid., pp. 234-37.

[4]Mark A. Noll, *The Rise of Evangelicalism: The Age of Edwards, Whitefield and the Wesleys* (Leicester, U.K.: Inter-Varsity Press, 2004), p. 15; Anon., *History of Revivals of Religion in the British Isles, Especially in Scotland* (Edinburgh: William Oliphant & Son, 1836), p. 3.

characteristics of the numerous revivals that were to take place in the English-speaking world during the next sixty years, maintaining a pattern already familiar from the days of Edwards, Whitefield, Wesley and their contemporaries. A crucial role was often played by a visiting itinerant preacher, but more as catalyst than sole cause. Preaching induced strongly emotional reactions from those who felt themselves convicted of sin, but the weeping and crying were merely the preliminary to true conversion, which was seen in the ecstatic rapture of the young woman described by Black. Converts came not only from the wholly unchurched but also from "backsliders": indeed, it has been argued that such occasional periods of intense personal renewal were a feature of evangelical spirituality at this period, at least in British North America.[5] Communions or love feasts provided a further focal point and stimulus to revival that highlighted its collective dimension, although personal responses were insisted upon. Even the revivalists themselves were prepared to ask serious questions as to the extent to which what we would now call psychological and social factors were operative, but they were in no doubt that at root revival was the work of the Holy Spirit.

Revivals were central to the expansion of evangelicalism between the 1790s and the 1840s. Their pattern and diverse specific forms will be surveyed by dividing the period into three main phases. In this chapter we shall first examine the 1790s, in which there were significant stirrings of revival in Britain, but relative stagnation in the United States. In the second phase, during the first two decades of the nineteenth century, there were widespread revivals in the United States, particularly with the spread of camp meetings. In Britain activity was now at a lower pitch, although this period did see the emergence of the new revivalistic Primitive Methodist denomination. The third phase, covering the development and impact of so-called new measures revivals from the 1820s onward, will be considered in chapter three.

THE 1790S

The very term "Second Great Awakening," when applied to the specific decade of the 1790s, is apt to mislead, insofar as it implies discontinuity with the first wave of the Evangelical Revival. Obviously there was generational change, both in

---

[5] G. A. Rawlyk, *The Canada Fire: Radical Evangelicalism in British North America, 1775-1812* (Montreal and Kingston: McGill-Queen's University Press, 1994), pp. 88-89.

the passing of the early leaders and in the growing up of younger people who had never encountered their ministry. There was also in specific localities, especially perhaps in England and New England, an apparent loss of initial fervor and a drift of Methodist societies and other evangelical groups into routine observance and even inertia and disintegration. On the other hand, taking the English-speaking world as a whole, revival was never absent. As we saw in the previous chapter, there was spectacular Methodist and Baptist expansion in the southern United States in the 1770s and 1780s. The usually more restrained Presbyterians were also touched by a revival in 1787 centered on their college at Hampden-Sydney in Virginia.[6] Irish Methodist membership more than doubled, from 6,109 in 1780 to 14,106 in 1790, with annual growth rates of 21.6 percent in 1785 and 32.3 percent in 1786, an indicator of significant revival activity during the decade.[7] These were also years of extensive revivalistic activity in the West Indies and the Maritimes. What happened in the 1790s and early 1800s is best seen as an acceleration and geographical expansion of a continuing undercurrent of revival.

The 1790s, however, saw something of a recession in revivals in North America, with the increase in Methodist membership dropping from 10.1 percent in 1790/91 to 2.52 percent in 1792/93 and an actual decline of 9.48 percent in 1794/95.[8] At this very time activity in Britain gathered new momentum. Two months after William Black's visit to Newfoundland, in October 1791, a revival broke out in the north Wales town of Bala. It was prompted by the preaching and educational ministry of the Calvinistic Methodist Thomas Charles, who described its onset as follows:

> Towards the close of the evening service, the Spirit of God seemed to work in a very powerful manner on the minds of great numbers present, who never appeared before to seek the Lord's face; but now, there was a general and a loud crying, "What must I do to be saved," and "God be merciful to me a sinner." And, about nine or ten o'clock at night, there was nothing to be heard from one end of the town to the other, but the cries and groans of people in distress of

---

[6]For an account see A. D. Thomas, "Reasonable Revivalism: Presbyterian Evangelization of Educated Virginians 1787–1837," *Journal of Presbyterian History*, 61 (1983): 321-24.

[7]David Hempton, *The Religion of the People: Methodism and Popular Religion, c. 1750-1900* (London: Routledge, 1996), p. 36.

[8]Richard Carwardine, *Transatlantic Revivalism: Popular Evangelicalism in Britain and America 1790-1865* (Westport, Conn.: Greenwood Press, 1978), p. 46.

soul. And the very same night, a spirit of deep conviction, and serious concern, fell upon whole congregations, in this neighbourhood, when calling upon the name of the Lord.[9]

The revival had a particular impact on older children and young adults "from eight or ten to thirty," and seemed for a time to transform the whole moral and cultural tone of the neighborhood. During the next two years its influence spread west into Caernarvonshire and the island of Anglesey, where enlarged congregations and a general spiritual awakening were observed, although the sense of "an extraordinary outpouring of the Spirit" was not experienced much beyond Bala itself. By early 1794 the immediate intensity of the movement was passing, but congregations were continuing to grow. Although a proportion of converts had fallen away, some of these had subsequently experienced a second renewal.[10] Meanwhile, a wider revitalization of Welsh religion was underway, notably among Baptists in the south whose recruitment peaked in 1795 when they baptized 822 converts. In Caerphilly, a Baptist minister was obliged to enter his church by the window as the body of the building was so full.[11]

In the year of the Bala revival William Bramwell (1759-1818), an earnest Methodist minister who had hitherto worked in Kent and his native Lancashire, was transferred to the Dewsbury circuit in Yorkshire. Bramwell was initially depressed by the spiritual state of the societies in his new posting, where, he wrote, "active religion scarcely appeared." Believing in the necessity of revival, which he further thought would be a panacea for current disunity in the circuit, his initial response was to engage in prolonged and impassioned personal prayer. He was joined in this endeavor by Ann Cutler, known as "Praying Nanny" (c. 1759-1794), a woman committed to a life of prayer. Both would rise to pray very early in the morning and, as one of Bramwell's biographers wryly observed, "Sleep there could be none for those who were within earshot

---

[9] Quoted in D. E. Jenkins, *The Rev. Thomas Charles of Bala*, 3 vols. (Denbigh: Llewelyn Jenkins, 1908), 2:89.

[10] Ibid., 2:90-102; cf. Michael R. Watts, *The Dissenters: Volume II: The Expansion of Evangelical Nonconformity* (Oxford: Oxford University Press, 1995), pp. 63-64.

[11] D. D. J. Morgan, "The Development of the Baptist Movement in Wales between 1714 and 1815 with particular reference to the Evangelical Revival" (D.Phil. thesis, Oxford University, 1986), pp. 185, 187.

of these clamorous suitors, when the spirit of supplication was strong."[12]

Bramwell's objective was initially not so much the conversion of unbelievers as the entire sanctification of professed believers, received by faith in a second experience of intense spiritual crisis, and leading to deeper zeal and holiness of life.[13] During the autumn of 1792, at prayer meetings and class meetings, a trickle of people began to profess sanctification, stirring a spiritual dynamism that then led to conversions of outsiders and an upsurge in membership. Bramwell emphatically believed that the revival was the work of God, in response to his own and Nanny Cutler's prayers, honoring him "by unstopping the sluices of heaven, and sending a mighty rain upon the land." After initial spiritual interest was stirred by sermons, actual conversions were usually secured in subsequent meetings for prayer, exhortation and counseling, which could continue for many hours.[14]

When Bramwell moved to the nearby Birstall circuit in 1793 he carried the movement with him, and it then spread out to affect nearly the whole of Yorkshire in 1794, when it was also beginning to touch other parts of the north of England. Bramwell's next move, to Sheffield in 1795, helped to strengthen the revival in that town. During 1795 and 1796 the revival gradually died down in Yorkshire, the loss of impetus being most apparent in the circuits first affected, but it continued for a while to spread outward, notably into Lancashire and the north Midlands. When Bramwell moved to Nottingham in 1798, he further assisted this process. There was an intensity of spiritual experience there that was recalled later by a child present when Bramwell preached: "The consciousness of a Deity, and the direct conviction of spiritual things, were so vividly expressed . . . that nothing will ever eradicate the impression." Certainly the impact on Methodist numbers was impressive: the membership of the Birstall circuit doubled during the two years that Bramwell ministered there, and during his first year at Sheffield membership increased from 1,750 to 3,000. Overall Methodist membership in Yorkshire increased from 10,397 in 1792 to 17,272

---

[12]*Memoir of the Life and Ministry of the Rev. William Bramwell*, by members of his family (London: Simpkin, Marshall & Co, 1848), pp. 38-39; William Bramwell, *A Short Account of the Life and Death of Ann Cutler* (Sheffield: John Smith, 1796).

[13]For analysis of sanctification in the Wesleyan tradition see David Bebbington, *Holiness in Nineteenth-Century England* (Carlisle: Paternoster Press, 2000), pp. 61-65.

[14]Ibid., pp. 40-43.

in 1796, although dropping back to 16,539 in 1797; in Lancashire it rose from 6,598 in 1792 to 10,963 in 1797. The revival was a key factor in producing an overall upsurge in Methodist membership in Britain: the growth rate increased from 1.04 percent in 1792/93, to 14.19 percent in 1793/94 and 8.47 percent in 1794/95. The converts were predominantly young people—for example, on one occasion fifty out of sixty new members at Armley near Leeds "seemed to be under twenty years of age."[15]

Events in the Hull area in early 1794 exemplify the dynamics of the Yorkshire revival at the local level. A stimulus came from awareness of the revival already underway some sixty miles to the west. The first response was prayer:

> When we heard of the great out-pouring of the Grace of God upon the Circuit in the West Riding . . . a very earnest desire was kindled in the hearts of the people, especially among the leaders, for a revival in our society, and which impelled us to address the Throne of Grace, both in public and private, with ardent importunity.

There was extensive prayer from January 1794 onward, but a sense of decorum proved an initial constraint. Nevertheless, at a prayer meeting on March 9, there was an atmosphere of great expectation, leading to a relaxation of order as two or three people started to pray at once. By the end of the meeting ten people professed conversion. On March 23, many from Hull attended a love feast at Beverley a few miles away and testified to what had happened, thus spreading expectation and excitement. At a further love feast in Hull on April 13, there was testimony from the new converts, and some then remained in prayer throughout the night. The climax came over the Easter weekend, from April 18 to 21: on Easter Day on April 20, there was a large congregation at 5 a.m., a still larger one at 7 a.m., and an evening service at 6 p.m. which turned into a prayer meeting that lasted until midnight. It was claimed that by this time there had been several hundred conversions in a few weeks, many of them children under fourteen. Activity continued at a high pitch until May 12, but thereafter there appears to have been a reaction and loss of momentum, prompted by concern about irregularities and complaints from both the families of par-

---

[15]Ibid., pp. 43-64; John Baxter, "The Great Yorkshire Revival of 1792-6: A Study of Mass Revival among the Methodists," *Sociological Yearbook of Religion in Britain* 7 (1974): 46-76; Carwardine, *Transatlantic Revivalism*, p. 46; Watts, *Dissenters*, pp. 64-68.

ticipants and the local magistrates about the socially disruptive effects of the prolonged evening meetings.[16]

The Yorkshire revival remained a regional rather than national movement. It was also specific to Methodism and did not directly affect other denominations. Methodism, however, also manifested its revivalistic potential elsewhere, notably in Cornwall, where a preaching tour by Joseph Benson in June 1794 stirred an enthusiastic response.[17] Revival broke out in west Cornwall at Christmas 1798, starting in a circuit love feast at Penzance, where "some who had been seeking the Lord for many years found him." Thus stirred, members carried "the flame of love" back to their local societies, and numerous conversions followed. At Redruth on New Year's Eve the preacher, John Hodgson, was overcome by a consciousness of the willingness of God to save sinners, and "almost the whole congregation were overwhelmed in tears." At St. Agnes in early March Hodgson was unable to make himself heard over the cries of the distressed, and the leaders turned to pray with those seeking divine pardon. The movement reached a climax in the 1799 Easter meetings at St. Ives, where membership of the society increased from 160 to 550 in a few weeks. At St. Just near Land's End "almost all the inhabitants seemed concerned for their souls." In all there were in a few months 3,600 new members in the Penzance and Redruth circuits. Here, too, the prominence of children among the converts was observed.[18] Similarly in Ireland, there was an upsurge in membership in the mid-1790s, and a more dramatic period of revival-led expansion at the turn of the century, concentrated particularly in the region around Lough Erne in southwest Ulster, where membership more than doubled from 3,950 in 1799 to 8,412 in 1801. The itinerant preachers believed that "the fire of the Lord attends us wherever we go."[19]

In the meantime there were stirrings of revival in Scotland, although there—in significant contrast to England, Wales and Ireland—they owed nothing to

---

[16] *The Arminian Magazine* 17 (1794): 603-7.

[17] Peter Isaac, *A History of Evangelical Christianity in Cornwall* (Gerrards Cross: WEC Press, n.d.), pp. 109-11.

[18] *The Methodist Magazine* 22 (1799): 409-11; 23 (1800): 44-47; Thomas Shaw, *A History of Cornish Methodism* (Truro: D. Bradford Barton, 1967), p. 65.

[19] Hempton, *Religion of the People*, p. 38; Thomas Coke, *Copies of Letters from the Missionaries who are Employed in Ireland* (Leeds: E. Baines, 1801), p. 43.

Methodism which, north of the border, remained a small movement with barely 1,000 members and did not expand at all during the 1790s.[20] Activity was rather on the fringes of Presbyterianism and was initiated notably by James Alexander Haldane (1768-1851), then a layman, who in the autumn of 1797 began a series of preaching tours of remote areas with visits to the far north of the mainland and the Orkney Islands. In common with the Highlands, this region had been touched by revival earlier in the eighteenth century. There was now a sense of general spiritual decline, although in a number of places parish fellowships and prayer meetings were "the chief means of maintaining and carrying forward the work of Christ." Haldane sought to proclaim the true gospel in the face of what he perceived as the worldly compromise of many Church of Scotland ministers. He drew large audiences notably in Orkney and Caithness, where he claimed that he preached to 3,000 in Kirkwall, 2,000-3,000 in Thurso and 4,000 in Wick. Although Haldane did not explicitly claim that mass conversions took place, his preaching had a profound impact on many. According to a later minister in Wick:

> Some have compared its operation to that of an electrical shock. Some have told me that there was an astonishing authority and a sort of indescribable evidence attending the word, which they could not resist.[21]

A more localized revival which developed at Moulin in Perthshire in 1798-1799 was later described by the parish minister, Alexander Stewart. According to Stewart, prior to the revival the people of the district had some knowledge of Christian doctrine, but in a "superficial and confused" way. There was an "almost universal" view that God's favor would be gained through one's own works.

> They were not, indeed, addicted to open vice, if we except lying and swearing. They were rather distinguished for sobriety, industry and peaceable behaviour. But they were destitute of religious principle.[22]

---

[20]Currie, Gilbert and Horsley, *Churches and Churchgoers*, p. 139.

[21]J. A. Haldane, *Journal of a Tour Through the Northern Counties of Scotland and the Orkney Isles in Autumn 1797* (Edinburgh: J. Ritchie, 1798); John MacInnes, *The Evangelical Movement in the Highlands of Scotland 1688-1800* (Aberdeen: Aberdeen University Press, 1951), p. 164 and passim.

[22]Alexander Stewart, *Account of a Late Revival of Religion in a Part of the Highlands of Scotland* (Aberdeen: G. Moir, 1801), p. 4.

Stewart himself had been minister at Moulin since 1786, and acknowledged that he had at first been perfunctory in his performance of his own duties. During the mid-1790s, however, he developed distinctive evangelical convictions through reading the works of men such as John Newton and Thomas Scott, and the biographical sketches in the *Evangelical Magazine*. His conversion was crystallized by a visit in June 1796 from the English evangelical leader Charles Simeon, "a man sent from God to me," who "preached in my church, and left a savour of the things of God which has remained with us ever since."[23] In 1797 Stewart began a series of sermons "on the fundamental doctrines of Christianity." Prayer meetings held in a "poor woman's little smoky hovel" were a further precursor of revival. Stewart's own spiritual and emotional temperature was further raised by his wife's death in February 1799, and in the following month he began to preach sermons on regeneration.[24] These proved to be the final trigger for revival.

> Seldom a week passed in which we did not see or hear of one, two, or three persons, brought under deep concern about their souls, accompanied with strong convictions of sin, and earnest enquiry after a Saviour. It was a great advantage to them that there were others on the road before them; for they were seldom at a loss now to find an acquaintance to which they could freely communicate their anxious thoughts. . . .
>
> It is observable, that the work of conversion has been begun and carried on among this people, in a quiet manner, without any confusion, and without those ungovernable agitations of mind, or convulsion of the body, or shrieking, or fainting which have often accompanied a general awakening in other places.[25]

Stewart estimated that there had been about seventy converts, the majority of them under thirty. There was also significant interest in religion among children, "but we find it difficult to form a decided opinion of their case."[26] There had been a general improvement in the moral tone of the neighborhood, with a cessation of swearing, profane talking and boisterous wakes.

The quiet revival at Moulin fits into a wider pattern in the 1790s of gentle but significant advance by evangelicals in the British state churches. This did not

---

[23]Ibid., pp. 6-11.
[24]Ibid., pp. 12-16.
[25]Ibid., pp. 18-19.
[26]Ibid., p. 20.

amount to revival in the narrow sense of the word, as there were no specific collective expressions of intense conviction. There was, indeed, ambivalence toward such occurrences, which had been voiced by John Newton in commenting on the Bala revival:

> There is generally much good done on such occasions of power: but we must not expect that every appearance will answer our wishes. There are many more blossoms on the tree in the spring, than apples in autumn; yet we are glad to see blossoms because we know that if there are no blossoms, there can be no fruit. Yet when sudden and general awakenings take place among people who are ignorant and unacquainted with scripture, they are more or less attended with blemishes and misguided zeal.[27]

However, through the regular preaching and writing of men such as Newton himself, Thomas Scott and Charles Simeon in the Church of England, and John Erskine and Stevenson Macgill in the Church of Scotland, influential people who would not have felt able to join in popular expressions of revival emotion were drawn toward evangelical convictions. Sir Walter Scott, the novelist, wrote of Erskine's preaching that "although the sermon could not be quoted as a correct specimen of pulpit eloquence, yet [the hearer] had seldom heard so much learning, metaphysical acuteness, and energy of argument brought into the service of Christianity."[28] The movement was further assisted by the publication of books such as Hannah More's *Thoughts on . . . the Manners of the Great* (1788) and *Estimate of the Religion of the Fashionable World* (1791) and William Wilberforce's *Practical View of the Religious System of Professed Christians* (1797). In works that achieved substantial sales these authors criticized the mores of fashionable society and called for a commitment to true Christianity. In particular Wilberforce's *Practical View* was instrumental in a number of high-profile conversions, including the writer Legh Richmond, the agriculturalist Arthur Young and the Scottish evangelical leader Thomas Chalmers.[29]

In the final years of the century there were fresh signs of revival in North America. In 1797-1798 there was a revival in Upper Canada (Ontario)

---

[27] Quoted in Jenkins, *Thomas Charles*, 2:95-96.
[28] Walter Scott, *Guy Mannering* (1815; London: Penguin Books, 2003), p. 212.
[29] John Pollock, *Wilberforce* (London: Constable, 1977), p. 149; Brown, *Chalmers*, pp. 55-56. For further discussion of Wilberforce and *Practical View* see below, pp. 160-61.

prompted by the preaching of Hezekiah Calvin Wooster, which, according to a subsequent revivalist, Nathan Bangs, was "in some sense, the beginning of that great revival of religion which soon after spread through various parts of the United States."[30] Earlier stirrings of revival in Connecticut associated particularly with the ministry of the Congregationalist Edward Dorr Griffin (1770-1837) developed in 1798-1799 into a more substantial movement in the vicinity of Hartford.[31] In 1799, before he traveled to Ireland, Lorenzo Dow reignited the embers of Wooster's revival in Canada.[32] Meanwhile, in the southern United States there was a mounting sense of expectation, particularly in the Cumberland region on the borders of Kentucky and Tennessee, where James McGready (c. 1758-1817), a Presbyterian minister, was inspiring his congregations to fast and pray for revival. The scene was being set for new and larger-scale movements.

THE ORIGINS OF CAMP MEETINGS

At the dawn of the nineteenth century Kentucky epitomized the ongoing expansion of the English-speaking world. Settlement in this and other regions across the Appalachians had only begun after independence twenty-five years before, but already the state had a population of 73,677 in 1790, which increased to 220,955 in 1800. It was admitted to the Union in 1792.[33] By 1800 the extreme violence and instability of pioneering days had passed, settled farming communities had been established and the state "bore a greater resemblance to the rest of rural America than to its frontier beginnings." Nevertheless, it was still a society experiencing significant political, economic and social stresses. Organized religious provision was taking shape in most districts, but churches were troubled by disunity and pastors were sometimes less than zealous. They had a particular difficulty appealing to younger people, a serious failing in a state where in 1800 an estimated 55 percent of the population was six-

---

[30]Quoted in Rawlyk, *Canada Fire*, p. 109.

[31]C. R. Keller, *The Second Great Awakening in Connecticut* (New Haven, Conn.: Yale University Press, 1942), pp. 37-41; David W. Kling, *A Field of Divine Wonders: The New Divinity and Village Revivals in Northwestern Connecticut 1792-1822* (University Park: Pennsylvania State University Press, 1993), pp. 2-3, 41-42.

[32]Rawlyk, *Canada Fire*, pp. 110-11.

[33]John B. Boles, *The Great Revival 1787-1805* (Lexington: University Press of Kentucky, 1972), pp. 43, 45.

teen or under. Church membership was static despite a rapidly rising population.[34]

McGready began his ministry in three small Presbyterian churches in Logan County in early 1797. Like Bramwell in Yorkshire a few years before, he was initially frustrated by the spiritual deadness of his flock, but his preaching began to inspire some conversions. He persuaded committed members of his congregations to covenant to fast and pray regularly "for the conversion of sinners in Logan county, and throughout the world."[35] Central to subsequent events was the tradition of the Communion season, which had developed in Scotland in the seventeenth century and had come with Presbyterianism to America. The Communion service itself marked the climax of a series of sermons and devotional meetings extending over a whole weekend. Such "holy fairs" drew large numbers, both of irregular worshipers and of the devout from neighboring churches.[36] There was a sense of awakening at Communion meetings in the summer of 1798, but zeal then appeared to fade again. In the late summer of 1799, however, revival at last began to gather momentum, with powerful manifestations, including physical prostration of converts, at Communion services at Gasper River and Muddy River. Again there was a lull in the following winter, but in June 1800 several hundred members of McGready's congregations gathered for the Communion season at his third church, Red River. On this occasion the gathering was joined by two ministers from neighboring Tennessee, William McGee and his brother John, a Methodist. It was John McGee, less inhibited than his Presbyterian colleagues, who, realizing that the congregation was already profoundly moved, "exhorted them to let the Lord God Omnipotent reign in their hearts, and to submit to Him." People began to cry and shout and, according to McGee, "the floor was soon covered with the slain."[37]

News of events at Red River spread and when Communion was held at Gasper River at the end of July, crowds came from long distances and from many different churches hoping to experience revival. They camped nearby.

---

[34]Ellen Eslinger, *Citizens of Zion: The Social Origins of Camp Meeting Revivalism* (Knoxville: University of Tennessee Press, 1999), pp. xv, 182-84.

[35]Quoted in Boles, *Great Revival*, p. 48.

[36]Leigh Eric Schmidt, *Holy Fairs: Scottish Communions and American Revivals in the Early Modern Period* (Princeton, N.J.: University Press, 1989), pp. 59-68.

[37]Quoted in Boles, *Great Revival*, p. 48.

Their own sense of anticipation heightened the intensity of the mood, and at the final Sunday evening service "awakening and converting work was to be found in every part of the multitude."[38] At Gasper River the traditional Communion season was beginning to evolve into the camp meeting, focused on the expectation of revival rather than the reception of the sacrament, and characterized by encampments of participants from extensive tracts of country who had left their homes and normal occupations for a few days in order to be present. Momentum was sustained at similar gatherings in late 1800 at other Communion seasons in nearby parts of southern Kentucky and northern Tennessee. Meanwhile, an apparently separate revival movement was gathering momentum among Baptists in the more thickly populated central "bluegrass" region of Kentucky some one hundred miles to the northeast.[39]

In 1801 these streams of revival came together. Barton Stone, the Presbyterian minister at Cane Ridge and Concord, not far from the state capital Lexington, first traveled to observe the revival in Logan County for himself, and on his return he began to inspire revival in his own churches. A summer of growing spiritual excitement reached its climax in a camp meeting at Cane Ridge, which began on Friday, August 8, 1801, and continued until the middle of the following week. The participants, whose numbers were variously estimated between 12,000 and 25,000, spread over the hillside for more than half a mile. A Communion on the Sunday was still the formal centrepiece of the gathering, but only 1,100 people, less than 10 percent of those attending, actually took the sacrament. It was impossible for such a large gathering to hear a single speaker, so the numerous ministers present—Baptists, Methodists and Presbyterians—set up stands in different places in the campground, gathering groups to listen to their preaching and exhortation. Many of those moved by such utterance—at least 1,000 during the course of the Cane Ridge meeting—fell suddenly to the ground, and then either lay still or stirred convulsively. When they recovered some converts then themselves joined in the exhortations, speaking to their friends and anyone else who would listen, proclaiming "the plain and essential truths of the gospel that they themselves have been powerfully convinced of . . . with all the feeling and pathos that human nature affected with

---

[38]Quoted in ibid., p. 57.
[39]Ibid., pp. 47-63; Eslinger, *Citizens of Zion*, pp. 192-201.

the most important objects is capable of."[40] Meanwhile, the multitude joined
in a cacophony of singing, praying, wailing and ecstatic acclamation. The extraordinary and chaotic atmosphere heightened the sense of spiritual immedi-
acy and implied a temporary suspension not only of church order but also of
normal social assumptions. Numerous children and young people, who were as
conspicuous by their presence at Cane Ridge as by their absence from normal
church services, were converted and joined in the exhortations. This unregulated explosion of intense popular Christianity was at one and the same time
both very encouraging and very disturbing for official church leaders.[41]

During the next two years revival spread across the South. The main inspiration came from Cane Ridge, but there were also other spiritual currents at
work, notably the ongoing revivalistic efforts of Methodist preachers. Indeed,
a key reason for the power of the revival was the effective convergence and cross-
fertilization of two denominational traditions: clerical-controlled Presbyterian
holy fairs associated with Communion seasons, and the less inhibited enthusiasm of lay Methodists. For example, on New Year's Day 1801, seven months
before Cane Ridge, there had been a powerful response to a Methodist sermon
in Accomack County on the Virginia eastern shore, when "the Spirit of the
Lord came as a rushing mighty wind—the people fell before it, and lay in heaps
all over the floor."[42] However, momentum increased substantially in late 1801
and early 1802. Notable camp meetings took place in October 1801 at Haw-
fields, North Carolina, and in April 1802 at Lancaster, South Carolina. By autumn 1802 revivalist excitement was also spreading across Georgia and Virginia. Attendances of many thousands at such gatherings were reported.[43] One
thoughtful observer of a camp meeting in Spartenburgh district, South Carolina, in July 1802 acknowledged that estimates of attendance varied widely, in
this case from 3,000 to 8,000, but he still thought 5,000 a realistic figure, in
view of reports that the surrounding country appeared depopulated during the
meeting. To him the "extraordinary work" among such crowds was manifestly

---

[40]Eyewitness account by the Rev. John Lyle, printed in Catharine C. Cleveland, *The Great Revival in the West 1797-1805* (Chicago: University of Chicago Press, 1916), p. 187.

[41]Ibid., pp. 183-89; Boles, *Great Revival*, pp. 63-69; Schmidt, *Holy Fairs*, p. 64; Eslinger, *Citizens of Zion*, pp. 206-12.

[42]Quoted in Wigger, "Taking Heaven by Storm," p. 183.

[43]Boles, *Great Revival*, pp. 73-89.

of divine origin and demonstrated the truth of Christianity. Conviction of sin came suddenly to those who had apparently lacked any prior knowledge of Scripture, and it seemed impossible that people would feign physical manifestations ranging from "mild swoons to convulsive spasms."[44]

The camp meeting was rapidly acknowledged as a new and valuable tool in bringing about mass revival, and the format quickly became more planned and controlled. At a revival held near Baltimore in September 1803, a trumpeter was used to call people to prayer at 8 a.m. Morning, afternoon and evening campfire services followed, at each of which exhorters followed the principal preachers, with the task of explicitly calling sinners to repentance and conversion.[45] There was, however, a growing caution toward the movement among those who perceived it as disorderly and those, particularly Presbyterians, who saw it as subversive of Calvinist orthodoxy. Thus as time went on, the impressive interdenominational unity apparent at Cane Ridge began to fracture, leaving the Methodists as the main exponents and beneficiaries of the movement. Among Presbyterians, on the other hand, the issue contributed to two local schisms. Barton Stone and others seceded in 1803 to form a new movement, initially calling themselves simply "Christians." Shortly afterward another group strongly committed to revivalism gained control of the Cumberland Presbytery, and when censured by the Synod of Kentucky they too seceded, eventually forming the separate Cumberland Presbyterian Church. Nevertheless, despite such tensions the Southern revival continued until around 1805-1806, by which time it is probable that most of the susceptible population had been reached. A reversion to more routine church life was therefore inevitable, although with memberships that had dramatically increased, especially among the Baptists and Methodists, in some areas by as much as threefold during the years of revival.[46]

An important aspect of the revival was its appeal to both black and white people. A consequence of the chaotic ecstatic atmosphere of the early camp meetings was that racial distinctions, together with ones of gender and age, appear to have been temporarily suspended: at least one black man was ob-

---

[44]Account by Ebenezer Cummins, printed in Cleveland, *Great Revival*, pp. 170-73.

[45]Terry Bilhartz, *Urban Religion and the Second Great Awakening: Church and Society in Early National Baltimore* (Cranbury, N.J.: Farleigh Dickinson University Press, 1986), p. 88; Eslinger, *Citizens of Zion*, pp. 236-37.

[46]Boles, *Great Revival*, pp. 143-64, 183.

served preaching at Cane Ridge.[47] Indeed, it is probable that black people, especially women, drawing on memories of traditional African religious dance, music and spirituality, often took the lead in expressing strongly emotional and physical responses to revival preaching, which then spread to whites.[48] Black converts, including women such as Jarena Lee and Zilpha Elaw, who then turned to preaching and exhortation played a crucial role as "mediators between Christian belief and the experiential world of the slaves."[49] Certainly the thirty years between 1785 and 1815 saw large-scale conversions among the slave and free black population, with Christians among them transformed from "an insignificant minority" to "a dominant religious influence."[50] A similar trend was apparent in the Caribbean, despite, or perhaps even because of, significant persecution by planters and the local authorities in the early nineteenth century. For example, Methodist membership in the West Indies increased from 6,570 in 1793 to 15,220 in 1815, progress that is the more impressive when it is recalled that here, unlike in Britain and the United States, overall population numbers were static. Here, as in the southern United States, this period saw the acceptance of evangelical Christianity as a central force in black culture, and its further diffusion through the agency of black people themselves. Further rapid growth was to come after the emancipation of the slaves in 1833, with Methodist membership in Jamaica doubling in the next seven years, and reaching over 54,000 in the West Indies as a whole in 1844.[51]

Camp meeting revivalism was particularly characteristic of dispersed rural districts, especially those that had only been settled within the last generation or so. Such conditions were also present in other parts of North America, notably upstate New York, where a three-day camp meeting at the village of West-

---

[47]Cleveland, *Great Revival*, p. 186.

[48]Wigger, *Taking Heaven by Storm: Methodism and the Rise of Popular Christianity in America* (New York: Oxford University Press, 1998), pp. 118-21; Lewis V. Baldwin, "New Directions for the Study of Blacks in Methodism," in *Rethinking Methodist History*, ed. Russell E. Richey and Kenneth E. Rowe (Nashville: Kingswood Books, 1985), p. 186.

[49]Albert J. Raboteau, *Slave Religion: The Invisible Institution in the Antebellum South* (New York: Oxford University Press, 1978), pp. 136-37; Wigger, *Taking Heaven by Storm*, p. 122.

[50]Sylvia R. Frey and Betty Wood, *Come Shouting to Zion: African American Protestantism in the American South and British Caribbean to 1830* (Chapel Hill: University of North Carolina Press, 1998), p. 118.

[51]Ibid., p. 149; Dayfoot, *Shaping of the West Indian Church*, pp. 140, 174.

ern helped to launch Methodism in the area.[52] In adjoining Upper Canada, the Hay Bay camp meeting in September 1805 drew 2,500 people, 5 percent of the population of the province. On this occasion people were seen gathering together in little groups to pray, experiencing an intense consciousness of fellowship with each other and oneness in Christ.[53] However, despite their Southern frontier origins, camp meetings became familiar across the United States, with an estimated 200-300 being held in 1804, increasing to 400-500 annually by 1811. The Methodists, whose leader Bishop Francis Asbury (1745-1816) was an enthusiastic advocate for camp meetings, were particularly instrumental in their spread outside the South. A camp meeting was held near Pittsburgh, Pennsylvania, in August 1803; in 1805 there was "a glorious camp-meeting upon Long Island" and "several" in New England; in 1806 Asbury heard of "eight or ten north of [New] York." A meeting near New York itself in 1806 seemed, like that near Baltimore in 1803, to be calculated to have an impact on the population of a major town, as well as on the rural districts.[54]

RESTRAINING REVIVAL

On the east coast, and above all in New England, quieter forms of revivalism predominated. Here much more long-standing settlements and ecclesiastical structures facilitated revival based on local churches, the converse of the spiritual ethos of the camp meeting which depended on removing people temporarily from their home communities. An initial stimulus came from Edward Griffin's ministry in the 1790s, and a central role was subsequently played by Timothy Dwight, president of Yale from 1795 to 1817, whose preaching inspired a revival on the university campus in 1802. Among Dwight's spiritually awakened students were the Congregational leaders of the next generation. Notable among them were Lyman Beecher (1775-1863) and Asahel Nettleton (1783-1844). Beecher was instrumental in revivals in his successive pastorates,

---

[52]Whitney R. Cross, *The Burned-over District: The Social and Intellectual History of Enthusiastic Religion in Western New York, 1800-1850* (Ithaca, N.Y.: Cornell University Press, 1950), p. 10.

[53]Rawlyk, *Canada Fire*, pp. 148-55.

[54]Nathan O. Hatch, *The Democratization of American Christianity* (New Haven, Conn.: Yale University Press, 1989), p. 257 n. 1; J. Manning Potts, Elmer T. Clark, Jacob S. Payton, eds., *The Letters and Journals of Francis Asbury*, 3 vols. (London: Epworth Press, 1958), 3:269-70, 311, 317, 321, 344, 346.

at East Hampton (Long Island) in 1807, Litchfield (Connecticut) in 1821 and Boston in 1826.[55] Nettleton labored as an itinerant revivalist between 1811 and 1822, supporting the work of local pastors. Such men worked for orderly revivals of the kind that had occurred at Moulin in Scotland. They eschewed the intense emotion and physical manifestations of the camp meetings, and sought rather to bring congregations to a quiet, solemn recognition of their spiritual need. Such an approach brought significant if unspectacular results: for example, in 1807 there were more than 200 converts in a revival at Litchfield, and at New Haven a further 310 "of all ages, and of all variety of characters which the town contained."[56] A similar ethos was apparent among more educated and respectable Presbyterians in Virginia, who were particularly stirred to serious spiritual concerns after the tragedy of a theater fire that killed seventy-two people in Richmond in 1811.[57] Revival of this kind also touched the Episcopal Church, notably at Bristol, Rhode Island, in 1812, under the ministry of Bishop Alexander Griswold. Griswold had not made any "unusual efforts," although he did think that his recent consecration to the episcopate had heightened his zeal in preaching and that his recent administration of confirmation had had an impact in the parish. A theological student recalled:

> All our assemblies at that time . . . were characterized by deep solemnity and thrilling interest, and a stranger coming into them could not fail to realize the pervading influence of the presence and power of God. There was no attempt made to excite the feelings or work on the passions, and yet it was manifest that "the fountains of the great deep" in the human heart were broken up; for here was seen the tear of godly sorrow coursing down the cheek of the penitent, and there the smile of joy irradiating the countenance of the pardoned sinner.[58]

Other Episcopalians, however, actively resisted the course of revivalism, a resistance that fueled the rise of a more distinct High Church party in the American church.

In North America the overall tone of this first phase of the Second Great

---

[55]Charles Beecher, ed., *Autobiography, Correspondence &c of Lyman Beecher, DD,* 2 vols. (London: Sampson, Low & Co., 1863), 1:38-39, 412; 2:75. On Nettleton see Carwardine, *Transatlantic Revivalism,* pp. 4-5.

[56]Keller, *Second Great Awakening in Connecticut,* pp. 41-54; Kling, *Field of Divine Wonders,* pp. 137-43.

[57]Thomas, "Reasonable Revivalism," p. 327.

[58]Quoted by E. Clowes Chorley, *Men and Movements in the American Episcopal Church* (Hamden, Conn.: Archon Books, 1961), p. 102.

Awakening was set more by the emotional and spiritual drama of the camp meet-ings than by the orderly preaching of men like Nettleton and Griswold. In Britain, however, the balance was a different one. Here the ethos of the state churches con-strained their evangelical ministers, who, like the New England Congregational-ists, sought to promote controlled revival by sustained preaching of the gospel rather than through any exceptional measures. Moreover, such an approach was also characteristic of evangelical Baptists and Congregationalists, who, although energetically expanding their ministry and founding numerous new chapels, did not in this period promote American-style revivals. Above all, the attitude of the English Methodist authorities was in stark contrast to their American counter-parts. In May 1806 Francis Asbury wrote to Thomas Coke in England extolling the virtues of camp meetings, which he perceived to be ushering in the millen-nium. Describing the recent meeting near New York, he wrote of

> the power of overwhelming power! upon the preachers, the members, the people
> of the world. We felt God was so great in the praying exercises that we could not
> call off the people to preaching . . . weeping, weeping on all sides.

Although Asbury claimed the meetings were marked by "harmony, zeal, and order," his enthusiasm was not reciprocated on the other side of the Atlantic, where the Methodist Conference coldly judged that "even supposing such meetings to be allowable in America, they are highly improper in England."[59] In their eyes, camp meetings seemed dangerously uncontrollable, chaotic and disorderly, at a time when Methodists, still nervous about persecution, were working hard to present themselves as a respectable movement that merited the countenance of the civil authorities.

The Methodist Conference was not, however, fully in control of the grass-roots of the movement. There significant strains of popular revivalism persisted, notably in Cornwall, which was sufficiently remote for the central authorities to feel unable to control them.[60] In Wales, too, the separate Calvinistic Meth-odists, as well as the Baptists, remained much more revivalistic than the Wes-leyan Methodists. In the north of England there were in the 1790s and early

---

[59] *Letters and Journals of Francis Asbury,* 3:343-44; Hatch, *Democratization,* p. 49; Valenze, *Prophetic Sons and Daughters,* p. 90.
[60] David Luker, "Revivalism in Theory and Practice: The Case of Cornish Methodism," *Journal of Ecclesiastical History* 37 (1986): 609-10.

1800s several small secessions of groups that espoused a revivalistic spirituality, sometimes drawing on the Quaker spiritual tradition of "inner light." These included the Independent Methodists in Lancashire, the Magic Methodists in Cheshire, and the "Kirkgate Screamers" in Leeds.[61] In 1803 William Bramwell, leader of the 1793-1795 Yorkshire revival, resigned from the Methodist Conference and made an unsuccessful attempt to develop a more united revivalist movement, but he was subsequently persuaded to rejoin the parent body. Jabez Bunting (1779-1858), then a young preacher in Macclesfield and destined to become the dominant figure in early nineteenth-century English Methodism, was particularly forthright in his condemnation of the revivalists:

> The people in this town are tired of parties and divisions: & in general equally of the rant & extravagancies of what is called Revivalism. . . . Revivalism as of late professed & practiced was [likely if] not checked to have gradually ruined genuine Methodism.[62]

Hence when, in December 1805, Lorenzo Dow made his second journey across the Atlantic, this time visiting the northwest of England as well as Ireland, internal Methodist tensions were already running high. Dow found his natural spiritual affinities to be with the Methodist dissidents rather than with the Wesleyan leadership, who, alarmed by Dow's republicanism as well as his revivalism, were almost as hostile to him as were the civil authorities. Dow, however, encouraged the seceders and, crucially, persuaded Hugh Bourne, leader of a group of revivalists at Harriseahead on the border of Staffordshire and Cheshire, to hold the first English camp meeting on the nearby hill of Mow Cop on May 31, 1807, attended by between 2,000 and 4,000 people and lasting from 6 a.m. to 8:30 p.m. Four preaching stands were erected and services carried on "with singing, prayer, preaching, exhortations, speaking experiences, relating anecdotes &c." According to Bourne, "a great solemnity rested on the people all the time." A second meeting on Mow Cop in July was extended to three days and saw more than sixty conversions, and a further three-day meeting was held at Norton-in-the-Moors in late August. The Methodist Conference banned the camp meetings, but Bourne was defiant, arguing that they were a

---

[61]Valenze, *Prophetic Sons and Daughters*, pp. 74-78, 205-41; W. R. Ward, *Religion and Society in England 1790-1850* (London: B. T. Batsford, 1972), p. 81.

[62]Quoted in Ward, *Religion and Society*, p. 80.

restoration of John Wesley's practice of field preaching, supporting it with praying services and a variety of other religious exercises. In the spring of 1808 he continued the movement with a gathering on the prominent Wrekin mountain in Shropshire on the first of May. This meeting was a conscious challenge not only to the Wesleyan authorities, but also to the popular pagan rituals that persisted in this place and were particularly associated with May Day. Bourne's expulsion from the Methodist Conference followed.[63]

Initially the various revivalistic groups associated with the camp meetings were not formally organized, but in 1811, after other dissidents, notably William Clowes (1780-1851), had also been expelled from Wesleyan Methodism, they united to form a new denomination, the Primitive Methodists. At first they remained a small group, concentrated in north Staffordshire where they had originated, but during the next decade the Primitives, who also became known as Ranters, extended their influence eastward into Derbyshire, Nottinghamshire and Lincolnshire, south into the industrial Midlands and north into Lancashire and Yorkshire. In the early 1820s they reached County Durham, where in 1822 they stirred revival in the northern dales and the coalfields. Although they did not succeed in stirring the kind of large-scale popular revivals seen in the United States, they continued to promote camp meetings and had a significant appeal to the lower classes in both rural and industrial districts.[64] They also maintained uninhibited revivalistic styles of worship, which disturbed outsiders. A local newspaper report of a service at their new chapel in Lincoln in 1819 noted the "phrenzy" of the speakers, and the way that "five or six" people began to "harangue" at one time. "What with the confusion arising from this circumstance, the cries and groans of the infatuated followers

---

[63]Hugh Bourne, *History of the Primitive Methodists Giving an Account of their Rise and Progress up to the Year 1823* (Bemersley, 1823), pp. 8-22; Julia S. Werner, *The Primitive Methodist Connexion: Its Background and Early History* (Madison: University of Wisconsin Press, 1984), pp. 59-65; Hatch, *Democratization*, p. 50; Carwardine, *Transatlantic Revivalism*, pp. 104-7.

[64]Werner, *Primitive Methodist Connexion*, pp. 68-134; James Obelkevich, *Religion and Rural Society: South Lindsey 1825-1875* (Oxford: Clarendon Press, 1976), pp. 225-27; R. W. Ambler, *Ranters, Revivalists and Reformers: Primitive Methodism and Rural Society: South Lincolnshire 1817-1875* (Hull: Hull University Press, 1989), pp. 28-45; Robert Colls, "Primitive Methodists in the Northern Coalfields," in *Disciplines of Faith: Studies in Religion, Politics and Patriarchy*, ed. Jim Obelkevich, Lyndal Roper and Raphael Samuel (London: Routledge and Kegan Paul, 1987), p. 325.

of the sect, and the noise of the others who were collected to see them, a tumult arose which defies all description."[65]

Meanwhile, on the border between Devon and Cornwall, another Wesleyan local preacher, William O'Bryan (1778-1868), was also finding himself at odds with the denominational authorities because of his irregular evangelistic activities. When the Wesleyans expelled him in 1815 he too formed a new denomination, the Bible Christians, which resembled the Primitive Methodists in its revivalistic ethos and close affinities with popular culture. The Bible Christians remained primarily concentrated in the southwest of England where, conversely, the Primitive Methodists had little impact. O'Bryan emigrated to the United States in 1831 and his influence therefore extended to North America, but the Bible Christians did not become a significant denomination there.[66]

In general, in Britain in the first quarter of the nineteenth century, in the face of the hostility and caution of the major evangelical denominations, revival was already being driven to the margins. In part these were social margins, as represented in the economically vulnerable lower-class constituency drawn to the Primitive Methodists, but they were also geographical ones. Cornwall experienced a major revival in 1814, but its full intensity was only felt in the western part of the county. In Scotland there were revivals in the Isle of Arran in 1804 and 1812-1813, in the Isle of Skye in 1805-1806 and 1812, and in the mountainous district of Breadalbane in 1816-1817.[67] Welsh Nonconformity remained strongly revivalistic, but was viewed with distaste by denominational leaders in England. Thus the Baptist William Richards, who had Welsh origins but ministered in King's Lynn for most of his life, was disgusted by Baptist revivals in Wales, "where there would be so much jumping, dancing, tumbling, embracing, roaring, raving etc. as was scarce ever equalled, and never exceeded among the most frantic lunatics."[68] In 1818 John Angell James (1785-1858), a prominent Independent, minister of Carr's Lane Chapel in Birmingham, witnessed a revival service near Bala. He was touched by the way that "hundreds

---

[65] Quoted in Ambler, *Ranters, Revivalists and Reformers,* p. 40; cf. Obelkevich, *Religion and Rural Society,* p. 225.

[66] Valenze, *Prophetic Sons and Daughters,* pp. 143-44; *BDEB,* pp. 837-38.

[67] Isaac, *Evangelical Christianity in Cornwall,* pp. 113-14; *Narrative of Revivals of Religion in Scotland, Ireland and Wales* (Glasgow, 1839); *History of Revivals of Religion in the British Isles,* passim.

[68] Quoted in Morgan, "Development of the Baptist Movement in Wales," pp. 202-3.

of people melted down to tears and groans by the simple and impassioned tones of a rustic [preacher]," but disturbed by the subsequent outbreak of howling and jumping, particularly by women. He was "quite alarmed" for his wife, and "often advised her to go out." James was in favor of revival in theory, but hostile in practice to "the irregularities and extravagances of some well-meaning but ignorant and fanatical persons in our own country, whose procedure has in many cases been no less opposed to decorum than to religion."[69]

In the United States suspicion of emotional excess in revival could easily acquire a racist dimension, as black people were, in general, more uninhibited than whites in their spiritual enthusiasm. Thus in 1819 one critic blamed African Americans for "gross perversions of true religion."[70] The very success of slaves and free blacks in assimilating Christianity to their African cultural and spiritual heritage meant that their religious expression took forms that could be very disconcerting to uncomprehending observers. Thus a Swedish visitor wrote of an African American Methodist church in Brooklyn in 1819:

> I cannot now describe for you the effect it had on me to see twenty or thirty Negresses, who thought they were full of the Holy Ghost, behave like regular furies. Their bellowing, dancing and jumping on benches was hideous and extremely barbaric.[71]

This was the same kind of spiritual ecstasy which two decades before had also transmitted itself to white people in the melting pot of Cane Ridge and its immediate aftermath, but it now seemed to require containment. In the rural Deep South white planters were indeed able, partially at least, to control the spiritual lives of their slaves in biracial churches, but in towns and among free black people in the Northern states many reacted by forming separate black churches where they could both escape white prejudice and develop their own expressions of Christianity. In 1816 a number of such black congregations in Pennsylvania, Maryland and elsewhere came together to form the African Methodist Episcopal Church, under the leadership of their first bishop Richard Allen, who had ministered at the Bethel black Methodist church in Philadel-

---

[69]R.W. Dale, ed., *The Life and Letters of John Angell James* (London: James Nisbet, 1861), pp. 221-23; John Angell James, *A Pastoral Letter on the Subject of Revivals in Religion* (London: F. Westley & A. H. Davis, 1829), p. 4.

[70]Quoted in Wigger, "Taking Heaven by Storm," p. 187.

[71]Quoted ibid., pp. 188-89; Frey and Wood, *Come Shouting to Zion*, pp. 144-45.

phia since 1794. The distinct African Methodist Episcopal Zion Church was formed in New York a few years later. There were also numerous black Baptist churches, but as these already enjoyed considerable congregational autonomy, they did not feel the need to form a separate national denomination.[72]

In North America there was something of a lull in revivals in the second decade of the nineteenth century, particularly around 1812-1815, as the stimulus of the early camp meetings faded and the War of 1812 operated as a distraction. However, here, unlike in Britain, the setback was a very temporary one and new momentum developed from 1816 onward, centered this time more on the north and east of the country than on the south. For example, in 1816 there was an awakening in the Baptist and Congregational churches in the Connecticut River valley in Vermont; there were revivals in Methodist and Presbyterian churches in Baltimore in 1817 and 1818; Bishop Griswold's church at Bristol, Rhode Island, again experienced revival in 1820. In February 1821 Lyman Beecher reported excitedly from Hartford, Connecticut, that "the city is greatly moved." Several hundred people had stayed behind after sermons for inquiry meetings, including some well-respected and influential gentlemen. Also in 1821 a camp meeting was held at East Hartford, with the attendance of around 1,000 swelling to an estimated 8,000 on the Sunday.[73] Even if the flames seemed sometimes to die down, there was still a lot of heat left in the revival fires

EVANGELICAL EXPANSION

It is impossible precisely to quantify the overall impact of revivals in this period. For most denominations calculations of numbers are scattered and often unreliable, although fortunately the Methodists kept detailed statistics, which give some insight into general trends. It is also difficult to distinguish the results of revival from more steady, if less spectacular, expansion through the gradual conversion and adherence of individuals. The pattern of revival was complex, with localized surges of enthusiasm in one district fading just as another one became awakened. Some converts did not sustain their commitment: the falling off in

---

[72]Ibid., pp. 177-81; Noll, *History of Christianity in the United States and Canada*, pp. 202-4.

[73]Randolph A. Roth, *The Democratic Dilemma: Religion, Reform and the Social Order in the Connecticut River Valley of Vermont, 1791-1850* (Cambridge: Cambridge University Press, 1987), pp. 81-82; Bilhartz, *Urban Religion*, p. 89; Chorley, *American Episcopal Church*, pp. 103-4; Beecher, *Autobiography, Correspondence*, 1:393; Keller, *Connecticut*, p. 199.

Methodist membership in Yorkshire in 1796-1797 has already been noted; in the Cornish revival of 1814 Methodist membership rose from 9,405 to 14,606 in a single year, but then fell back to 14,296 in 1815.[74] Across the Atlantic in the Delmarva peninsula Methodist membership rose from 8,705 in 1800 to nearly 25,000 in 1807, but then declined to 22,000 in 1810 and 21,000 in 1820.[75] Such local fluctuations tended, however, to cancel each other out, and overall Methodist numbers on both sides of the Atlantic showed year-to-year increases between 1800 and 1820, except in Britain in 1799-1801 and in America in 1814.[76] Table 3 compares the two countries.[77]

Table 3: Methodist Growth in United States and Great Britain

	US (1800)	US (1820)	US (1850)	GB (1801)	GB (1821)	GB (1851)
Methodist Membership (000s)	65	257	1,185	94	227	504
As % of Population	1.2	2.7	5.1	0.8	1.5	2.4

Thus, although growth in Britain was impressive by any other standards, it was significantly outpaced in the United States, an indication perhaps that divergent attitudes to revivals had implications for church growth. In Ireland, moreover, after the dramatic revivalism at the turn of the century, Methodist growth lost momentum, only increasing relatively slowly from 24,233 in 1801 to 29,388 in 1814. There was, though, a further significant upsurge in 1819 and 1820, taking numbers to 37,100 in 1821.[78] In British North America, on the other hand, where the "Canada fire" of revivalism had continued to blaze in the early nineteenth century, evangelical denominations continued to be numerically strong relative to population.[79] Revivals did not on their own account for the expansion of evangelicalism, but they were showing themselves to be an important factor in its growth.

---

[74]Isaac, *Cornwall*, p. 114.

[75]Williams, *Garden of American Methodism*, pp. 73, 81-82.

[76]Carwardine, *Transatlantic Revivalism*, pp. 46-47.

[77]British figures are from Currie, Gilbert and Horsley, *Churches and Churchgoers*, pp. 139-40. They do not include the separate Calvinistic Methodists in Wales, for whom no figure is available before 1838, when they had 37,576 members. They had 52,600 in 1848; if this figure were added to the 1851 total the percentage of Methodists in the population would increase to 2.7 percent. American figures are from Noll, *America's God*, p. 169.

[78]Hempton, *Religion of the People*, p. 36.

[79]Rawlyk, *Canada Fire*, p. 122.

3

"NEW MEASURES" REVIVALS, 1820-1850

In the second half of our period, from the mid-1820s onward, there was a new upsurge of revivalism in America, which was spread and sustained by the advance of the so-called new measures associated with Charles Grandison Finney. These made populist and spontaneous movements more institutionalized and socially respectable, and strengthened a consciousness of a transatlantic revivalist movement shaping both British and American evangelicalism.

FINNEY AND THE "NEW MEASURES"

The initial geographical center of a new upsurge of revivals in the 1820s was in the western and northern parts of New York State, which, like Kentucky at the time of Cane Ridge, was a region of comparatively recent settlement. During the years since independence numerous land-hungry New Englanders had, like their counterparts to the south, been crossing the mountains to build new lives for themselves in the fertile country beyond. Among the migrants in 1794 or 1795 were Sylvester and Rebecca Finney from Warren, Connecticut. They brought with them a large family, including their two-year-old seventh child Charles Grandison.[1] The Finneys settled first near Utica, but later moved north to a farm near Henderson close to the eastern shore of Lake Ontario. When Charles grew up he stayed in the locality, where he worked initially as a teacher and then in a lawyer's office. In 1821 he experienced a dramatic conversion, fol-

---

[1] For details of Finney's life see Keith J. Hardman, *Charles Grandison Finney 1792-1875: Revivalist and Reformer* (Grand Rapids: Baker, 1987).

lowed by "the most profound spiritual tranquility," a sense of meeting Jesus face
to face like "any other man" and "a mighty baptism of the Holy Ghost" that
seemed to go through him "like a wave of electricity." Immediately Finney left
his legal work, announcing to an astonished client that "I have a retainer from
the Lord Jesus Christ to plead his cause, and I cannot plead yours."[2] In 1824,
now a licensed Presbyterian preacher, Finney began to stir revival in the remote
rural districts along the St. Lawrence, close to the Canadian border. Then in
1825-1826 his career as the leading revivalist in the mid-nineteenth-century
English-speaking world was decisively launched when his preaching inspired
large-scale revival in the more densely populated Oneida County around Utica.

Mark Noll has argued that there is "a good case" for ranking Finney as one
of "the most important public figures in nineteenth-century America," and certainly that he was "the crucial figure in white American evangelicalism after
Jonathan Edwards."[3] His impact was indeed profound. Nevertheless, it is essential to see his personal role in the context of a wider spiritual and social landscape. Western New York in Finney's formative years was itself a society growing
to maturity and subject to significant stresses and upheavals. The building of the
Erie Canal, completed in 1825, the very year of the outbreak of the Oneida revivals, brought the promise of increased prosperity, but also the unsettling presence of numerous construction workers and other social pressures that came
with rapid economic change. There was also a history of religious excitement and
innovation. The migrants tended to come from the less developed parts of New
England that had been particularly receptive to earlier waves of revival. Contacts
with original home districts persisted and churches there invested significantly
in mission and church-planting in the newly settled areas. Moreover, significant
migration directly from Europe and Canada further increased the social and religious diversity of the region. There had been significant revival in 1799-1800,
and local awakenings continued in subsequent years. Contemporary with
Finney's early career, the region was giving birth to other even more radical religious movements: at Low Hampton William Miller was pursuing his study of
biblical prophecy that led him in 1828 to announce that the second coming

---

[2]Garth M. Rosell and Richard A. G. Dupuis, eds., *The Memoirs of Charles Grandison Finney*
(Grand Rapids: Zondervan, 1989), pp. 22-23, 27.
[3]Mark A. Noll, *A History of Christianity in the United States and Canada* (Grand Rapids: Eerdmans, 1992), p. 176.

would take place in 1843, and it was near Palmyra that Joseph Smith claimed to have discovered the golden plates published as the Book of Mormon in 1830. The frequency and intensity of the religious movements associated with western New York have led to it being labeled the "burned-over district."[4]

The "new measures" associated with Finney's revivals have been summarized as follows by Richard Carwardine:

> In new measure revivalism, preaching was often more direct, specific and theatrical and was often conducted by preachers who itinerated with the avowed intention of stirring churches and winning converts. Prayers were sustained over long periods, sometimes with specific requests for named individuals. At "social" or "promiscuous" prayer meetings, women might prove as vocal as men. In addition to the more reputable enquiry meetings, the "anxious seat" was employed. This was a pew set aside at the front of the congregation where those in a state of concern over their souls could go to be exhorted and prayed for by the minister and where a public commitment might be expected. . . . In these high pressure conditions, the roused emotions found in any revival could explode uncontrollably. . . . Protracted meetings held over three or four days—or even much longer—served only to increase the likelihood of emotionalism. In general there was no rigid procedure, and the methods employed could vary from revival to revival. What was constant was the boldness, frenetic activity, emphasis on public pressures, and general readiness to experiment that marked the exponents of the new-measure revivalism.[5]

In reality the "new measures" were by no means entirely new. Many features of them had been apparent in the camp meetings and in the Methodist revivalism of recent decades. Moreover, even some other Congregationalists and Presbyterians were already adopting some similar techniques. In 1826, contemporary with Finney's campaign in Oneida, Lyman Beecher was stirring revival at Hanover Street Congregational Church in Boston. Here, as he had done at Hartford a few years before, Beecher used repeated meetings to awaken interest, and also sustained prayer.[6]

---

[4]Whitney R. Cross, *The Burned-over District: The Social and Intellectual History of Enthusiastic Religion in Western New York, 1800-1850* (Ithaca, N.Y.: Cornell University Press, 1950), passim.

[5]Richard Carwardine, *Transatlantic Revivalism: Popular Evangelicalism in Britain and America, 1790-1865* (Westport, Conn.: Greenwood Press, 1978), p. 8.

[6]Charles Beecher, ed., *Autobiography, Correspondence &c of Lyman Beecher, DD*, 2 vols. (London: Sampson, Low & Co., 1863), 2:72-78, 89-90.

Nevertheless, Finney was initially viewed with considerable suspicion by leading New England revivalists such as Beecher and Nettleton. To a significant degree the divergence is best understood as one of style rather than substance: Nettleton sought to stir conversions in "hushed mysterious stillness," whereas Finney's approach was much more flamboyant, "bold, striking [and] demonstrative." Beecher and Nettleton in their published criticisms of Finney emphasized particularly the brashness of his manner and the harsh and severe nature of his preaching, which they feared would divide churches and needlessly antagonize potential converts.[7] When Finney and his critics met at New Lebanon on the border of Massachusetts and New York in July 1827 in an endeavor to reach an understanding, it was indeed apparent that the theological differences were not substantial. Independently of Finney, Beecher, together with his friend, the leading Yale theologian Nathaniel Taylor, had already been edging away from traditional Calvinism toward a position that acknowledged and advocated a positive role for human agency in the work of conversion and moral reform. Hence there was ready agreement that Finney's revivals were to be welcomed as a means to "the preservation and extension of true religion in our land." The New Lebanon convention was more divided on the specific "new measures" adopted, but crucially for Finney it did not impose any obstacles to their use. Controversy continued for another year, until in 1828 there was an agreement "to cease from all publications, correspondences, conversations, and conduct designed or calculated to keep those subjects before the public mind."[8] The outcome was a somewhat uneasy but nevertheless effective assimilation between the New England tradition of restrained, respectable revivalism as developed by Beecher, and the popular mass revivalism associated with Finney's "new measures." The real loser in the process was Asahel Nettleton, whose conservative Calvinism and particularly low-key approach to revivalism were now decidedly out of fashion. He sought new audiences in a visit to Britain in 1831 and 1832, from where it was reported that "he seemed to have a special faculty for sending people to sleep."[9]

---

[7] Ibid., 2:94; *Letters of the Rev. Dr. Beecher and Rev. Mr Nettleton on the "New Measures" in Conducting Revivals of Religion* (New York, 1828). A tendency to see the differences as a clash of generations is misleading: Finney was only nine years younger than Nettleton.

[8] Beecher, *Autobiography, Correspondence*, 2:93-108.

[9] Carwardine, *Transatlantic Revivalism*, p. 67.

During the late 1820s and early 1830s the revivals in the United States spread rapidly. Finney was but the most prominent of a number of itinerant evangelists who carried the movement across northern New York and into nearby states, notably Vermont to the east and Ohio to the west. Meanwhile, Finney himself took revival to the cities of the eastern seaboard, beginning in Wilmington, Delaware, in December 1827, and moving on to Philadelphia in 1828 and New York City in 1829-1830. In September 1830 Finney returned to western New York, launching the most successful of all his urban revival campaigns in the boom town of Rochester, where he continued to work until March 1831. While Rochester itself was a relatively small place, the renown of Finney's preaching drew people from a wide area around, thus spreading the impact of the revival. Moreover, as newspaper reports spread news of the apparent spiritual and moral transformation of a previously turbulent and materialistic town, revival was stimulated elsewhere and the early 1830s saw an upsurge in church growth across the nation. Such a response was immediate because Finney's approach suggested that church people should themselves work directly to instigate revival rather than relying primarily on prayer to stir the supernatural intervention of the Holy Spirit. Thus, for example, in 1831 revivals in Vermont "took a more self-conscious tone."[10]

The Rochester revival also marked the maturing of Finney's revivalistic techniques and the completion of his move toward evangelical respectability. According to his own recollections, this was the first time that he made extensive use of the "anxious seat," which he thought helped to overcome the reticence of "the higher classes especially."[11] It was indeed a powerful tool. Members of the congregation stirred to spiritual concern by the revivalist's preaching were urged at the end of the sermon to make an immediate response by coming forward to the anxious seat, where they would be subject to further exhortation, counseling and prayer, in full view of the rest of the congregation. Concluding a revival address in Vermont in late 1835 or early

---

[10]Hardman, *Charles Grandison Finney,* pp. 150-211; Paul E. Johnson, *A Shopkeeper's Millennium: Society and Revivals in Rochester, New York, 1815-1837* (New York: Hill and Wang, 1978); Randolph A. Roth, *The Democratic Dilemma: Religion, Reform and the Social Order in the Connecticut River Valley of Vermont, 1791-1850* (Cambridge: Cambridge University Press, 1987), pp. 189-90.

[11]Rosell and Dupuis, *Memoirs of Finney,* p. 306.

1836, Jedediah Burchard, an imitator of Finney, presented the invitation to the anxious bench and the very call of God:

> The Spirit and the bride say come! Then come forward, while the wind of the Spirit is blowing. Many have felt its influences since this meeting commenced, who would gladly come out and say amen, and testify that what I have stated is true! And now I want every man, woman and child to come forward and take the front seats and be talked and prayed with.[12]

Such a technique forestalled procrastination, and revival momentum was increased by very public conversions.

Moreover, by the time of the Rochester revival, Finney's preaching, although still dramatic and compelling, had lost something of the earlier backcountry roughness that had offended Beecher and Nettleton, and became more attuned to educated urban congregations. He recalled:

> In this revival at Rochester I am not aware that there was ever any complaint of any fanaticism, or anything that was to be deplored in its results. The revival was so powerful that it gathered in such great numbers of the most influential class in society, it made so clean a sweep, that it created a great excitement far and near.[13]

Finney's growing acceptability was indicated by his decision to hold his next major revival campaign in Boston, starting in August 1831, and meeting his erstwhile critic Lyman Beecher on his home ground. Some tensions persisted and the New England capital proved stony ground compared with Rochester, but Beecher later magnanimously wrote that Finney "did very well."[14]

Then in 1832, now weary of an itinerant lifestyle, Finney accepted a settled pastorate at Chatham Street Chapel in New York, in a strategic location at the commercial heart of the city, offering the opportunity to preach to numerous visitors as well as residents. The chapel was an adapted former theater, offering Finney the perfect environment for his dramatic style of preaching, with better lines of sight for members of the congregation than in a conventional church-building. When in 1835 Finney's supporters built the Broadway Tabernacle for

---

[12]C. G. Eastman, *Sermons, Addresses & Exhortations by Rev Jedediah Burchard* (Burlington, Vt.: Chauncy Goodrich 1836), p. 44.

[13]Rosell and Dupuis, *Memoirs of Finney*, pp. 323-24.

[14]Beecher, *Autobiography, Correspondence*, 2:89-108.

him, the innovative circular design was reminiscent as much of a theater as of a church.[15] That year also saw the publication of Finney's *Lectures on Revivals of Religion*, which enjoyed enormous sales on both sides of the Atlantic. It was a highly practical handbook of advice to ministers and others, premised on the conviction that human agency was crucial in preparing the ground for revivals. For Christians passively to await the miraculous intervention of God was as absurd as it would be for a farmer to expect God miraculously to provide a crop if he did not cultivate his fields. Granted that conversion required "God's special agency by his Holy Spirit," the agency of man was also essential. The book was important not only in ensuring the wide dissemination of Finney's approach to evangelism, but in reinforcing the ongoing evangelical reaction against traditional Calvinism that was implicit in the adoption of "new measures" revivalism.[16]

Whereas the camp meeting revivalism of the early nineteenth century achieved its greatest successes in the Southern states, the "new measures" were primarily a Northern movement. Finney himself never campaigned any further south than Delaware. His importance lay in transmitting to the more spiritually cautious and socially respectable churches of the North and Northeast a comparable revivalistic energy to that which had already in the previous generation transformed the Baptist and Methodist churches of the South.[17] Women were usually in the majority over men among the converts: the English writer Fanny Trollope, who witnessed a revival in Cincinnati in about 1828, observed that "all who obeyed the call to place themselves on the 'anxious benches' were women, and by far the greater number, very young women."[18] There was indeed a tendency, particularly in later phases of revival, for converts to be disproportionately teenagers and young people in the twelve to twenty-five age group,

---

[15]Jeanne Halgren Kilde, "Church Architecture and the Second Great Awakening: Religion, Space and Politics," in *Embodying the Spirit: New Perspectives on North American Revivalism*, ed. Michael J. McClymond (Baltimore: Johns Hopkins University Press, 2004), pp. 84-92.

[16]Charles Grandison Finney, *Lectures on Revivals of Religion*, ed. William G. McLoughlin (Cambridge, Mass.: Belknap Press, 1960), pp. ix-x, 14, 17-18.

[17]Cf. Marianne Perciacannte, *Calling Down Fire: Charles Grandison Finney and Revivalism in Jefferson County, New York, 1800-1840* (Albany: State University of New York Press, 2003), pp. 37-39, 72-79.

[18]Fanny Trollope, *Domestic Manners of the Americans*, ed. Richard Mullen (1832; Oxford: Oxford University Press, 1984), p. 67.

presumably because most susceptible adults had already been converted. In Vermont, however, the presence of children and especially of young people aged fifteen to nineteen in their households apparently influenced older men to convert. In Rochester, although women continued to make up the majority of church members, the proportion of men increased during the revivals. Due both to the intensity of the efforts used to secure conversions and the youth and consequent material, moral and spiritual instability of some of the converts, there were quite high rates of falling away from church commitment in the years after the revivals. In Vermont this tendency was particularly apparent in the later years of the revival—between 1834 and 1843—when efforts to reach outside the circle of existing church attenders were probably at their most intensive. It has also been observed that, without gainsaying the importance of Finney's achievement in bringing large-scale revival to the major cities, his achievements in Boston, New York and Philadelphia were somewhat ambivalent, and that, in common with earlier revivalists, his most profound impact was in rural and small-town America.[19]

Although Finney's spectacular career overshadowed the camp meetings, it did not supersede them. These continued, especially among the Methodists, and became more closely institutionalized and regulated. Campgrounds became semi-permanent, being used for regular annual meetings in successive summers, the sexes were segregated to forestall charges of immorality, and blacks were separated from whites. George Metzger described a camp meeting of the Methodist Episcopal Church which he attended in Ohio in summer 1836. An acre and a half of woodland had been thinned to allow the erection of rows of tents on each side of the campground. At one end was the preacher's tent with a pulpit nearby. The congregation was seated in the middle, with men on one side and women on the other. The meetings lasted five to seven days, with preaching for four hours each day. Attendance was "upwards of 600" during the week, rising to more than 3,000 on the Sunday. At daybreak there was

---

[19] Roth, *Democratic Dilemma*, pp. 187-219; Mary P. Ryan, *Cradle of the Middle Class: The Family in Oneida County, New York, 1790-1865* (Cambridge: Cambridge University Press, 1981), pp. 75-83; Johnson, *A Shopkeeper's Millennium*, pp. 102-8; Curtis D. Johnson, *Islands of Holiness: Rural Religion in Upstate New York 1790-1860* (Ithaca, N.Y.: Cornell University Press, 1989), pp. 61-63; Marion L. Bell, *Crusade in the City: Revivalism in Nineteenth-Century Philadelphia* (Cranbury, N.J.: Associated University Presses, 1977), pp. 43-94.

worship in each tent, and then a bugle called the congregation together:

> Before Sermon a hymn is sung and a Prayer is offered up. After Sermon any
> one of the Preachers gets up and exhorts and in connexion with his exhorta-
> tion he urges the people with the strongest persuasion he can make use of to
> come forward to the Mourners bench; if some come he leaves the pulpit and
> resorts to that bench and others such as Leaders and Exhorters and people be-
> longing to the Church join him—they now "compel" them to come in by the
> most urgent invitations and with those that come they engage in prayer. The
> longer they are engaged in this exercise the more lively and noisy the meeting
> gets . . . and this exercise continues until the bugle sounds again for preaching.
> . . . After the mourners have been in agony and prayer for a while they are asked
> how they feel and when they express that they found peace, others exclaim
> "Glory to God etc. etc."[20]

This account shows that the mourners' bench, an alternative term for the
anxious seat, was also being used in camp meeting revivalism by the mid-
1830s.[21]

BRITISH DEVELOPMENTS

In Britain, meanwhile, developments during the 1820s and early 1830s served
to reinforce the predominant evangelical caution toward revivals. The Primitive Methodists established themselves as a new denomination with a strongly
revivalistic ethos, but remained relatively small, having 35,535 members in
1830 compared with 232,074 Wesleyans.[22] Jabez Bunting, who as a young
preacher had shown himself an implacable opponent of revivalists, rose by the
1820s to become the dominant figure in Wesleyan Methodism. The Arminian
theology and revivalistic tradition of Methodism ensured that intermittent revivals nevertheless continued, notably in Cornwall, but also in the 1820s in
the north of England.[23] Such movements, though, lacked the encouragement

---

[20] Cf. Dickson D. Bruce, *And They All Sang Hallelujah: Plain-Folk Camp-Meeting Religion 1800-
1845* (Knoxville: University of Tennessee Press, 1974), pp. 70-90.

[21] There is debate as to whether this stemmed from Finney's influence, or whether in fact
Finney himself had originally adopted the idea from the Methodists.

[22] Robert Currie, Alan Gilbert and Lee Horsley, *Churches and Churchgoers: Patterns of Church
Growth in the British Isles Since 1700* (Oxford: Oxford University Press, 1977), p. 140.

[23] Peter Isaac, *A History of Evangelical Christianity in Cornwall* (Gerrards Cross: WEC Press, n.d.),
pp. 114-18; Carwardine, *Transatlantic Revivalism*, p. 103.

from the national leadership that they received in America.

During the 1820s some younger Anglican and Church of Scotland Evangelicals sought to present a more radical challenge to secular society than had been offered by the Clapham Sect generation. They were fired by revivalistic aspirations and influenced by continental European developments, notably an ongoing awakening *(réveil)* in the Swiss Protestant churches.[24] In 1822 James Haldane Stewart published a pamphlet calling on Christians to engage in special prayer for the outpouring of the Holy Spirit as a means to "increase the zeal, and love and holiness of all true Christians, and give spiritual life and light to sinners now dead in trespasses and sins."[25] Edward Irving (1792-1834), an exact contemporary of Charles Finney,[26] took a prominent role, as a minister of a Church of Scotland congregation in London from 1822. Like Finney, he had a commanding presence and was a powerful preacher, and by the mid-1820s had gained considerable fame and influence and drew large fashionable crowds to his church. Excitement mounted in the late 1820s as Irving and others met in a series of conferences at Albury Park, the country home of Henry Drummond (1786-1860), to study unfulfilled biblical prophecy. Then in 1830 there was an outbreak of speaking in tongues at Row in Dumbartonshire, the Clydeside parish of Irving's friend John McLeod Campbell. Similar manifestations occurred in Irving's church the following year, with apparently Spirit-led utterances reminiscent of American camp meetings. Drummond reported that "I found persons wholly uninstructed in the Schools of Theology, pouring out a mass of doctrine condensed into a few abrupt sentences such as no living divine could do." He himself experienced an "extraordinary anxiety for the souls of men."[27]

Closely linked to Irving and his circle was the "Second Reformation" movement, which during the 1820s promoted the vision of wholesale conversions to Protestantism among the Roman Catholic population in Ireland. This objec-

---

[24]For a detailed account see Timothy C. F. Stunt, *From Awakening to Secession: Radical Evangelicals in Switzerland and Britain* (Edinburgh: T & T Clark, 2000).

[25]James H. Stewart, *Thoughts on the Importance of Special Prayer for the General Outpouring of the Holy Spirit* (London: Religious Tract Society, 1822), p. 4.

[26]Both were born in August 1792.

[27]New College, Edinburgh, Thomas Chalmers Papers, CHA 4.178.17-20, Drummond to Chalmers, April 25, 1832. For Irving's career see M. Oliphant, *The Life of Edward Irving* (London: Hurst and Blackett, 1862).

tive was pursued through educational and Bible societies, and then from 1827 onward by the British Society for Promoting the Religious Principles of the Reformation. Protestant hopes were boosted by a surge of conversions in 1826-1827 centered on Lord Farnham's estates in County Cavan, which were being run on an aggressively evangelical basis. The movement, however, never became large scale, and it rapidly faltered against a background of rising political tension which meant that Catholics became even less receptive than they had been. Revivalism in Ireland proved unable to extend its impact beyond the Protestant minority. Even among Protestants it was liable to be constrained by a sense of vulnerability to the Catholic majority, which, for example, led many Methodists to prefer conservative solidarity with the Church of Ireland to unregulated revivalistic expansion. That tendency was most strongly expressed in 1819 when the Primitive Wesleyans, who saw themselves as "Church Methodists" and were opposed to forming a wholly independent church, split from the Irish Methodist Conference.[28]

There was, moreover, a crucial difference between these stirrings in Britain and Ireland and the contemporary rise of "new measures" in the United States. Common to both movements was an undertone of millennial expectation, a conviction that such evidence of the presence and power of the Holy Spirit presaged radical transformation in human society. For the American revivalists, though, the vision was a postmillennial one in which these changes were to be achieved primarily through human agency, paving the way for the eventual (but still remote) second coming. For Irving, Drummond and their associates, on the other hand, current spiritual excitements were interpreted as signs of the imminent premillennial advent of Christ. This starker vision implied pessimism about the potential of human activity to achieve large-scale conversions and predisposed them to a sectarian retreat from mainstream evangelicalism, rather than an endeavor to remold it on their own terms. In addition Irving's personal position was weakened when he exposed

---

[28]Stewart J. Brown, *The National Churches of England, Ireland and Scotland 1801-46* (Oxford: Oxford University Press, 2001), pp. 120-36; John Wolffe, *The Protestant Crusade in Great Britain 1829-1860* (Oxford: Clarendon Press, 1991), pp. 33-41; David Hempton, *The Religion of the People: Methodism and Popular Religion, c. 1750-1900* (London: Routledge, 1996), pp. 19-20; David Hempton and Myrtle Hill, *Evangelical Protestantism in Ulster Society 1740-1890* (London: Routledge, 1992), pp. 76-78.

himself to charges of heresy by so strongly emphasizing the human nature of Christ that he appeared to question his sinlessness. Potential sympathizers were alienated by what the leading Congregationalist John Angell James termed "the wild luxuriance of all sorts of novelties."[29] Hugh McNeile (1795-1879), the moderator at the Albury conferences and one of the most energetic evangelical Anglican clergy of his generation, turned against his former associates in the early 1830s.[30] Thomas Chalmers, leader of the Evangelicals in the Church of Scotland, was open to millennial and revivalist ideas and sought and received information from Drummond about the manifestations, but he too remained aloof.[31]

Hence for Irving, unlike Finney, the sequel to a meteoric rise to evangelical fame in the 1820s was nemesis rather than sustained influence. While Finney was acclaimed in New York, Irving found himself locked out of his London church in 1832, deposed from the Church of Scotland ministry in 1833, and died, a broken man, the following year. The movement he had helped to inspire continued under the leadership of Drummond and others, but far from fulfilling their initial aspirations to transform the existing churches, its adherents left the state churches to form the small Catholic Apostolic Church. There was a parallel movement in the early 1830s among other radical Evangelicals. John Nelson Darby (1800-1882) had been a curate in Ireland in the 1820s and was a leading participant in a series of conferences on prophecy at Powerscourt, County Wicklow, between 1827 and 1833. His subsequent uneasy alliance with Benjamin Wills Newton (1807-1899) led to the development of the (Plymouth) Brethren, for whom extensive growth proved similarly elusive. Such potent new wine could not be contained within the old wineskins of the state churches, but when it was removed from them it lost its potential to ferment large-scale revival.[32] On the other hand, it was also during the 1830s that other

---

[29]Robert William Dale, ed., *The Life and Letters of John Angell James* (London: James Wisbet, 1861), p. 261.

[30]Hugh McNeile, *Letters to a Friend who has Felt it his Duty to Secede from the Church of England and who Imagines that Miraculous gifts of the Holy Ghost are Revived Among the Seceders* (London, 1834).

[31]Stewart J. Brown, *Thomas Chalmers and the Godly Commonwealth in Scotland* (Oxford: Oxford University Press, 1982), pp. 215-17.

[32]For more detail see C. G. Flegg, *"Gathered under Apostles": A Study of the Catholic Apostolic Church* (Oxford: Oxford University Press, 1992); H. H. Rowdon, *The Origins of the Brethren 1825-1850* (London: Pickering and Inglis, 1967).

Anglican clergy who had previously been Evangelicals, notably John Henry Newman and William Dodsworth, came to the conviction that the best means of reviving the Church of England was through reasserting her Catholic rather than Protestant identity, thus giving an impetus to the Oxford Movement and the subsequent development of Anglo-Catholicism.[33]

With indigenous revivalistic impulses repressed or marginalized, those who hoped for revival in Britain now looked to the United States for inspiration. John Angell James wrote in February 1828 to William Patton, a revivalistic Presbyterian minister in New York, that

> of Revivals, properly so-called, I am sorry to say, we know nothing in this coun-try. It is true that religion is, I think, steadily advancing, but it is more in the way of silent and unmarked progress, than in that of conspicuous and noticeable movements.[34]

James was subsequently encouraged by a visit from Patton which helped to stimulate interest in revivals among English Nonconformists, and in 1829 himself published a pamphlet to promote the cause. With an eye to a broad evangelical constituency uneasy with "irregularities and extravagances," he de-fined revival in generalized terms as "a greater increase of true piety in those who are already sincere Christians, and in the number of those who are truly converted to God, than we have been accustomed to witness." Nevertheless, in 1831, as revival swept across the United States, James judged that in Britain "the little stir that was made about two years ago has nearly all died away."[35]

The 1830s did, however, see something of a recovery of momentum in Britain. The cholera epidemic of 1832 stimulated revival in some districts, especially northeast England and the Black Country.[36] There was also a steady stream of American evangelical visitors to Britain who heightened awareness

---

[33]Sheridan Gilley, *Newman and His Age* (London: Darton, Longman and Todd, 1990); Stephen Young, "William Dodsworth and the Origins of Tractarianism in London" (Ph.D. thesis, Open University, 2004).

[34]Dale, *John Angell James*, p. 244.

[35]Carwardine, *Transatlantic Revivalism*, p. 59; John Angell James, *A Pastoral Letter on the Subject of Revivals in Religion* (London: F. Westley & A. H. Davis, 1829), p. 4; Dale, *John Angell James*, p. 261.

[36]R. J. Morris, *Cholera 1832: The Social Response to an Epidemic* (London: Croom Helm, 1976), pp. 144-45.

of developments across the Atlantic. Fact-finding tours to the United States were made by the Congregationalists Andrew Reed and James Matheson in 1834 and the Baptists Francis Cox and James Hoby in 1835, and heightened British awareness of revival across the Atlantic. Reed and Matheson gave even-handed accounts of American revivals, and Reed found himself a somewhat unwilling but nevertheless effective preacher at a camp meeting in Virginia.[37] On his return Cox summarized some of the lessons that he thought his compatriots could learn from the "energetic and progressive" piety of the Americans:

> If churches relapse into a low state, they are not satisfied long to continue so; but they begin to inquire into the cause of this declension and the means by which it may be remedied. They entertain confidence in the success of suitable means, and are often at once sagacious in the discovery and prompt in the application of them to the condition of particular congregations. Should plans be suggested which have for their object to awaken professors from a state of slumber, and arouse the unconverted from their sleep of death, objections are not urged against them because they are new; they do not restrain zeal, lest it should produce innovation; and are more afraid of incurring the guilt of lukewarmness than of being charged with the extravagance of enthusiasm.[38]

He recommended a range of measures that had proved effective in the United States, including efforts by individuals in their own social circles, organized prayer, inquiry meetings, the cultivation of juvenile piety, associations of mothers to work for the conversion of their children, the planting of new churches, itinerant evangelists and protracted meetings. He was, however, critical of "injudicious" camp meetings as disruptive of normal pastoral provision, and the "anxious seat" as liable to induce ill-considered conversions.[39]

The momentum of revival faltered somewhat in the United States in the

---

[37] Andrew Reed and James Matheson, *A Narrative of the Visit to the American Churches by the Deputation from the Congregational Union of England and Wales* (London: Jackson and Walford, 1835), pp. 58-60, 135-37, 249-51, 270-87; Carwardine, *Transatlantic Revivalism*, pp. 66-68.

[38] F. A. Cox, *Suggestions Designed to Promote the Revival and Extension of Religion Founded on Observations Made During a Journey in the United States of America in the Spring and Summer of 1835* (London: Thomas Ward & Co, 1836), p. 4.

[39] Ibid., pp. 5-23; F. A. Cox and J. Hoby, *The Baptists in America: A Narrative of the Deputation from the Baptist Union in England to the United States and Canada* (London: T. Ward, 1836), pp. 520-21.

mid-1830s, but when activity resumed around 1837, the echo in Britain was
stronger than it had been hitherto. Finney's *Lectures on Revivals of Religion* was published in Britain in January 1838 and had to be reprinted several times during
the next two years. Already in September 1838 there was an expectation that it
would "find its way into the abode of every class of Christian" and give "a considerable impetus to Christian zeal."[40] Individual Baptist and Congregational
churches began to work actively for revival, applying "new measures" such as
the protracted meeting held over numerous successive days. Valuable assistance
came from American visitors, notably the Presbyterian Edward Norris Kirk,
who arrived in Britain in 1837 and offered an orderly style of revivalism that
appealed to middle-class English Congregationalists. William Patton made a
return visit in 1839 accompanied by Nathaniel Beman, who had been an early
and controversial supporter of Finney's "new measures." The Methodist James
Caughey, who had been converted in a Finney revival in Troy, New York, in
1830, arrived in Britain in 1841 and remained until 1847, having a substantial
impact on Wesleyan congregations in the north of England. Among Baptists,
home-grown itinerant evangelists played an important part, in particular
Thomas Pulsford and Charles Roe, an Irishman who worked in Britain in the
1820s, '30s and '40s before subsequently emigrating to the United States.[41]

Such activity contributed to an acceleration of growth in Baptist numbers in
the late 1830s. It is probable that Congregationalists showed a similar trend, although one that cannot be documented. Caughey's campaigns had a substantial
short-term impact on Wesleyan membership in the localities where he worked,
but momentum was not sustained and at a national level numbers remained static.
During the 1830s and 1840s the more revivalistic Primitive Methodists propor-
tionally grew much more rapidly than the Wesleyan Methodists.[42]

These years also saw quite extensive revivals in Scotland and, above all, Wales.
Following some stirrings during the 1830s, a more full-blooded revival movement began in Scotland in the summer of 1839 at Kilsyth, originating in tradi-

---

[40]Charles G. Finney, *Lectures on Revivals of Religion*, 9th ed. (London, 1839), advertisement.
The British Library also holds a thirteenth edition (London: Simpkin and Marshall,
1840). American editions were included in this count, but British sales evidently
amounted to many thousands.

[41]Carwardine, *Transtlantic Revivalism*, pp. 71-77.

[42]Ibid., pp. 80-82, 107-33; Currie, Gilbert and Horsley, *Churches and Churchgoers*, pp. 140-41.

tional Presbyterian fashion in a Communion season, and stirred particularly by
the powerful outdoor preaching of the parish minister's son, William C. Burns, a
prospective overseas missionary. It transformed life in the parish and rapidly attracted large crowds from the Glasgow area, ten miles to the southwest.[43] During
the next year revivals spread more widely. In Dundee the catalyst was Burns's temporary ministry at St. Peter's in autumn 1839, but the ground had been prepared
since 1836 by the outstanding ministry of the parish minister Robert Murray
McCheyne (1813-1843). According to a contemporary observer, "the cries and
disquietude of arrow-stricken souls drew multitudes from every street and ally of
a crowded city of 60,000 inhabitants." The movement also touched Perthshire
and Angus, spreading west into Breadalbane, south into the Borders and north
into Strathbogie and Rossshire.[44] At Rosskeen on the Cromarty Firth the parish
minister wrote that the revival had especially affected the young, that "numbers"
had been "savingly converted," and that he was "enabled to preach frequently on
week days to attentive, impressed and weeping congregations."[45]

Wales in the early nineteenth century had been more revivalistic than any
other part of Britain except Cornwall, with periods of particular activity occurring in 1807-1809, 1815-1820 and 1828-1832.[46] Even here, however, the
mid-1830s saw a perceptible lull. Then in 1839 a Welsh translation of Finney's
Lectures appeared, fuelling a substantial new upsurge, which was popularly
known as "Finney's revival" although the American evangelist was not to cross
the Atlantic in person for another decade. Other factors at work included the
exertions of a Welsh-American itinerant evangelist, Benjamin Chidlaw, the enduring receptivity of Welsh churches to revivalism, and social and religious conditions that were arguably more comparable to those in the United States than
were those in other parts of Britain. This revival appears to have been relatively

---

[43]*Narratives of Revivals of Religion in Scotland, Ireland and Wales*, No. XI; Carwardine, *Transatlantic Revivalism*, pp. 94-97; Brown, *Thomas Chalmers*, pp. 324-26.

[44]Andrew Bonar, *The Life of Robert Murray McCheyne* (1843; Banner of Truth, 1960), p. 153; Alexander Smellie, *Biography of R. M. McCheyne: A Shining Light* (1919; Fearn: Christian Focus, 1995), p. 234.

[45]Quoted in Thomas Brown, *Annals of the Disruption* (Edinburgh: MacNiven and Wallace, 1892), p. 11.

[46]Thomas Rees, *History of Protestant Nonconformity in Wales* (London: J. Snow, 1861), p. 460; E. T. Davies, *Religion in the industrial revolution in South Wales* (Cardiff: University of Wales Press, 1965), p. 55.

subdued, by Welsh standards, "not being accompanied by the usual excitement and noisy manifestation of feeling."[47]

British North America in the second quarter of the century also maintained a strongly revivalistic religious culture, reminiscent both of recently settled regions of the United States, notably adjoining upstate New York, and of remoter parts of Britain, such as Cornwall, Wales and the west of Scotland. Extensive immigration from Britain ensured close links to movements at home. The Methodists were the primary driving force in Canadian revivals, but like the British Wesleyans they sought to control wilder manifestations. There was a surge of revival in Upper Canada in 1817-1818, and during subsequent decades itinerant preaching and camp meetings proved very effective in spreading and sustaining revivalism in sparsely populated regions. In a revival in 1841 Mathilda Chapel was described as "covered with the spiritually slain." Other denominations were also touched. The Presbyterians developed their distinctive pattern of revivals associated with Communion seasons and in 1831 also began to hold Finney-style protracted meetings. The Baptists in eastern Ontario experienced a series of powerful revivals, beginning in 1834-1836.[48]

In its final phase, between 1837 and 1844, the Second Great Awakening came closer than at any earlier date to becoming a genuinely international movement across the English-speaking world, shaped above all by the impact of Charles Finney. To some it might therefore seem ironic that in 1837 Finney himself appeared to retreat somewhat from the center of events by moving away from New York to Oberlin College in Ohio, which was to be his base for the rest of his life. Finney's move, though, reflected a preoccupation among American evangelicals at this period with the proclamation of the gospel on the western frontier. It can also be seen as more broadly symbolic of the important place of revivalism at the expanding edge of the English-speaking world. Although settled in the west, Finney returned to lead further

---

[47]Richard Carwardine, "The Welsh Evangelical Community and 'Finney's Revival'," *Journal of Ecclesiastical* History 29 (1978): 463-80; Rees, *Protestant Nonconformity in Wales*, p. 460.

[48]Marguerite Van Die, " 'The Double Vision': Evangelical Piety as Derivative and Indigenous in Victorian English Canada," in *Evangelicalism: Comparative Studies of Popular Protestantism in North America, the British Isles and Beyond, 1700-1990*, ed. Mark A. Noll, David W. Bebbington and George A. Rawlyk (New York: Oxford University Press, 1994), pp. 256-58; S. D. Clark, *Church and Sect in Canada* (Toronto: University of Toronto Press, 1948), pp. 90-172; *The Methodist Magazine* 2 (1818): 33-38.

revivals both on the east coast and in Rochester during the early 1840s. These were in some respects climactic years, with a return in the Methodist Episcopal Church at least to rates of growth not seen since the early years of the century. The spiritual atmosphere was an intense one, fueled in America by the approach of 1843, the year in which the Millerites proclaimed the second coming would take place, and in Britain by the tensions that culminated in the Disruption of the Church of Scotland in that very same year. Thereafter excitement subsided quite abruptly, although in 1849-1851 Finney was at last to visit England. Although he had a positive impact in the churches and districts where he preached, notably in a sustained campaign in London in 1850-1851, he failed to stir the kind of wider revival that had been triggered by his work in the United States two decades before. Finney had perhaps delayed this visit too long: by 1849 he was no longer a young man, but, more important, on both sides of the Atlantic the flames of revival had now, in most places, died down to an extent that was beyond even his skill to rekindle fully. Nevertheless, local and regional outbreaks continued—for example in Wales in 1849—and in the late 1850s there was to be a further great international upsurge, demonstrating that, although revivals ebbed and flowed, they remained a central feature of transatlantic evangelicalism.[49]

REVIVALS IN CONTEXT

A substantial historical, sociological and theological literature has been generated in attempts to explain and contextualize revivals.[50] One can identify a whole spectrum of presuppositions, from those that treat the supernatural intervention of the Holy Spirit as axiomatic and the motivations of participants as almost entirely

---

[49]Carwardine, *Transatlantic Revivalism*, pp. 51-53, 134-55; Rosell and Dupuis, *Memoirs of Finney*, passim.

[50]Good starting points for further reading are William G. McCloughlin, *Revivals, Awakenings and Reform: An Essay on Religion and Social Change in America* (Chicago: University of Chicago Press, 1978); Carwardine, *Transatlantic Revivalism*, pp. 54-56; David Hempton, "Evangelicalism in English and Irish Society, 1780-1840," in *Evangelicalism: Comparative Studies of Popular Protestantism in North America, the British Isles and Beyond, 1700-1990*, ed. Mark A. Noll, David W. Bebbington and George A. Rawlyk (New York: Oxford University Press, 1994), pp. 156-76; and, most recently, Michael J. McClymond, "Issues and Explanations in the Study of North American Revivalism," in *Embodying the Spirit: New Perspectives on North American Revivalism*, ed. Michael J. McClymond (Baltimore: Johns Hopkins University Press, 2004), pp. 1-46.

spiritual, to those that perceive revivals as merely a reflection of underlying economic and social tensions with specifically religious motivation barely acknowledged and divine action inconceivable. In the middle ground lay approaches that in varying measure acknowledge that human beings exist in a material and social world and are shaped by their environment, while at the same time recognizing that their religious and spiritual lives have a dynamic of their own, grounded for many in a conviction of the reality of personal encounter with the living God. For those operating in this intermediate intellectual territory, "social" approaches are viewed as complementary rather than antagonistic to "spiritual" ones: indeed, claims for the transformative impact of revival are more plausible if they are grounded in a convincing analysis of prior social patterns. It is worth noting, too, that in part at least recent historiographical debate mirrors the contemporary mid-nineteenth-century controversy about "new measures": can revivals be explained primarily in human terms, or should they rather be seen as the mysterious and unpredictable interventions of the Almighty? Now as then, there is room for legitimate difference of opinion among evangelicals themselves, as well as in the wider world of historical study.

Three more specific points are worthy of emphasis. First, revivals did not occur in a spiritual vacuum. When one looks closely there were always some preparatory factors at work, for example intense prayer by individuals or groups (as in Yorkshire in 1792-1793), a mounting crescendo of devotional or evangelistic activity (as in Kentucky in 1799-1801), or an awareness of revivals already underway elsewhere (as in the Southern United States in the early 1800s and the Northern United States in the early 1830s). In some regions and periods of time such conditions were almost continuously present, leading to self-fulfilling expectations of further revivals.

Second, material circumstances and events could be a significant catalyst. Communities experiencing economic difficulty, such as Yorkshire in the 1790s and Vermont in 1816, "the year of no summer," proved receptive to revival. The crash of 1837 appears to have been an important trigger for the notable upsurge of revival in the United States in that year. Alarm at cholera stimulated revival in 1831-1832 and again in 1849. More local factors such as fishing disasters in coastal communities or pit accidents in mining communities could also be significant. Conversely, economic prosperity or political excitement, such as popular radicalism in Britain in the 1790s, the war of 1812 in North

America, or agitation over slavery in the early 1830s, could dampen and divert revivalistic energies.

Third, revivals were inherently a time-limited and cyclical phenomenon. In the short term it was impossible for communities, sometimes on the margins of subsistence, to maintain intensive religious activity indefinitely when normal occupations required attention. Successful revivalists recognized the need to plan their gatherings by the calendar, holding camp meetings in the earlier part of the summer before the harvest, or protracted campaigns—such as that in Rochester in 1830-1831—in the winter, when scope for other activities was limited. In the medium term, surges of revival would burn themselves out when the supply of potential converts was exhausted, only to reignite a decade or two later when a new cohort of young people had reached a susceptible age and older people felt the need to have their faith reawakened. In the long term, the very success of the Second Great Awakening could not be sustained indefinitely. Reaction was inevitable from those who questioned the validity and utility of revivalistic styles of religious experience. Fanny Trollope, in her widely read *Domestic Manners of the Americans*, published in 1832, was scathingly critical of revivals and camp meetings, particularly because she thought women were manipulated into making public exhibitions of intense emotion. Even writers more sympathetic to evangelicalism raised significant questions and concerns.[51] At the same time the spectacular growth of new and revived denominations carried with it a creeping institutionalization and a growing caution toward unregulated spiritual impulses. In British North America the very success of revivals meant that by the 1830s, the Baptists and the Methodists had acquired substantial social influence and now sought to present themselves as respectable rather than radical movements. A similar trend was apparent among Methodists in the United States.[52] Finney's "new measures" were an appropriate

---

[51]Trollope, *Domestic Manners*, pp. 61-67, 137-45; James D. Bratt, "From Revivalism to Anti-Revivalism to Whig Politics: The Strange Career of Calvin Colton," *Journal of Ecclesiastical History* 52 (2001): 63-82.

[52]Michael Gauvreau, "Protestantism Transformed: Personal Piety and the Evangelical Social Vision," in *The Canadian Protestant Experience 1760-1990*, ed. George A. Rawlyk (Kingston and Montreal: McGill-Queen's University Press, 1990), p. 61; William Westfall, *Two Worlds: The Protestant Culture of Nineteenth-Century Ontario* (Kingston and Montreal: McGill-Queen's University Press, 1989), pp. 50-81; John H. Wigger, *Taking Heaven by Storm: Methodism and the Rise of Popular Christianity in America* (New York: Oxford University Press, 1998), pp. 190-95.

and powerful response to this development insofar as they made revivalism itself more institutionalized, predictable and controllable. However, while Finney's influence was crucial in prolonging the awakening into the 1830s and 1840s, he delayed rather than averted the loss of momentum that occurred in the middle of the century. Meanwhile, in the South, unvisited by Finney, the large-scale revivals of the early years of the century died down into limited local movements. Biracial Baptist churches were socially and religiously dominated by whites, offering little scope for revivalist black spirituality.[53] Under the leadership of Daniel Payne, who became bishop in 1852, even the African Methodist Episcopal Church was to move firmly down the path of ordered institutionalization.[54]

It remains to review the contribution of revivals to the wider process of evangelical expansion. Fluctuations in membership reveal that by no means all revival converts remained committed churchgoers. Conversely, much evangelical church growth occurred through the slow but steady recruitment of individuals rather than through the mass conversions associated with revivals. Such a pattern of marked but unspectacular expansion was in general characteristic of British evangelicalism in the early nineteenth century. It was also initially replicated in British colonies in the Southern Hemisphere, where both in Australia and Cape Colony evangelical church structures usually only developed gradually as the fruit of hard pastoral and missionary labor. There were, though, some localized outbreaks of revival in Australia from the mid-1830s onward, notably in Parramatta in 1840 where "many were converted," presaging an era of significant revivalism and numerical growth in Australian Methodism in the third quarter of the century.[55] In Britain and America, however, it was evident

---

[53]Samuel S. Hill, "Northern and Southern Varieties of American Evangelicalism in the Nineteenth Century," in *Evangelicalism: Comparative Studies of Popular Protestantism in North America, the British Isles and Beyond, 1700-1990*, ed. Mark A. Noll, David W. Bebbington and George A. Rawlyk (New York: Oxford University Press, 1994), p. 280; John B. Boles, ed., *Masters & Slaves in the House of the Lord: Race and Religion in the American South, 1740-1870* (Lexington: University Press of Kentucky, 1988), pp. 9-11.

[54]James T. Campbell, *Songs of Zion: The African Methodist Episcopal Church in the United States and South Africa* (New York: Oxford University Press, 1995), pp. 38-41.

[55]G. Mears, *Barnabas Shaw: Founder of South African Methodism* (Rondebosch: Methodist Missionary Department, 1957); W. D. Hammond-Tooke, *The Journal of William Shaw* (Cape Town: A. A. Balkema, 1972); Stuart Piggin, *Evangelical Christianity in Australia: Spirit, Word and World* (Melbourne: Oxford University Press, 1996), pp. 39-43.

as the period wore on, that the importance of revivals came to lay as much if not more in stirring and sustaining a sense of living faith among existing churchgoers and their children than in recruiting from previously untouched groups. Nevertheless, in its earlier, more explosive and uncontrolled phase, the Second Great Awakening had been a crucial catalyst giving evangelical Christianity a central role in cultures where its penetration had hitherto been limited or nonexistent, notably in Wales and among blacks in America. In general it was a movement that popularized and democratized evangelicalism: theologically, by its implicit and eventually explicit movement away from exclusive Calvinism, and socially, by drawing in working-class men and women whose faith was validated by their experience despite their lack of education.

The overall trend throughout the first half of the nineteenth century was continuing striking numerical expansion of evangelicalism, both in absolute numbers and relative to population. The Methodist figures for 1850 (see p. 70 above) show that there had been a further doubling in membership in Britain since 1820, and a quadrupling in the United States. In both countries Methodism also markedly increased its share of the population. As in earlier decades, though, the greater extent of Methodist progress in America may well be attributable, at least in part, to a more universal and enthusiastic embrace of revivals. A similar point can be made about the Baptists. Whereas their numbers grew strongly in England, to an estimated 122,000 Particular Baptists in 1851, this expansion was still dramatically overshadowed by that of their American counterparts, who had a reported membership of 622,478 in 1843. Also noteworthy was the increase in Welsh Baptist numbers to an estimated 35,000 in 1848, a much larger proportion of population than in England, and an indication that here, as in America, greater revivalism was helping to fuel expansion. On the other hand, among Congregationalists, whose relative caution toward revivals was evident on both sides of the Atlantic, growth rates were much more comparable, with memberships estimated at 160,000 in the United States in 1843 and 165,000 in England in 1851.[56]

Revivals also had an important impact on evangelical denominational structures, particularly where attitudes to them were divided, as they were among Presbyterians on both sides of the Atlantic and among Methodists in

---

[56]Currie, Gilbert and Horsley, *Churches and Churchgoers*, pp. 148, 151; Robert Baird, *Religion in the United States of America* (Glasgow and Edinburgh: Blackie and Son, 1844), p. 600.

Britain. The initially local splits among Kentucky Presbyterians in the early 1800s proved to have a lasting and widespread impact. Barton Stone's "Christians" eventually merged in 1832 with another radical group, the "Disciples of Christ," led by Alexander Campbell (1788-1866). This new denomination grew strongly, particularly in the upper South and lower Midwest, in the 1830s and 1840s, having an estimated membership of between 150,000 and 200,000 in 1843. In that year the Cumberland Presbyterians had a further 70,000 communicants. Meanwhile, in 1837-1838 the mainstream Presbyterians, whose overall strength was estimated at 243,000 in 1843, had split into "Old School" and "New School" churches.[57] The bitter disputes between these factions were driven by a range of theological and organizational issues, as well as by different attitudes to slavery, but "New School" support for Finney's revivalism was a significant factor in the schism. Similarly in Scotland, the upsurge in revival from 1839 was a factor stiffening the resolve of the Church of Scotland Evangelicals, who were currently defying the civil courts. In the Disruption of 1843 many of them were to secede to form the Free Church of Scotland. In this context McCheyne saw revival and the spiritual freedom of the church as opposite sides of the same coin. When in Strathbogie (Aberdeenshire) in the winter of 1839-1840 a court order in effect excluded Evangelical ministers from the churches, their defiant open-air preaching assumed a strongly revivalistic character.[58]

American Methodism was not immune to division. In addition to the separate black Methodist churches, in 1828-1830 the Protestant Methodists seceded because of their discontent at lack of lay representation in the decision-making processes of the Methodist Episcopal Church. Until conflict over slavery led to division on north-south lines in the 1840s, however, Methodism appeared more united in America than it was in Britain. Here the minor secessions at the turn of the nineteenth century and the larger-scale movement that was to become Primitive Methodism were followed from 1815 onward by the development of the Bible Christians in the west of England, in 1828 by the breakaway of the Protestant Methodists in Leeds, and in 1836 by the secession of the Wesleyan Methodist Association. Then around 1850 the departure of

---

[57]Figures from ibid.
[58]Smellie, *Biography of R. M. McCheyne*, p. 246. See below, pp. 220-21, for further explanation of the background to these events.

numerous Wesleyan Reformers reduced mainstream Wesleyan membership by over 50,000. Whereas conflicting attitudes to revivals were an important factor in the divisions with the Primitives and the Bible Christians, they were not so explicit in later splits. Nevertheless, the underlying tensions that gave rise to such repeated and painful divisions owed something to the legacy of a revivalistic tradition that had given ordinary Methodists a sense of spiritual dignity and empowerment, leading them to confront the perceived authoritarianism of the connectional leadership.

Not only did revivals transform evangelicalism itself, but they were also a crucial point of contact between the movement and the wider society, as a catalyst not only for individual spiritual renewal and commitment, but also for collective acceptance of profound changes in the social order. Thus they have been seen by historians as instrumental in, for example, both "the making of the English working class" and American adaptation to "the new market economy." In British North America, too, revivals led to "the dedication of entire communities to a new spirit of Christian behaviour and action."[59] Some aspects of these transformations will be explored further in later chapters of this book. They were the product of an impulse that, in North America at least, seemed to have become an intrinsic, albeit sometimes controversial, feature of evangelical Christianity. In 1843, the American Presbyterian Robert Baird wrote that revivals

> have become . . . a constituent part of the religious system of our country. Not a year has passed without numerous instances of their occurrence, though at some periods they have been more powerful and prevalent than at others. . . . There exists, indeed, a diversity of opinion as to the proper means of promoting them. . . . But, while these differences exist . . . all, or nearly all, agree that such a revival is an inestimable blessing: so that he who should oppose himself to revivals, *as such*, would be regarded by most of our evangelical Christians as *ipso facto* an enemy to spiritual religion itself.[60]

---

[59]E. P. Thompson, *The Making of the English Working Class* (Harmondsworth, U.K.: Penguin, 1968), pp. 385-440; Mark A. Noll, *America's God from Jonathan Edwards to Abraham Lincoln* (New York: Oxford University Press, 2002), pp. 188-89; Gauvreau, "Protestantism Transformed," p. 61.

[60]Baird, *Religion in America*, p. 456.

4

SPIRITUALITY
AND WORSHIP

I love Thy kingdom, Lord
The house of Thine abode,
The Church our blest Redeemer saved
With His own precious blood . . .

Beyond my highest joy
I prize her heavenly ways
Her sweet communion, solemn vows,
Her hymns of love and praise.[1]

Thus wrote Timothy Dwight, President of Yale, in what was to become one
of the most popular American hymns of the period, first published in 1801.
His lines point to both the personal and corporate dimensions of evangelical
relationships with God, which will be explored in this chapter. The subject is a
vast and complex one. Despite the apparent commonalities in evangelical convictions and religious experience, it is essential also to acknowledge and respect
the uniqueness of the interior spiritual lives of countless different human beings. In the majority of cases, of course, recollection of such personal struggles
and triumphs, exaltation and despair, faithfulness and backsliding, died with
the individuals who lived through them. Nevertheless, there remains a very ex-

---

[1] *Church Hymnary,* no. 462. Its popularity is indicated by its high frequency of publication in
compilations, as shown in figures presented by Stephen Marini to the "Hymnody in American Protestantism" conference at Wheaton College, Wheaton, Illinois, in May 2000.

tensive body of evidence available to historians in published memoirs, autobiographies and obituaries, and in manuscript letters and diaries. Exploration of this rich and as yet little studied material can, however, only be illustrative and not systematic. Similarly, corporate worship took many and diverse forms. Dwight's verses are especially evocative of the orderly but nonliturgical worship of New England Congregationalists, but in other places evangelical worship was shaped rather by the structures of Anglican liturgy, or the spontaneity of popular revivals. The physical environment of worship included ancient English and Scottish parish churches, the newer churches and meeting houses of American Protestants and British Nonconformists, and also the cottage and open-air meetings of the Methodists. Such diversity can be readily recognized, but its full delineation would require a substantial book in its own right.

THE CHRISTIAN LIFE

A survey of evangelical spirituality could readily take its starting point from David Bebbington's four identifying characteristics of evangelicalism: conversionism, biblicism, activism and crucicentrism. It is, indeed, easy to offer instances of these qualities at work in individual lives. For example, Sterling Coleman Brown, a native of Brunswick County, Virginia, born in 1795, was converted on October 9, 1817, when "the light of heaven shone into his heart" and he "found redemption through the atoning blood of Jesus."[2] Biblicism was powerfully apparent in the obituary of Lydia, a poor woman in the English Midlands who died in her mid-eighties in 1825. She retained the use of her eyes almost to the last and "employed much of her time in reading that book of books, as she often termed it, the Bible." She perceived it as her guide through life and trusted that "it will conduct me to eternal glory."[3] Joshua Hill, endeavoring to bring about moral and spiritual reform on Pitcairn Island in the South Pacific, was a formidable activist in his small and remote sphere. He arrived on October 28, 1832, and on March 25, 1833, reported to the Church Missionary Society that he had already established a Temperance Society to combat drunkenness, a "Maundy Thursday Society," monthly prayer meetings, a juvenile society with about a dozen youths, and a Peace Society. He was hold-

---

[2] *The Methodist Magazine* 5 (1823): 85.
[3] *The Christian Observer* 26 (1826): 126-27.

ing regular church services and had established a school of twenty to thirty children between ages four and seventeen. No one, surely, would dispute his claim that "I am doing all I can."[4] An eloquent implicit expression of crucicentrism is found in the lines of the hymnwriter James Montgomery, written in 1818:

> Faith in the only Sacrifice
> That can for sin atone,
> To cast our hopes, to fix our eyes,
> On Christ, on Christ alone.[5]

A picture of evangelical spirituality based merely on such particularly salient characteristics would, however, be liable to be a fragmentary and distorted one. In order to develop a more rounded picture, the subject will be approached through an overview of phases in the evangelical life cycle, before we turn in the next section to specific illustration by means of case studies.

The experience of the early years of life are inevitably visible primarily only through the eyes of parents and other adults, and through those of often distorted much later recollection. Children, though, from the very beginning, were liable to be the focus of intense spiritual concern by evangelical parents. Lyman Beecher prayed in 1800 on the birth of his first child, Catharine:

> Jesus! Thou former of the body and father of the spirit, accept as Thine the immortal soul Thou has ushered into life. Take, O take it to be Thine before it cling around my heart, and never suffer us to take it back again. May it live to glorify Thee on earth, and to enjoy Thee forever in heaven. Now, Lord, we look to Thee for grace to help us rear it for Thee,—may it be Thine forever, Amen and Amen.[6]

John Angell James recollected his mother "pouring her fervent and pious breathings over my infant head."[7] The variable moods of childhood could be variously interpreted as symptomatic of original sin or precocious spiritual and moral growth: thus the future leading Anglican evangelical Edward Bickersteth

---

[4]CMS, G/AC/15/75.

[5]Maurice Frost, ed., *Historical Companion to Hymns Ancient & Modern* (London: William Clowes & Sons, 1962), p. 312.

[6]Quoted in Marie Caskey, *Chariot of Fire: Religion and the Beecher Family* (New Haven, Conn.: Yale University Press, 1978), p. 71.

[7]Robert William Dale, ed., *The Life and Letters of John Angell James* (London: James Nisbet, 1861), p. 15.

(1785-1850) then gave "little promise of what he was afterwards to become," having "much natural obstinacy" and "affections somewhat cold." He recollected that when he was seven or eight he did of his own accord pray three times a day, "but this I soon neglected."[8] On the other hand, his fellow Anglican William Marsh (1775-1864) had a "tender sensitiveness" and even as a small child was thought to have "steadfastness and power of self-sacrifice," evidenced by his readiness to hand over his own toys to stop his siblings quarrelling.[9] Indications of precocious spiritual and moral development in young children could be a great source of comfort in the event of their early deaths, as they were taken as evidence that they had a place in heaven.[10]

Although ages at conversion in a sample of English Nonconformists ranged from eight to eighty, the great majority of conversions took place in the later teens and early twenties, with a tendency for the age at conversion to decrease somewhat in the later part of the period. In a post-Freudian age, it seems natural to note the coincidence with puberty and to speculate that sexual guilt played a part in the overwhelming consciousness of sin that led up to conversion.[11] Contemporary sources, though, presented awareness of sin in much more generalized terms: for example, a Lancashire girl named Margaret Parr became conscious of "guilt and danger" because "she was occasionally led by her companions, to places of public and worldly amusement, and to join in singing carnal songs, and practising sinful sports."[12] Conversion could be an almost instantaneous datable experience, as in the case of Sterling Coleman Brown, but for others it was more prolonged and less intense. John Angell James recalled that for him "there was no pungent conviction of sin, no poignancy of godly sorrow, no great and rapid transition of feeling, nor any very clear illumination of knowledge, but there were many evidences of a real

---

[8]T. R. Birks, *Memoir of the Rev. Edward Bickersteth*, 2 vols. (London: Seeleys, 1852), 1:4, 10.

[9]Catherine Marsh, *The Life of the Rev. William Marsh, DD* (London: James Nisbet, Hatchard, 1867), p. 2.

[10]For example, see the account of a small boy fatally injured in a road accident, who in his dying moments recited the Lord's Prayer and affirmed, "I am going to heaven," *Christian Observer* 25 (1825): 263-64.

[11]Michael R. Watts, *The Dissenters, Vol. II: The Expansion of Evangelical Nonconformity* (Oxford: Oxford University Press, 1995), p. 57; Linda Wilson, *Constrained by Zeal: Female Spirituality Among Nonconformists 1825-1875* (Carlisle: Paternoster, 2000), pp. 69-99.

[12]*The Primitive Methodist Magazine* 24 (1843): 46.

change."[13] For some conversion was followed by a sense of clear-cut, irrevocable commitment, articulated in quasi-legal language by one Episcopalian freshman at Brown University:

> I, Benjamin Clark Cutler, of Boston, now at Providence, December 13th, 1818, in the twenty-first year of my age, in firm health, and sound mind—feeling that I received all that I possess from God, having publicly professed the faith . . . do hereby solemnly (with death, judgment and eternity in view) give, covenant, and make over myself, soul and body, all my faculties, all my influence in this world, all the worldly goods with which I may be endowed, into the hands of my Creator, Preserver and constant Benefactor, to be his for ever, and at his disposal.[14]

Cutler was following the advice of the eighteenth-century English Congregationalist Philip Doddridge, whose *Rise and Progress of Religion in the Soul* had been republished in America in 1816, to engage in "an express act of self-dedication to the service of God."[15] For others initial conversion was less decisive and was followed by an extended period of backsliding or spiritual uncertainty. For example, William Sellars (b. 1791), later a Primitive Methodist local preacher in the Barnsley (Yorkshire) circuit, was initially converted at "about seventeen years of age" but subsequently was perplexed by intermittent "darkness and unbelief" for a period of eleven years. Only in 1820 did he secure "deliverance from his . . . captivity" through the visit of Primitive Methodist missionaries to his neighborhood.[16]

Just as conversion experiences differed, subsequent spiritual lives varied. Mary Ann Peaco, from Annapolis, Maryland, had been converted at the age of sixteen in the 1770s, but was "subject to a spiritual instability" until "about seven or eight years" before her death in 1817.[17] In 1814 Daniel Wilson, minister of the key Anglican chapel of St. John's, Bedford Row in London, heard that one of his protégés, John King, now a missionary in New Zealand, was wa-

---

[13]Dale, *John Angell James*, p. 34.

[14]Quoted in E. Clowes Chorley, *Men and Movements in the American Episcopal Church* (Hamden, Conn.: Archon Books, 1961), p. 54.

[15]Philip Doddridge, *The Rise and Progress of Religion in the Soul* (Brattleborough: John Holbrook, 1816), pp. 160-70.

[16]*The Primitive Methodist Magazine* 24 (1843): 241-42.

[17]*The Methodist Magazine* 1 (1818): 273.

vering from his first commitment. He addressed a passionate letter to King urging him to "remember your first love." Wilson did not mean to imply he was doing anything "positively wrong," but "I am still afraid you are less zealous, less devoted, less modest, less teachable than you were!"[18] For some, though, such fluctuations were normal and indeed spiritually creative. The Welsh hymn-writer Ann Griffiths (1776-1805) struggled with a sense of her persistent sinfulness and distance from God, an experience she graphically characterized as "spiritual whoring." Her verse, however, testified to the intensity of her spiritual and mystical experience when her prayers for divine support and refreshment were answered:

> Though it crosses human nature,
> this perplexing path I trace,
> I will travel on it gladly,
> while I see your precious face;
> take the cross as crown and gladly,
> through oppression and dismay,
> seek the city of fulfillment,
> by the straight though tortuous way.
> (From the Welsh "Er mai cwbwl groes i natur")[19]

Similarly, following his initial spiritual awakening, Edward Bickersteth wrote in February 1810 of experiencing much "coldness and deadness of my heart," but by late April he found he was enjoying "much of God's presence" and affirmed, "Come life, come death, come poverty, want, or disease; in Jesus Christ all is mine, and I am Christ's, and Christ is God's."[20]

Intense post-conversion spiritual experience was variously interpreted. For Bickersteth and his biographer it was seen merely as "a season of peculiar spiritual refreshment," which although symptomatic of ongoing growth in his inner life, did not mark any radical new departure.[21] For others, especially Method-

---

[18]Hocken Library, Dunedin (read on microfilm at Birmingham University Library), Samuel Marsden Papers, vol. 54, no. 34 (March 18, 1814).

[19]Ann Griffiths, *Hymns and Letters*, trans. Alan Gaunt and Alan Luff (London: Stainer and Bell, 1999), pp. 11, 56; A. M. Allchin, *Ann Griffiths: The Furnace and the Fountain* (Cardiff: University of Wales Press, 1987), pp. 25-35.

[20]Birks, *Bickersteth*, 1:103-5.

[21]Ibid., 1:104.

ists, feelings of this kind could be viewed as marking a distinctive new phase, in which by faith the believer received entire sanctification and renewed assurance of salvation.[22] More unusually for this period, Henry Drummond, the proto-charismatic and founder of the Catholic Apostolic Church, explicitly believed that he had received the baptism of the Holy Spirit. He described his experience as follows:

> I am . . . as conscious, as I am of my own existence, of a power within me yet distinct from me, not using me as a mere machine, but bending my will and affections to love to glorify Jesus; giving me a peace, and joy, and love for God and man passing all understanding so that while upon me I could willingly lay down my life for men.[23]

Such an unclouded experience of God could fuel an activist commitment that was absolute and unwavering. Following his own conversion Sterling Coleman Brown was fired with love for God and "an earnest desire to see sinners converted." He reportedly thought and spoke of nothing else. He began a frantic ministry as a Methodist preacher, which, although still only in his midtwenties, reduced him to exhaustion within four years. He died shortly afterward, affirming that this was preferable to living and not being able to preach the gospel. His obituarist commented, "Our brother Brown may properly be styled a martyr in the work of God."[24] Such cases of ministerial burnout arising from a sense of an overwhelming spiritual imperative to preach were "extremely common" in the United States, especially in periods of revival. A contrasting attitude, however, was voiced by the leading Presbyterian William Sprague, who thought such a pattern of behavior was irresponsible, if not positively sinful, because it threw away potential "years of usefulness." It had, he suggested, "less of the glory of martyrdom than of the guilt of suicide."[25]

Conscientious observance of Sunday was an important focal point of many

---

[22]For example, Nathan Bangs, a leading figure in American Methodism, regarded his sanctification on February 6, 1801, as more significant than his earlier conversion (George A. Rawlyk, *The Canada Fire: Radical Evangelicalism in British North America, 1775-1812* [Montreal and Kingston: McGill-Queens University Press, 1994], p. 115). See above, p. 49; David W. Bebbington, *Holiness in Nineteeth-Century England* (Carlisle: Paternoster Press, 2000), pp. 61-65.

[23]Chalmers Papers, CHA.4.178.25-26, Drummond to Chalmers (April 25, 1832).

[24]*Methodist Magazine* 6 (1823): 86-89.

[25]25 Chalmers Papers, CHA.4.228.69, Sprague to Chalmers (November 3, 1834).

spiritual lives, although, perhaps significantly, evidence on this point is more explicit for middle-class than for working-class evangelicals, for whom seclusion from the pressures of weekday life would often have been less practicable. Edward Bickersteth believed that his period of spiritual difficulty in 1809-1810 had begun with "a neglected Sabbath." Subsequently he resolved to spend Saturday evening in preparation, and considered ceasing to dine out with friends on Sunday evenings so that he could "stay at home, and employ my time more immediately on things relating to God."[26] George Barrell Cheever, a New England Congregationalist then visiting Britain, wrote to his mother on Sunday October 8, 1837, that the day had been "so sweet a Sabbath" and "so precious a season of the Lord's goodness" that he felt impelled to record something of "the Lord's mercies towards me." He resumed the letter the following Saturday, expressing his prayer that "the morrow be a blessed day, a precious Sabbath to us all."[27] Such sources highlight the mainspring of evangelical Sabbath observance as laying in the desire of individuals to secure and protect time with God. It was also perceived as a time for affirming and cultivating family life: the day when the roving Cheever turned his thoughts and prayers to his mother and sister in far-off Maine, and which William Wilberforce, despite the pressures of public life, always spent "in the midst of his family." "Never," his sons later recalled, "was religion seen in a more engaging form than in his Sunday intercourse with them."[28]

Throughout life, consciousness of the reality of death and eternity was never far away, and in due course the manner of a believer's death was perceived to be the ultimate test of his or her faith, and a source of vital testimony and inspiration to the living. Thus narratives of deathbeds were a crucial part of biographies. In his preface to the American edition of Charles Simeon's biography, the Bishop of Ohio, Charles Pettit McIlvaine, urged the reader to "direct his attention very particularly to Simeon's last hours," which he believed to be "peculiarly edifying."[29] A similar sentiment was

---

[26]Birks, *Bickersteth*, I:101, 103.

[27]American Antiquarian Society, Worcester, Mass., Cheever Papers, George Barrell Cheever to Charlotte Barrell Cheever (October 8, 14, 25, 1837).

[28]Quoted in Christopher Tolley, *Domestic Biography: The Legacy of Evangelicalism in Four Nineteenth-Century Families* (Oxford: Oxford University Press, 1997), p. 24.

[29]William Carus, *Memorials of the Right Reverend Charles Pettit McIlvaine* (London: Elliot Stock, 1882), p. 114.

voiced by *The Primitive Methodist Magazine:*

> The deathbed scenes of those who die in the Lord possess deep interest, and af-
> ford many solemn lessons to living christians. When the dying believer rejoices
> in the "full triumph of faith," we have evidence that his religious life has not been
> professional merely. Of all the inquiries respecting a man, that of "How did he
> die?" is the most important. What he was—who he was—how great—how tal-
> ented—how famed—how rich, are inquiries which sink into nothingness, com-
> pared with that of "How did he die?"[30]

Obituaries in Methodist periodicals characteristically dealt briskly with
events up to the onset of terminal illness and then recounted the final days and
weeks in great detail. The deathbed was perceived as the ultimate class meeting,
as an occasion for triumphant testimony to saving faith and the ritual affirmation of continuing fellowship in the hereafter.[31] Dying people themselves appear to have been well aware of the expectations placed upon them, and did
their best not to disappoint. Thus a soldier, fatally wounded in a shooting incident in Leicestershire in 1793, spoke of his vision of the loving, bleeding
Jesus, and somehow found the energy to preach at some length to those gathered round his bed.[32] Mrs. Hannah Howe, of Brandon, Vermont, who developed consumption in May 1812, was initially "much engaged with God in
prayer for resignation to his will." She came to speak about her impending
death with composure, affirmed that there was "mercy in Christ," and, as her
husband held her hand questioning her as to whether her confidence still held
out, "said 'Yes' and fell asleep in Jesus without a struggle or a groan."[33]

THREE CASE STUDIES

In order to give more specificity to discussion of evangelical spirituality, we turn
to three examples from strongly contrasting backgrounds: the prominent New
England Congregational minister Lyman Beecher (1775-1863), his first wife
Roxana (d. 1816) and their daughter Harriet (1811-1896); the pioneer black
Methodist evangelist Zilpha Elaw (c. 1790-c. 1850); and Anthony Ashley-

---

[30] *The Primitive Methodist Magazine* 24 (1843): 44.

[31] A. Gregory Schneider, "The Ritual of Happy Dying among Early American Methodists,"
Church History 56 (1987): 348-63.

[32] *The Arminian Magazine* 16 (1793): 647-50.

[33] *Methodist Magazine* 1 (1818): 23-24.

Cooper (Lord Ashley, later Earl of Shaftesbury, 1801-1885), the English philanthropist and social reformer. Any such choice of individuals is to some extent arbitrary and unrepresentative, but this one does cover the obvious distinctions of American and British, male and female, rich and poor, black and white, Anglican, Congregationalist and Methodist.

Lyman, the son of a prosperous blacksmith and farmer in New Haven, Connecticut, had a conventionally pious upbringing which produced a "serious-minded, conscientious" young man with "a settled fear of God and terror of the day of judgement."[34] He was converted in 1796 during his third year as a student at Yale. He recalled the process in classic evangelical terms as an initial despairing recognition of his sinfulness and lack of love for God, followed by a period of turmoil during which he "had no guidance but the sermons of Dr Dwight," then in his first year as president. Beecher struggled particularly in "the sloughs of high Calvinism," apparently believing himself under divine condemnation. Eventually "the light did not come in a sudden blaze, but by degrees" and he suffered continuing "alternations of darkness and discouragement."[35]

In 1797 Beecher, now settled on ordination, began his divinity studies under Dwight. He felt that "the conversion of the world to Christ was near" and saw himself as an agent of the divine purpose, following the "leadings of Providence" and "harnessed to the chariot of Christ." He paid attention to the writings of "great and good men," but always commenced his "investigations of Christian doctrines, duty, and experience with the teachings of the Bible."[36] Meanwhile, he had begun to court Roxana Foote, who had been brought up in the Episcopal Church, and during 1798 the two young people pursued an intense spiritual correspondence. Lyman continued to be tortured by intermittent despair at his own lack of genuine love for God and his fear that Roxana, who had professed conversion as a little girl, "had not had a true change of heart." At this time, her spiritual experience seemed sunnier and more secure than his. On August 13, she acknowledged an "extreme propensity to see everything in the most favourable point of view" and wrote that "I feel, I can-

---

[34]Charles Beecher, ed., *Autobiography, Correspondence &c of Lyman Beecher, DD,* 2 vols. (London: Sampson, Low & Co., 1863), I:22.

[35]Ibid., I:32-34.

[36]Ibid., I:51-54.

not help feeling a hope so strong that it has almost the effect of a certainty, that helpless myself, I shall have help from God." By August 31, Lyman, still feeling "like the troubled ocean, continually ebbing and flowing," had become anxious that in his efforts to verify the reality of her faith he was in fact disturbing it. He asked, though, whether her sense of joy came from resignation to God's will, or merely because of her sense of God's goodness to her. The latter, he implied, would be a selfish faith that would evaporate in the face of affliction. Roxana, however, found the distinction a false one:

> When recollection brings back the past, where can I look that I see not his good-
> ness? What moment of my life presents not instances of merciful kindness to me,
> as well as to every creature, more and greater than I can express—than my mind
> is able to take in? How then, can I help loving God because He is good to me?
> . . . I am not sensible that I ever in my life imagined anything but good could
> come from the hand of God. From a Being infinite in goodness everything must
> be good, though I do not always comprehend how it is so. . . . Sensible that af-
> flictions are but "blessings in disguise" I would bless the hand that with infinite
> kindness wounds only to heal, and equally love and adore the goodness of God
> in suffering as in rejoicing.

Lyman, it seems, was comforted and reassured. More than half a century later, long after her death, he was to endorse on this letter "Roxana beloved still." More whimsically, when the letters were read back to him, he said, "But if I had had *him* and *her* in one of my enquiry meetings, I could have set them right in half an hour."[37]

The mature Lyman Beecher did indeed exude spiritual clarity and confidence. His son recalled that "he went to men in the full and sublime conscious-ness of power, by the Spirit's aid, to show them that they were wrong and God right, and that all their complaints, cavils, objections, and accusations could be completely answered." When he left his first pastorate at East Hampton in 1810, he gave the congregation a brisk summary of his doctrinal beliefs, which showed a clear leaning to Calvinism, although he did not explicitly refer to them as such. It was essential to him, though, that assent to such teachings was supported by "credible evidence given of a change of heart, and saving faith, and evangelical repentance." He was no systematic or philosophical theologian,

---

[37]Ibid., 1:59-70.

but pursued a life of vigorous activism, convinced that his most profound in-
sights came not in the seclusion of his study, but in the spiritual white heat of
participation in revival. His outlook was also deeply biblicist: "No one ever felt
more deeply than he the fullness and sufficiency of the Bible and that by it the
man of God was thoroughly furnished to every good work."[38]

In September 1816, after seventeen years of happy marriage and the births
of numerous children, Roxana died of consumption. She had had presenti-
ments of death, saying to Lyman the previous winter that she had had a vision
of heaven and "I do not think I shall be with you long." As she lay dying, she
experienced an overwhelming sense of anticipation of heaven and said that "her
Saviour had constantly blessed her; that she had peace without a cloud." It was
reported that in the face of his bereavement Lyman "counts up all his mercies,
and talks of the goodness of God continually." Nevertheless, in the ensuing
months "great emptiness" set in and he prayed earnestly that God would either
take him too or "restore to me that interest in things and susceptibility to mo-
tive I had before."[39]

Harriet, the seventh of Lyman's and Roxana's children, was only five when
her mother died. In 1825, when she was fourteen, she was converted through
listening to one of her father's sermons, in which he spoke powerfully of the
friendship of Jesus for every human being. Although aware that she had not experienced the conviction of sin, that standard evangelical teaching held to be
the essential preliminary to conversion, she decided that if this was necessary,
Jesus would give it to her. Her "whole soul was illumined with joy" and she
went to her father in his study and told him, "I have given myself to Jesus, and
He has taken me." She never forgot his "sweet . . . gentle" expression, and the
way in which he held her silently and wept for joy. He had now learned the wisdom of not probing too painfully into the faith of those close to him. Others,
though, were not so sensitive, and when the following year Harriet began to attend church in Hartford, Connecticut, ill-judged questions from the pastor left
her feeling that "my sins take away all my happiness." She remained for some
time in a "dark, desolate" state, but, counseled by her brother Edward, she
turned back to God and "felt as if restored, nevermore to fall." Her initial

---

[38]Ibid., 1:169-71; 2:581-85.
[39]Ibid., 1:257-64.

happy experience of Jesus' friendship remained elusive, however, and she now found herself wondering whether it was possible to experience the presence of God in a manner such "that He can supply the place of earthly friends."[40] Her sense of spiritual realities was a profound and growing one, however: in 1830, as a healthy nineteen-year-old, who had more than six decades of life in front of her, she wrote of her sense of the shortness of life and of living on the verge of the eternal world. Nevertheless, she admitted that she could not sustain a high spiritual pitch indefinitely: she hoped that there would be laughter, in heaven and reflected that "a smiling face recommends religion more than almost any thing I can name."[41]

Harriet's subsequent life and spiritual experience were to be associated more with suffering than with laughter. Marriage to Calvin Stowe in 1836 brought her fulfillment of a kind, but also money worries, a hypochondriac husband, and the devastating early deaths of two of their children, Charles in infancy in 1849, and Henry, her beloved eldest son, who drowned in 1857 before he had made public profession of his faith. In the meantime, the sufferings of the slaves in the Southern United States inspired her in 1851-1852 to write *Uncle Tom's Cabin,* the great novel that projected her to immediate transatlantic fame and was arguably a major factor contributing to the growth of anti-slavery feeling in the decade before the American Civil War. The climax of the novel comes as the saintly and grossly maltreated slave Uncle Tom finds "victory" over his sufferings through the vision "of one crowned with thorns, buffeted and bleeding," and the face of that same Jesus bending toward him and speaking the words of Revelation 3:21, "He that overcometh shall sit down with me on my throne." Herein was a profoundly crucicentrist spirituality, but one that dwelt more on the suffering of Christ as the supreme exemplar for humanity than on its significance in satisfying the wrath of God against human sinfulness, the emphasis of mainstream evangelical belief. By the 1850s Harriet's ideas, in common with those of several of her siblings, were thus exploring more liberal and romantic varieties of Christianity. She retained, however, some of her spiritual moorings to her father's evangelicalism, including his intense sense of the reality

---

[40] Annie Fields, *Life and Letters of Harriet Beecher Stowe* (London: Sampson Low, 1897), pp. 50-53, 61-62.

[41] Stowe-Day Library, Hartford, Conn., Harriet to George Beecher (February 20, 1830[?], July 21, 1830, March [1831?]).

of God and of the prospect of heaven for believers.[42]

Powerful and moving as it was, Harriet Beecher Stowe's portrayal of slave religious experience was a second-hand and fictional one and, despite the very real hardships she faced, her circumstances were comfortable and secure in comparison to the situation of most African Americans, whether slaves or free. The autobiography of Zilpha Elaw, born in the Philadelphia area probably around 1790, gives some contrasting first-hand insight into the life and spiritual experience of an African American woman.

Zilpha was one of twenty-two children, only three of whom survived infancy. By the time she was fourteen both her parents had also died, and she was living as a servant with a family to whose care her father had consigned her. Her teenage conversion was prompted by a frightening dream of the day of judgment, and then by the conviction that Jesus appeared to her while she was milking a cow, a manifestation that also seemed to affect the animal. During the next few years she experienced "habitual communion with . . . God," an "overflowing stream of love" in her soul, and a sense of spiritual adoption. Meanwhile, in 1808 she joined a local Methodist society, and in 1810 married Joseph Elaw.[43]

Zilpha's marriage brought tensions with it, as she judged that her husband, despite his professed Christianity, "had never tasted of the pardoning love of God through the atonement of Jesus Christ." Nevertheless, now living in Burlington, New Jersey, she attended a Methodist class meeting and "grew in grace daily." The next landmark in her spiritual life came in 1817, when at a camp meeting she experienced a "trance or ecstasy" in which she felt overpowered by the presence of God and sank prostrate on the ground. It seemed that her spirit ascended "into the clear circle of the sun's disc" and she heard a voice saying, "Now thou art sanctified: and I will show thee what thou must do." Before the meeting closed she felt the Holy Spirit reveal to her a calling to visit families and to speak to them "of the salvation and eternal interests of their souls." At a subsequent camp meeting, in about 1821, she again fell into a trance and

---

[42]Caskey, *Chariot of Fire*, pp. 169-207; Harriet Beecher Stowe, *Uncle Tom's Cabin*, ed. Ann Douglas (New York: Penguin, 1986), p. 554.

[43]"Memoirs of the Life, Religious Experience, Ministerial Travels and Labors of Mrs Zilpha Elaw," reprinted in *Sisters of the Spirit: Three Black Women's Autobiographies of the Nineteenth Century*, ed. William L. Andrews (Bloomington: Indiana University Press, 1986), pp. 53-61.

heard a voice speaking to her: "Thou must preach the gospel; and thou must travel far and wide."[44]

Zilpha's husband died in January 1823, leaving her with burdensome debts and a young daughter. She worked as a servant and then opened a school with a view to raising funds as well as educating colored children. When, however, after two years her financial situation still remained difficult, she decided that she must obey God's command to go and preach the gospel, "whatever might become of me." Leaving her daughter with a relative, she began an extensive and powerful itinerant Methodist ministry taking her to many parts of the United States and eventually, in 1840, across the Atlantic to England. In Zilpha's worldview supernatural forces were never far away: she clearly believed the course of her journeyings to be guided by God, and saw the success of her ministry as evidence of divine favor. Opposition or discouragement, such as her well-founded fear of being arrested and sold into slavery when she visited the Southern states, was seen as the work of Satan. Her language and Christian experience were steeped in scriptural resonances: for example, God's initial word to her that she would eventually go to London, "that great city," to preach the gospel carried an obvious echo of the divine command to Jonah (Jon 1:2; 3:2) to go to Nineveh.[45]

Zilpha published her memoirs in London in 1846, announcing in the dedication her intent to return to "the occidental land of my nativity." Nothing, however, is known of her subsequent life and she may well have died in obscurity before arriving back in the United States. The memoirs, indeed, were consciously valedictory and concluded with a summary of her spiritual priorities. She urged her Christian friends to take every opportunity for "attendance on the means of grace." She extolled particularly the value of class meetings, which she believed resembled the meetings of the primitive church, as a means by which "the weary soul is invigorated, the doubting mind confirmed, the dismayed heart encouraged: the tempted are instructed, the heedless are admonished, and the lukewarm stimulated." She affirmed her conviction that there "is but one church of Jesus Christ in this wilderness," destined amidst the ominous signs of the times soon to stand forth in its true beauty and

---

[44]Ibid., pp. 61-82.
[45]Ibid., pp. 84-159.

power. In the dedication she further urged Christians to shun the love of money, to clothe themselves with humility and to avoid "an infidel, obscene or disloyal newspaper press." They should focus rather on the study of the Scriptures, seeking to follow the pattern and teaching of Christ and the apostles, "that you may become His true and finished disciples, perfect and entire, lacking nothing, but complete in all the will of God."[46]

Anthony Ashley-Cooper's material circumstances were strikingly different both from the genteel poverty of the Beechers and from the real hardship faced by Zilpha Elaw. Born in 1801 into the English aristocracy, he enjoyed wealth and security. He was styled Lord Ashley from boyhood and in 1852 was to succeed his father as Earl of Shaftesbury. His spiritual experience also varied significantly, in that he had no specifically dated conversion experience and did not develop distinctively evangelical views until he was in his early thirties. Nevertheless, his early years did have an important formative impact on his spiritual life. As an emotionally deprived child, with cold and distant parents, he was strongly influenced by a family servant named Maria Millis, who gave him genuine affection and early religious teaching. He grew into an intelligent and introspective young man, who entered parliament in 1826. His diary showed strong but unfocused ambition to change his country for the better, and a firm but doctrinally unspecific commitment to "religion" which, he believed, must be "our guide . . . our beginning [and] . . . our end." He also had "a great mind to found a policy upon the Bible" and was inspired by meditating upon it.[47]

Ashley served as a junior government minister from 1828 to 1830, married Emily ("Minny") Cowper in 1830, and in 1832 began his involvement in the factory reform campaigns with which his name was to be associated. It was only in 1834, though, that his diaries and writings began to show a clear-cut identification with evangelicalism, expressed in his conviction of the depravity of the human heart and "of the great, necessary and most comfortable doctrine of the Atonement." His reverence for the Bible increased, he became more scrupulous about observance of the Sabbath, and noted his scorn for those who treated religion as "an acquaintance lately introduced whom they treat with ci-

---

[46]Ibid., pp. 51-52, 159-60.

[47]Edwin Hodder, *The Life and Work of the Seventh Earl of Shaftesbury, K.G.*, 3 vols. (London: Cassell, 1886), 1:54, 71, 76 (diary entries for October 13, 1825; August 9, November 4, 1827).

vility, but are rather pleased to get rid of." In 1835 Ashley met Edward Bicker-steth, now a respected leader of Anglican Evangelicals, whose theology had a strong influence on him, particularly in leading him to adopt a belief in the premillennial advent of Christ. Ashley's evangelicalism, like Bickersteth's, was integrated with a firm commitment to continuing the links between church and state and to sustaining the liturgy of the Church of England, including the "soul-inspiring worship" of the great cathedrals as a means of diffusing due reverence for God.[48]

For Ashley, as for Lyman Beecher and Zilpha Elaw, evangelical spirituality fueled an intense activism, reflecting his conviction of divinely appointed calling to labor for "the advancement of His ever-blessed name, and the temporal and eternal welfare of all mankind."[49] For him, however, the chosen sphere of action was politics rather than preaching. He had a strong sense of accountability to God, both for his own decisions and stewardship of time, and on behalf of the nation, which he believed must be prompted to act in accordance with Christian principles. Hence his interests extended from domestic social reform to questions of imperial and foreign policy. His mental and spiritual temperament was an introspective and at times depressive one, in which his faith was no security against discouragement. He was also strikingly lacking in the impulsive quality that led other evangelicals to follow their sense of the direct guidance of the Holy Spirit. An observer wrote of him in 1838, "All that Lord Ashley does seems to be done from conviction and principle, and not even a muscle dares to move without an order from head-quarters."[50]

Family life revealed different aspects of Ashley's nature. Minny identified with his evangelicalism, while lightening the intense and somber side of his nature. It was a marriage of deep happiness, but was later to be clouded by tragedy, notably in the death in 1849 at the age of sixteen of their second son, Francis. Ashley's moving diary account of this event gives a revealing insight into the spiritual lives of both father and son. In the earlier stages of the illness, when there was still realistic hope of recovery, Ashley was consoled by his son's sense

---

[48]Geoffrey B. A. M. Finlayson, *The Seventh Earl of Shaftesbury* (London: Eyre Methuen, 1981), pp. 103-5; Hodder, *Shaftesbury*, 1:203, 279, 288-89 (diary entries for December 10, 1834; October 15, 1839; January 23, 1840).

[49]Hodder, *Shaftesbury*, 2:359 (diary entry for December 25, 1851).

[50]Quoted in ibid., 1:228.

of his sin and unworthiness. They "read and talked much of the free and full mercy of God in Christ Jesus." Francis professed himself reconciled to God and thanked his father for the religious upbringing that meant his repentance was no mere deathbed matter. When Francis died, his father was devastated but resigned, convinced that "the child . . . is with Christ, which is far better." He speculated on God's purposes in the bereavement, seeing it as a potential means of awakening faith in others, both among his son's schoolfellows and his family, as a striking demonstration of divine grace, but also, paradoxically, as a kind of chastisement to himself. In the end, though, he returned to the conviction that "my own dear, precious, darling son is taken to everlasting glory." On Francis's gravestone was inscribed a central tenet of evangelicalism—"he only sought forgiveness in the free love and mercy of God through the atonement of a crucified Saviour"—and in his own unshaken confidence in the reality of eternal life for the believer Ashley affirmed another cornerstone of early nineteenth-century evangelical spirituality.[51]

WORSHIP

The development of evangelical worship in this era of rapid expansion involved particularly acute tensions between inherited structures and pressures for innovation and adaptation. Church-buildings and furnishings themselves imposed constraints and assumptions, about the authority of leaders and preachers and the extent of congregational participation, about the relative prominence of liturgy and preaching, and about the role and nature of music in services. There was, of course, no straightforward distinction between private spirituality and public worship. It is more appropriate to think in terms of a spectrum, from solitary devotion at one end to large gatherings, whether Sunday services or camp meetings, at the other. In between was a plethora of more or less formal activities, including prayer meetings, Methodist class meetings and mid-week services and sermons from itinerant preachers. Such gatherings played a crucial part in the spread and maintenance of evangelical convictions and devotion. Paradoxically, too, there were also occasions, above all in the intensity of the early camp meetings, when encounter with God could simultaneously be very public, in the context of an assembly of thousands of people, and very private,

---

[51]Ibid., 2:283-88 (diary entries for May 21 to June 7, 1849).

in the depth of individual spiritual experience. Moreover, hymns also served powerfully to link collective and personal affirmations of faith.

For Anglicans and Episcopalians the basic structure of worship was determined by the liturgy of the *Book of Common Prayer.* In general Evangelicals appear readily to have accepted and even to have welcomed this constraint. Charles Simeon and other Anglicans were devoted to the liturgy, and in the late eighteenth and early nineteenth centuries Evangelicals took the lead in reviving and extending observance of holy Communion in the Church of England.[52] In Maryland, when in 1822 the High Church Bishop Kemp charged Evangelical clergy with attempting to "mutilate and change the Liturgy," they responded by arguing that their variations in practice, which included the use of hymns and informal prayers, were confined to matters "which every man's own judgement must regulate for himself." In 1838 the Evangelical Bishop Meade of Virginia described the *Book of Common Prayer* as "the most perfect of all liturgies."[53]

Among Methodists, too, the initial legacy of John Wesley was one of structured liturgical worship, as set out in his *Sunday Service of the Methodists*, a modified version of the *Book of Common Prayer*, which he first drew up in 1784. This publication was intended particularly for use in America, but it was in Britain that it was most rapidly repudiated, immediately after Wesley's death, in the *Discipline* of 1792. Directions were here given for a much simpler form of morning service, consisting of "singing, prayer, the reading of a chapter out of the Old Testament, and another out of the New, and preaching." Such a form of service was obviously better suited to the frontier congregations of early American Methodism.[54] In Britain, on the other hand, there was more lasting adherence among Wesleyan Methodists not only to Wesley's service book but also to the *Book of Common Prayer* itself. Practice varied, however, and other Methodist traditions, such as the Bible Christians and the Primitives, followed from the outset a similar non-liturgical form of worship to the Americans. On both sides

[52]Horton Davies, *Worship and Theology in England III: From Watts and Wesley to Maurice, 1690-1850* (1961; Grand Rapids: Eerdmans, 1996), pp. 223-24.

[53]Chorley, *Men and Movements*, pp. 86-87.

[54]Raymond George, "The People called Methodists—4. The Means of Grace," in *A History of the Methodist Church in Great Britain*, ed. Rupert Davies, A. Raymond George and Gordon Rupp, 4 vols. (London: Epworth Press, 1965), 1:259-73; Karen B. Westerfield Tucker, *American Methodist Worship* (New York: Oxford University Press, 2001), pp. 8-9.

of the Atlantic Methodism professed a devotion to the Lord's Supper that was greater than contemporary Anglican practice. Wesleyans in Britain were exhorted in 1806 to attend "at least once in every month," whether in their own chapels or at Anglican churches. An American direction of 1791 even advocated weekly Communion, although this rapidly gave way to the more realistic "at every opportunity," which for many would have been only at quarterly intervals. American Methodists also abbreviated and simplified the Anglican Communion service. Greater informality was also apparent among non-Wesleyan Methodists in Britain who, while sharing a commitment to regular observance of the sacrament, did not follow prescribed liturgies at all. Meanwhile, alongside rituals inherited from Anglicanism, Methodists enthusiastically adopted a rich range of other rituals, including love feasts, covenant services and watch-night services. These "great festivals" of Methodism were fertile soil for revivals.[55]

Congregationalists and Presbyterians were less constrained than Anglicans in respect of the precise detail of public worship, and indeed rejected liturgy as such, but they were still under pressure to conform to overall expectations of order and decorum. There was little difference in styles of worship between the United States and Britain, although an American visitor to England in 1828 was struck by the "solemn pause" that occurred at the end of the service in Dissenting chapels there, which he thought much preferable to the "bustle and confusion" in churches at home, as the congregation got up immediately to leave.[56] The development of the early camp meetings out of Presbyterian Communion seasons was testimony to unrealized potentialities in the tradition, but subsequent measures to control them indicated the limits of flexibility. Tensions continued to be very much apparent, especially among Presbyterians, both in Scotland and in the United States, where differing approaches to worship were a significant factor in the split into Old School and New School churches in 1837. Broadly speaking, the Old School emphasized what they held to be scriptural principles of restraint and good taste, while the New

---

[55]Norman P. Goldhawk, "The Methodist People in the Early Victorian Age: Spirituality and Worship," in *A History of the Methodist Church in Great Britain*, ed. Rupert Davies, A. Raymond George and Gordon Rupp, 4 vols. (London: Epworth Press, 1978), 2:123-38; Tucker, *American Methodist Worship*, pp. 60-81, 125-26.

[56]W. B. Sprague, *Letters from Europe in 1828* (New York, 1828), p. 91.

School sought to enhance their evangelistic impact through measures such as more fervent preaching and congregational hymn-singing.[57]

Indeed, the preeminence given to preaching was a universal feature of evangelical worship, and during this period hymn-singing became an almost equally dominant characteristic. Preaching the gospel was the central and defining role of Methodist itinerants, to which other aspects of worship were ancillary. Thus when Nathan Bangs itinerated in Upper Canada in the early years of the nineteenth century, he introduced himself to congregations as follows:

> I am bound for the heavenly city, and my errand among you is to persuade as many as I can to go with me. I am a Methodist preacher; and my manner of worship is to stand while singing, kneel while praying, and then to stand while I preach, the people meanwhile sitting.[58]

In evangelical churches and chapels the pulpit was usually the most conspicuous physical feature of interiors. It was positioned so as to allow the preacher maximum opportunities for eye contact with the congregation, and in a galleried building it would be raised well above the floor so as to ensure a good view for those seated on the upper level. This consideration was taken to its extreme in the theater-like interiors used by Charles Finney during his New York ministry.

Obituaries and other accounts of leading evangelical ministers consistently showed a strong interest in their performance in the pulpit, which was a matter of spiritual and emotional style quite as much as theological and intellectual substance. In his later years, in the midst of his endless traveling around the United States, Bishop Francis Asbury's preaching suffered from lack of preparation time, being characterized more by "weighty and judicious thoughts" than by "sustained or consecutive course of argument," but there was no doubt that "he spoke out of a heart warmed with the love of souls, and moved by the powers of the world to come." Asbury once urged a colleague to "feel for the power, feel for the power, brother."[59] Robert Hall (1764-1831), a revered English Baptist preacher, initially seemed unprepossessing, but, "His manner, as he

---

[57]Julius Melton, *Presbyterian Worship in America: Changing Patterns since 1787* (Richmond, Va.: John Knox Press, 1967), pp. 28-58.

[58]Quoted in Rawlyk, *Canada Fire*, p. 119.

[59]Ibid., pp. 18, 22; quoted in John H. Wigger, *Taking Heaven by Storm: Methodism and the Rise of Popular Christianity in America* (New York: Oxford University Press, 1998), p. 77.

advanced, became powerfully impressive . . . and his burning thoughts seemed
to brighten every feature of his countenance, and nerve every muscle of his
frame." His eloquence was not contrived, but "seemed rather the natural and
simple operation of a mind, which could not move without leaving behind it a
track of glory."[60] When, after a period of illness, Charles Simeon was able to
return to preaching, "the prospect of again standing there to speak for his
Lord" was to his soul like "honey and the honeycomb." When he preached,
"his countenance was heavenly" and "he seemed perfectly absorbed in devotional meditation."[61] A similar quality was perceived in the preaching of the
American Methodist Wilbur Fisk (1792-1839):

> You could not hear him preach without being deeply impressed with the convic-
> tion that every word that he uttered came from his inmost soul; and his simple
> earnest utterances would produce an effect upon you that no tricks of oratory
> ever could produce.[62]

Successful evangelical preachers adapted their style to their audience and situation. Educated urban congregations expected and generally received relatively
intellectual and theologically sophisticated sermons from university and college
graduates. Thus when Timothy Dwight, formerly minister of Greenfield, Connecticut, was elevated to the presidency of Yale in 1795, he reportedly elabo-
rated "his pulpit efforts more than he had found necessary in the comparatively
retired station, which he had previously occupied." In his preaching Dwight
bore in mind above all "that man is an intellectual being."[63] On the other hand,
preachers who aimed primarily at a popular constituency, and often themselves
had limited education, adopted a much more informal style. Hugh Bourne, the
founder of Primitive Methodism, recalled that, tongue-tied when preaching his
first sermon, "it came to my mind to preach as if speaking to one person."[64]
Primitive Methodist preachers were urged not to allow the "excellency of

---

[60]Sprague, *Letters from Europe*, pp. 111-12.

[61]Carus, *Memorials of McIlvaine*, p. 56.

[62]W. B. Sprague, *Annals of the American Methodist Pulpit* (New York, 1861), p. 586 (quoting
Nathan Bangs).

[63]William B. Sprague, *Life of Timothy Dwight*, in *The Library of American Biography Vol. XIV* (Boston, 1845), pp. 282, 286-87.

[64]John Walford, *Memoirs of the Life and Labours of the Late Venerable Hugh Bourne* (London, 1855),
pp. 76-77.

speech or wisdom" to obscure the simple "truth as it is in Jesus."[65] Successful popular preachers developed their own distinctive techniques to hold a congregation's attention. Lorenzo Dow engaged in sometimes crude humor and repartee, and would smash chairs for effect or arrange for a trumpet to blow. Charles Finney gripped the urban professional classes with logical argument that reflected his legal training, punctuated by moments of high drama such as his vivid evocation of the smoke of the torment of sinners in hell, prompting the audience to imagine that they could see it themselves.[66]

In the first volume of this series, Mark Noll emphasized the importance of hymns as an individual and corporate expression of the characteristic spiritual emphases of early evangelicalism.[67] Nevertheless, during the eighteenth century legal constraints and the conservatism of congregations had limited their presence in formal Sunday worship, especially among Anglicans and Presbyterians. In the later eighteenth century Evangelicals in the Church of England, such as John Newton, were probably more comfortable using hymns in mid-week devotional meetings than in public church services. In many places congregational singing was still restricted to texts directly based on Scripture, metrical psalms and paraphrases of other biblical passages (for example, Nahum Tate's "While shepherds watched"). Although the hymns of Isaac Watts (1674-1748) were gaining increasing acceptance, as much if not more in America than in his native England, even these were too innovative for some. For example, the Third Presbyterian Church in Philadelphia started to use Watts's hymns in 1788, but the Presbyterians in small-town Carlisle, Pennsylvania, 100 miles to the west, did not do so until 1824.[68]

---

[65] *Primitive Methodist Magazine* 24 (1843): 293.

[66] Nathan O. Hatch, *The Democratization of American Christianity* (New Haven, Conn.: Yale University Press, 1989), p. 130; Keith J. Hardman, *Charles Grandison Finney 1792-1875: Revivalist and Reformer* (Grand Rapids: Baker, 1987), pp. 201-2, 207.

[67] Mark A. Noll, *The Rise of Evangelicalism: The Age of Edwards, Whitefield and the Wesleys* (Leicester, U.K.: Inter-Varsity Press, 2004), pp. 260-69.

[68] Bruce Hindmarsh, *John Newton and the English Evangelical Tradition* (Oxford: Clarendon Press, 1996), pp. 258-66; John Wolffe, " 'Praise to the Holiest in the Height': Hymns and Church Music," in *Religion in Victorian Britain V: Culture and Empire*, ed. John Wolffe (Manchester: Open University/Manchester University Press, 1997), pp. 62-63; Henry Wilder Foote, *Three Centuries of American Hymnody* (Cambridge, Mass.: Harvard University Press, 1940), p. 154.

In the period between 1790 and 1850, however, hymns gained much more general acceptance. Their dissemination was facilitated by pioneering compilations, above all John Wesley's *Collection of Hymns for the Use of the People Called Methodists* (1780) and the Baptist John Rippon's *Selection of Hymns from the Best Authors* (1787). Both works went through numerous reprints and were widely used on both sides of the Atlantic.[69] In the Church of England a key role was played by Thomas Cotterill, an Evangelical clergyman in Sheffield, who compiled a hymnbook that went through numerous editions. Cotterill argued that all members of congregations should join in singing and that, although a choir was useful in providing a lead, they should not be "sole performers." When in 1819 Cotterill, in collaboration with the hymnwriter James Montgomery, brought out an eighth "considerably enlarged" edition of his book, he provoked legal action from members of his own congregation. The eventual decision of the archbishop of York in 1820 in Cotterill's favor in effect gave authoritative sanction to the inclusion of hymns in Sunday worship, thus opening the door to their much wider adoption in the second quarter of the century.[70] Cotterill's collection was superseded in 1833 by Edward Bickersteth's *Christian Psalmody*, which rapidly came to dominate the Anglican market, selling 226,000 copies by the time of its compiler's death in 1850.[71] Meanwhile, American Episcopalians had already included a few hymns in their 1790 prayer book, and in 1827 published their own approved hymnbook.[72]

The acceptance of hymns among Presbyterians and Congregationalists in the United States followed a similar chronology. While British Congregationalists benefited from Rowland Hill's *Collection of Psalms and Hymns* (1784) and Ralph Wardlaw's *Selection of Hymns for Public Worship* (1803), an initial landmark in America was the publication of Timothy Dwight's edition of Watts in 1801, which also included some of his own paraphrases, notably "I love thy kingdom

---

[69]John Julian, ed., *A Dictionary of Hymnology* (London, 1907), pp. 112, 727-27; Foote, *American Hymnody*, p. 171.

[70]T. Cotterill, *A Selection of Psalms and Hymns for Public and Private Use, Adapted to the Services of the Church of England*, 8th ed. (Sheffield, 1819), pp. xiv, xv; Julian, *Dictionary of Hymnology*, pp. 334; Wolffe, "Praise to the Holiest," p. 63.

[71]Edward Bickersteth, *Christian Psalmody, A Collection of Above 900 Psalms, Hymns and Spiritual Songs Selected and Arranged for Public, Social, Family and Private Worship* (London: Dean & Son, 1850), title page.

[72]Foote, *American Hymnody*, pp. 167, 193-95.

Lord." It was produced at the request of the Congregational General Association of Connecticut and subsequently approved by the General Assembly of the Presbyterian Church. Asahel Nettleton's *Village Hymns for Social Worship* (1824) did not gain such official sanction, but was still popular and influential in New England, giving currency to hymns from more recent writers than Watts. Scottish Presbyterians, though, were in this respect noticeably more conservative than their American counterparts. Here a refusal to move beyond metrical psalms and paraphrases was still widespread even in the middle of the nineteenth century, although Presbyterian Dissenters, such as the Relief Synod, were more progressive in this matter than the Church of Scotland.[73]

Quite apart from legal obstacles and denominational inertia, the diffusion and acceptance of new hymns was a slow process. Initial publications were likely to have a limited circulation or to be ephemeral in character, and wider use was crucially dependent on their inclusion in the compilations that appeared in increasing numbers during this period. When in the 1830s Wesley's 1780 collection was still being republished in the United States with little revision and no American hymns at all, it had become a force for conservatism rather than innovation. By contrast, the 1827 Episcopalian hymnbook gave space to recent American compositions, but did not give much recognition to any English hymnwriters later than Wesley.[74] During the second quarter of the nineteenth century, compilations on both sides of the Atlantic began to give more space to newer hymns, but in most cases there would have been a further time lag before these became generally available and accepted by congregations. Thus in the first half of the nineteenth century the hymns most widely sung by evangelicals were eighteenth-century rather than contemporary ones, with Watts and early Methodist writers such as John Cennick and Charles Wesley continuing very popular. Later eighteenth-century hymns, such as the *Olney Hymns* (1779) of William Cowper and John Newton, including "Amazing Grace" and "O for a Closer Walk with God," only fully established their popularity in this period. For "Amazing Grace" the crucial breakthrough did not come until 1835, when in his best-selling tunebook *Southern Harmony* William Walker linked it to the folksong tune "New

---

[73]Julian, *Dictionary of Hymnology*, p. 259; Foote, *American Hymnody*, pp. 164, 189-90; J. S. Andrews, "Hymnology, Scottish," in *DSCHT*, pp. 412-13.

[74]Foote, *American Hymnody*, pp. 194, 230-31.

Britain," a compelling combination that secured its enduring popularity in the United States.[75] Similarly, although important hymns by contemporary writers such as the Englishwoman Charlotte Elliott (1789-1871), the Scot Horatius Bonar (1808-1889) and the Americans Leonard Bacon (1802-1881) and Samuel Smith (1808-1895) were first published before 1850, they did not reach their maximum impact until later in the century. This time lag had particular implications in the United States where few hymns had been written before the nineteenth century, and hence the predominance of British writers in the hymnbooks, and hence probably in worship itself, continued until after the Civil War.

Alongside the hymns by educated and theologically sophisticated writers, gradually gaining acceptance in the more formal and established churches, popular revivalism in America generated its own powerful tradition of sacred song. This initially derived from religious dissidents in eighteenth-century New England, but gained much greater strength and richness through Methodism and camp meetings, which facilitated their rapid diffusion. Some were written by identifiable preachers and laypeople steeped in popular religious culture, but others have no known author and were initially handed down by oral tradition. Some were lengthy compositions, but others consisted merely of a "wandering verse" sung as a refrain to other hymns, relating them to popular experience.[76] Asahel Nettleton had such songs in mind when he observed that "there is a numerous class of hymns which have been sung with much pleasure and profit in seasons of revival, and yet are entirely destitute of poetic merit."[77] They did, however, powerfully express popular spiritual experience, with characteristic motifs including vivid expectation of heaven, a sense of this life as a time of trial and difficulty, emphasis on the redeeming power of the cross, and affirmation of the personal presence of Jesus with the believer:

> We have a howling wilderness
> To Canaan's happy shore,

---

[75]Steve Turner, *Amazing Grace: John Newton, Slavery and the World's Most Enduring Song* (Oxford: Lion, 2005), pp. 152-58.

[76]Dickson D. Bruce, *And They All Sang Hallelujah: Plain-Folk Camp-Meeting Religion 1800-1845* (Knoxville: University of Tennessee Press, 1974), p. 122; Eileen Southern, *The Music of Black Americans: A History* (New York: W.W. Norton, 1997), p. 86.

[77]Asahel Nettleton, *Village Hymns for Social Worship* (New York, 1831), p. vi.

A land of drought, and pits, and snares,
While chilling winds do roar,

But Jesus will be with us
And guard us by the way;
Though enemies examine us,
He'll teach us what to say.[78]

The impact of these spiritual songs in Britain was limited in comparison to that in America, but the Primitive Methodists adopted some of them, and earned their nickname of "Ranters" by their hearty singing. Hugh Bourne even celebrated their own history and denominational experience in verse that seemed closer to a ballad than a hymn:

The Lord a glorious work begun,
And thro' America it run,
Across the sea it flies;
This work is now to us come near,
And many are converted here,
We see it with our eyes.

The little cloud increases still,
That first arose upon Mow hill,
It spreads along the plain:
Tho' men attempt to stop its course,
It flies in spite of all their force,
And proves their efforts vain.

Sinners at first an uproar made,
And formalists were sore afraid,
Because it broke their rules:
'Twould bring religion in disgrace
Begun by men so mean and base,
And either knaves or fools.

Yet still these simple souls rejoice,
And on the hills they raise their voice,

[78] Albert Christ-Janer, Charles W. Hughes and Carleton Sprague Smith, *American Hymns Old and New* (New York: Columbia University Press, 1980), p. 301; Bruce, *And They All Sang Hallelujah*, pp. 96-122.

Salvation to proclaim;
They preach, exhort, and sweetly sing,
While hills and dales with praises ring,
And sound the Saviour's name.[79]

Camp meetings were also an important catalyst for the development of the parallel and related tradition of spirituals among black people. Although both slaves and free blacks shared the enthusiasm of whites in America for traditional formal hymns, above all those of Watts, they added to them their own distinctive songs combining African poetic and musical idioms with biblical motifs of redemptive suffering and liberation. The verses were very straightforward and repetitive, sometimes giving a simplified and adapted version of ideas in formal hymns, as was appropriate for a largely illiterate population with strong oral traditions.[80] Like poorer whites, slaves sang of the trials of the present life and of their hopes for a better one beyond death, but with language colored particularly by biblical motifs of exodus and liberation that linked their material and spiritual situations:

When Israel was in Egypt's land,
Let my people go:
Oppressed so hard they could not stand,
Let my people go.

Chorus:
Go down Moses,
Way down in Egypt land—
Tell ole Pharoh—
Let my people go.

O let them all from bondage flee,
Let my people go;
And let us all in Christ be free,
Let my people go.

Chorus

---

[79]Hugh Bourne, *A General Collection of Hymns and Spiritual Songs, for Camp-Meetings, Revivals, &c.* (Hull, 1821), pp. 41-42; George Pullen Jackson, *White and Negro Spirituals: Their Life Span and Kinship* (New York: J. J. Augustin, 1943), pp. 90-98.

[80]Southern, *Music of Black Americans*, pp. 82-89, 127-31, 178-90.

We need not always weep and moan,
Let my people go;
And wear these slavery chains forlorn,
Let my people go.

Chorus[81]

As African American Methodism became more developed and institution-alized, however, the leadership moved to marginalize the use of such spiritual songs in public worship in favor of official Methodist hymnody, a policy that was in tension with the wishes of congregations. There were similar develop-ments among Primitive Methodists in Britain.[82]

Congregational experience of hymns was, of course, shaped by the music as well as the words. In the eighteenth century there had been two main forms of singing. On the one hand there was "lining out," when a clerk or precentor would give out each line in turn, which was then repeated by the congregation. It was a system well suited to semi-literate and musically un-sophisticated congregations, but it was at best cumbersome and at worst musically excruciating. On the other hand there were elaborate fuguing tunes, normally sung by choirs with the majority of the congregation not participating. Harriet Beecher Stowe recalled their use in her father's church at Litchfield, Connecticut:

> But the glory in the execution of those good old billowy compositions called fuguing tunes, where the four parts that compose the choir take up the song, and go racing around one after another, each singing a different set of words till at length, by some inexplicable magic, they all come together again, and sail smoothly out into a rolling sea of harmony! I remember the wonder with which I used to look from side to side when treble, tenor, counter, and bass, were thus roaring and foaming, and it verily seemed to me as if the psalm were going to pieces among the breakers, and the delighted astonishment with which I found that each particular verse did emerge whole and uninjured from the storm.[83]

The main musical trend in evangelical worship during the early nineteenth century was the development of a middle way between the austerity of lining

---

[81]Christ-Janer, Hughes and Smith, *American Hymns*, p. 314.
[82]Campbell, *Songs of Zion*, pp. 42-43; Jackson, *White and Negro Spirituals*, p. 97.
[83]Quoted in Fields, *Harriet Beecher Stowe*, pp. 8-9.

out and the elaboration of fuguing. These were straightforward tunes that were closer to the singing capability of ordinary congregations than fuguing tunes, while avoiding the tedium of lining out. Their diffusion was assisted on both sides of the Atlantic by the introduction of simplified musical notation and the work of itinerant singing masters, who would visit towns and churches for a few weeks to provide elementary musical training before moving on.[84] Compilers of hymnbooks, for example Edward Bickersteth, urged the duty of singing hymns as enjoined in Scripture and as a means of spiritual benefit. "It tends to store the memory with the precious truths of God's word, and thus assists in maintaining spirituality of mind and constant communion with our God."[85] Meanwhile, organs were gradually introduced to assist congregational singing, although these were sometimes controversial, notably in provoking a local Methodist schism in Leeds in the 1820s. They were not authorized in the main Scottish Presbyterian churches until the second half of the century.[86]

African American Christians developed their own distinctive forms of music and worship. Lining out persisted among them, but in the context of a musical tradition that made much of effective repetition, it was a creative rather than stultifying device. At Bethel Church in Philadelphia in 1811 psalms were chanted antiphonally by men and women in turn. In 1820 an observer recorded:

> After the sermon they began singing merrily, and continued without stopping, one hour, till they became exhausted and breathless. . . . While all the time they were clapping hands, shouting and jumping, and exclaiming "Ah Lord! Good Lord! Give me *Jasus!* Amen."

Such worship practices were most fully developed in the "shout," a practice that owed much to African tradition, in which spirituals were sung to accompany ritual dance, perceived as a means of communicating with God and gaining the empowering of the Holy Spirit.[87]

---

[84]Turner, *Amazing Grace*, pp. 148-49.

[85]Bickersteth, *Christian Psalmody*, p. ix.

[86]David Hempton, *Methodism and Politics in British Society 1750-1850* (London: Hutchinson, 1984), p. 197; K. R. Ross, "Musical Instruments in Worship," in *DSCHT*, pp. 615-16.

[87]Southern, *Music of Black Americans*, pp. 78-79, 181-83.

Hymns were thus an adaptable and diverse medium, providing an important bridge between collective worship and individual spirituality, and between diverse religious cultures. Some recalled their lines as readily as they did favorite texts of Scripture. As Mrs. Anne Dow of Belleville, New Jersey, lay dying in December 1822, her husband repeated to her the apt lines of one of her favorite hymns: "The world recedes, it disappears/Heaven opens on my eyes, my ears/ with sounds seraphic ring." Similarly, Harriet Beecher Stowe visualized Uncle Tom in the final crisis of his life drawing inspiration and comfort from a modified version of John Newton's "Amazing Grace" and Isaac Watts's lines:

> When I can read my title clear
> To mansions in the skies,
> I'll bid farewell to every fear,
> And wipe my weeping eyes.[88]

Verses such as this had become the common spiritual currency of English-speaking evangelicalism.

---

[88]Stowe, *Uncle Tom's Cabin*, pp. 555-57; Turner, *Amazing Grace*, pp. 174-75.

5

WOMEN, MEN AND
THE FAMILY

By sweet experience now I know,
That those who knock shall enter in;
God doth his gifts and grace bestow,
On Women too, as well as men . . .

While men with eloquence and fame,
The silver trumpet manly blow,
A plainer trump we humbly claim,
The saving power of God to show.

These verses titled "The Female Preacher's Plea" first appeared in the *Primitive Methodist Magazine* in 1821.[1] They were written by Catherine O'Bryan, wife of the founder of the Bible Christians. She affirmed the spiritual equality of men and women, and her conviction that God gave spiritual gifts, including a divine call to preach, to both sexes. She acknowledged, though, that men's and women's roles differed in practice. Eloquent and famous preaching seemed to her an attribute of manliness and she, in common with most other early nineteenth-century women preachers on both sides of the Atlantic, accepted continuing male monopoly of the ordained ministry.[2] Nevertheless, she firmly

---

[1] *The Primitive Methodist Magazine* 2 (1821): 191-92; cf. Deborah M. Valenze, *Prophetic Sons and Daughters: Female Preaching and Popular Religion in Industrial England* (Princeton, N.J.: Princeton University Press, 1985), p. 150.

[2] Cf. Harriet Livermore's conclusion *Scriptural Evidence in Favour of Female Testimony in Meetings for Christian Worship* (Portsmouth, N.H., 1824), p. 120 that ordination "belongs only to the male sex." On the Bible Christians, see above, p. 67.

asserted women's capacity to fulfill the essential evangelical and evangelistic task of proclaiming the "saving power of God."

Catherine O'Bryan's perception that the spiritual experience of female evangelicals did not differ significantly from that of men has been confirmed by recent research.[3] Social constraints, however, meant that only a small minority of evangelical women preached in public, and as the period went on even these were progressively marginalized and eventually excluded. Numerous other women, though, shared their sense of vocation, even if they did not apply it literally. The eighteen-year-old Harriet Beecher wrote to her brother:

> You see . . . that I was made for a preacher—indeed I can scarcely keep my letters from turning into sermons, but my "dear hearer" in consideration that you are the only one you must excuse me if I am somewhat lengthy. Indeed in a certain sense it is as much my vocation to preach on paper as it is that of my brothers to preach viva voce.[4]

Harriet was to become the first major—and arguably the greatest—American woman novelist. Her life and writing should be seen in parallel with her English contemporaries, Charlotte (1816-1854), Emily (1818-1848) and Anne (1820-1849) Brontë and George Eliot (Marian Evans 1819-1880), all of whom also had strong early connections with evangelicalism. Moreover, these enduringly famous mid-nineteenth-century women novelists should be seen not only as successors in the standard literary canon to Jane Austen (1775-1817), but as following in a tradition of writing by evangelical women. These included notably Hannah More (1745-1833) and, in the next generation, Mary Martha Sherwood (1775-1851), Charlotte Elizabeth Tonna (1790-1846) and the poet and hymnwriter Charlotte Elliott (1789-1871). The latter authors are relatively little read nowadays, but were enormously popular and influential in their time: they are therefore significant not only as examples of female achievement, but as articulators of models of evangelical womanhood.

Writers, like preachers, were, however, exceptional. For the large majority of

---

[3] Linda Wilson, *Constrained by Zeal: Female Spirituality Among Nonconformists 1825-1875* (Carlisle: Paternoster Press, 2000), pp. 64-65.

[4] Hartford, Conn., Stowe-Day Library, Harriet Beecher to George Beecher (February 20, 1830). Harriet's father, Lyman, believed female delicacy was incompatible with "public perfomance" (Catherine A. Brekus, *Strangers and Pilgrims: Female Preaching in America, 1740-1845* [Chapel Hill: University of North Carolina Press, 1998], p. 153).

evangelical women in this period, as for their unconverted sisters, life was limited by domestic and family demands, and by successive pregnancies throughout young adulthood. Repeated childbearing carried with it the danger not only of immediate sudden death, but of the creeping exhaustion and semi-invalidism that afflicted many women from early middle age onward. In the United States in 1846 "the number of those whose health is crushed before the first few years of married life are passed, would seem incredible to one who has not investigated the subject."[5] For such women circumstances rather than gender as such meant that their contribution to evangelicalism was a largely passive one, although their need for social and spiritual support in the physical and material challenges that they faced, and their awareness of the fragility of life, helped to ensure that they made up a larger proportion of congregations than their menfolk did, in general from 55 percent to 70 percent of the total. Moreover, in New England Congregation-alism at least, the proportion of women increased during the period, from 59 per-cent of new members between 1730 and 1769, to 64 percent between 1770 and 1799, and 69 percent between 1800 and 1835.[6]

When health, time and energy allowed for greater activity, philanthropic and educational activity became a central concern. There was a spectrum of en-deavor. There was casual good-neighborliness, the informal work of women like Lydia Finney, wife of the revivalist, and Mary Johnson, the first free European woman to live in Australia, in supporting their respective husbands' public min-istries, and the involvement of women in local organizations such as Sunday schools and visiting societies. There were also high-profile careers, such as those of the prison reformer Elizabeth Fry (1780-1845) in England and the slavery abolitionist Lucretia Mott (1793-1880) in the United States, both evangelical Quakers, a denomination that was exceptional in the extent to which it recog-nized and supported public ministry and activity by women.

Given the numerical dominance and importance of women in evangelical-

---

[5]Catharine E. Beecher, *The Evils Suffered by American Women and American Children* (New York: Harper & Bros., 1846), p. 13.

[6]Gail Malmgreen, "Domestic Discords: Women and the Family in East Cheshire Method-ism, 1750-1830," in *Disciplines of Faith*, ed. J. Obelkevich, Lyndal Roper and Raphael Sam-uel (London: Routledge & Kegan Paul, 1987), p. 60; Richard D. Sheils, "The Feminiza-tion of American Congregationalism, 1770-1835," in *Religion*, Volume 13, History of Women in the United States, ed. Nancy F. Cott (Munich: K. G. Saur, 1993), p. 5.

ism, their contribution is acknowledged throughout this book rather than being limited to a single chapter. In particular, women's vital contribution to reforming and missionary endeavors will receive fuller attention in the next chapter, which is concerned with evangelical efforts to transform society. First, though, it is appropriate to focus in the following pages on issues relating specifically to women to explore how their role changed during the period. In the first half of this chapter we shall consider the active contribution to evangelicalism made by female preachers and writers, before turning in the second section to explore the situation of women in their perceived primary roles in home and family. This discussion will also lead us to consider the status and image of men in evangelicalism, and to discuss interactions between the sexes and between parents and children.

PREACHERS BY VOICE AND PEN

Harriet Beecher Stowe's sense of herself as a preacher on paper linked her and other middle-class literary women to the literal preaching activity of other women, generally drawn from lower-class and less well-educated backgrounds, which was at its height on both sides of the Atlantic in the first quarter of the nineteenth century. A similar link was implicitly made by George Eliot when she began her first full-length novel, *Adam Bede*, published in 1859 but set in 1799, with an extended evocation of a sermon by a female itinerant, Dinah Morris. "The chararacter of Dinah," Eliot wrote, "grew out of . . . recollections" of her own aunt Elizabeth Tomlinson, who had been a notable preacher in her youth at the turn of the century, and to whom, in 1839, she had talked about her "inward life" at a time when her own early evangelical convictions were beginning to loosen. Even as Eliot, by 1859, had turned her back firmly on evangelical theology, her portrait of Dinah remained a powerfully sympathetic one, of a woman of great courage, compassion and quiet dignity, who had a profound influence on her hearers and their scattered rural communities. Indeed, in the character of Dinah Morris, Eliot was not only paying tribute to her aunt but recapturing something of her own earlier evangelical self.[7]

From the outset women played an important organizational role in grass-

---

[7]George Eliot, *Adam Bede*, ed. Stephen Gill (London: Penguin, 1985), p. 586, quoting Eliot's journal for November 30, 1858; Frederick Karl, *George Eliot: A Biography* (London: Harper Collins, 1995), pp. 41, 278-80.

roots evangelicalism. There was only one Countess of Huntingdon (d. 1791), who had used her wealth to found her own denomination, but there were many women like Alice Cross, who in the middle of the eighteenth century led a class meeting at the village of Booth Bank in Cheshire and set up the main room of her house as a place of worship.[8] For a few such women there was a natural progress from leading small meetings, praying and exhorting to fully fledged preaching. Such activity was encouraged by John Wesley himself, even though he stopped short of formally accepting women as itinerant preachers. He reasoned that if women were manifestly being used by God to convert sinners, he would be resisting the Almighty by standing in their way. Mary Bosanquet (1739-1815), while living at Leytonstone, northeast of London, began to "exhort, and to read, and expound the scriptures." In 1771 Wesley acknowledged that she had an "extraordinary call" as a preacher, and she exercised an unofficial ministry first in the Leeds area, and then in Shropshire after her marriage to John Fletcher of Madeley, a staunch supporter of Methodism even though he was an Anglican clergyman. In 1810, now aged over seventy, she was still regularly preaching five times a week.[9] On Long Island, Sarah Wright Townsend similarly made the transition from exhorter to preacher, and gave sermons to a Separate Baptist church between 1759 and the 1770s.[10]

The revivalistic upsurge of the 1790s and 1800s was associated with a marked increase in female preaching. Ann Cutler and Mary Barritt played central roles in the Yorkshire revival of the mid-1790s. Barritt married a fellow itinerant, Zachariah Taft, in 1802, and adverse reaction to her continuing ministry in 1803 led the increasingly conservative Wesleyan Methodist Conference to prohibit female preaching. Mary, however, defied this decision, and her husband not only strongly supported her, but published his own works advocating and publicizing the ministry of women, notably two volumes of biographical sketches published in 1825 and 1828. Taft's compilation covered seventy-eight women, including some historical exemplars such as Margaret Fox and Susannah Wesley, and the Latvian Madame de Krudener, but the great majority of

---

[8]Malmgreen, "Domestic Discords," pp. 57-58.

[9]*BDEB*, p. 394; Z. Taft, *Biographical Sketches of Lives and Public Ministry of Various Holy Women* (1825, facsimile reprint Peterborough: Methodist Publishing House, 1992), pp. ii-iii, 24, 26.

[10]Marilyn J. Westerkampf, *Women and Religion in Early America 1600-1850: The Puritan and Evangelical Traditions* (London and New York: Routledge, 1999), p. 98.

them active in England in his own day. Intriguingly, William Bramwell, another male Wesleyan supporter of female preachers, believed that the only reason there were not more of them was that some women were not faithful to their call.[11] Their hesitation was understandable in the light of the personal costs and opposition encountered.

The popular Methodist secessions, however, initially placed fewer obstacles in the way of women, and such activity was extensive in the early decades of Primitive Methodism. Between 1827 and 1841 there were at least twenty-eight women preachers active in only six counties in central southern and southwest England, and a count across the whole country and the whole period would undoubtedly yield substantially larger numbers. In a slum district of Leeds the "Female Revivalists," led by the redoubtable Ann Carr, set up their own chapel in 1825. It flourished until Carr's death in 1841.[12] Dorothy Ripley, who had been born in Yorkshire around 1767, had a remarkable career of a different kind, in the United States as well as Britain, crossing the Atlantic ten times by 1825, and preaching effectively to African and Native Americans as well as to whites. Such a solitary female traveler became the inevitable subject of unfounded gossip and salacious rumors.[13]

Female preaching similarly increased in North America from the 1790s onward. Women such as the Methodist Episcopalian Eliza Barnes (1796-1887) and the Bible Christian Elizabeth Dart (1792-1857) made an important contribution to the spread of evangelicalism in Canada.[14] Catherine Brekus has counted more than 100 women preachers in the United States in the period between 1740 and 1845, with the greatest activity occurring in the early nineteenth century. As in England, mainstream Methodism was relatively unsympa-

---

[11]Valenze, *Prophetic Sons and Daughters*, pp. 56-64; Taft, *Holy Women*, p. 150.

[12]Valenze, *Prophetic Sons and Daughters*, pp. 52-64, 113-14, 187-204; D. Colin Dews, "Ann Carr and the Female Revivalists of Leeds," in *Religion in the Lives of English Women, 1760-1930*, ed. Gail Malmgreen (London: Croom Helm, 1986), pp. 68-87.

[13]Dorothy Ripley, *The Bank of Faith and Works United* (Whitby, 1822); Taft, *Holy Women*, pp. 205-41; Christine Leigh Heyrman, *Southern Cross: The Beginnings of the Bible Belt* (New York: Alfred A. Knopf, 1997), p. 182.

[14]Elizabeth Gillan Muir, "Beyond the Bounds of Acceptable Behaviour: Methodist Women Preachers in the Early Nineteenth Century," in *Changing Roles of Women within the Christian Church in Canada*, ed. Elizabeth Gillan Muir and Marilyn Färdig Whiteley (Toronto: University of Toronto Press, 1995), pp. 161-82.

thetic, producing only nine of the total, and in effect banning women from the pulpit altogether in 1830. Women, however, fared better among Methodist secessions and radical popular groups such as the Christians, the Freewill Baptists and the Millerites. The African Methodists were also more initially accepting of the preaching of women such as Jarena Lee and Zilpha Elaw (discussed in the previous chapter[15]) than was the Methodist Episcopal Church. It was, though, a white woman, Harriet Livermore (1788-1868), brought up as a Congregationalist but subsequently eschewing denominational structures, who had the distinction of delivering sermons to Congress on four occasions between 1827 and 1843, an indication of the degree of transient acceptability gained by women preachers in this period.[16]

The Capitol in Washington, to which Livermore gained access by virtue of her superior education and political connections, was, however, far removed from the normal sphere of women's preaching. Typically they operated among a popular lower-class constituency in religious groups that valued a sense of first-hand spiritual experience more than an informed theological teaching that was impossible for women with limited educational opportunities. George Eliot's characterization of Dinah Morris rings true in relation to real-life women preachers: "She was not preaching as she heard others preach, but speaking directly from her own emotions, and under the inspiration of her own simple faith." Ann Cutler seldom preached in an expository fashion, but she sought "to impress the minds of the people with a powerful and lively conviction of the *omniscience* and *omnipresence* of God; that the LORD . . . *was in the midst* and that HE was there, to do the people good—to save souls." She then outlined the essential evangelical doctrines of human depravity, atonement, repentance and salvation. Nevertheless, these women were also steeped in knowledge of the Bible, which they quoted extensively. They also tended to see their own life stories in prophetic biblical terms.[17]

Alongside itinerant female preachers were other women who exercised informal leadership in evangelical churches through their organizational abilities, their readiness to host cottage meetings and visiting preachers, and their pastoral role as "mothers in Israel," a status commonly attributed to them in the

---

[15]See above, pp. 108-10.

[16]Brekus, *Strangers and Pilgrims*, pp. 1ff., 133-35, 270.

[17]Eliot, *Adam Bede*, p. 72; Taft, *Holy Women*, p. 302; Brekus, *Strangers and Pilgrims*, pp. 172-73.

late eighteenth and early nineteenth centuries. In the American South, where women preachers were denied even the degree of acceptance accorded to them in the North and in England, such activities were a particularly important parallel channel of influence. Such women could be looked up to, even by male ministers, as individuals of great sanctity and spiritual authority. In Derbyshire, Hannah Yeomans served as a supporter and facilitator for generations of Primitive Methodist preachers, feeding and housing them, but also praying with them and promoting connectional activity in the locality. A similar status as a "mother in Israel" was accorded to "Mother Smith" in Cape Town. She encouraged and supported the missionaries passing through the colony and, after she died in 1821, was judged to have had an evangelistic impact greater than ten male missionaries.[18]

Female preaching declined in the middle decades of the nineteenth century. As even radical lower-class denominations like the Primitive Methodists and the African Methodist Episcopal Church acquired tighter organizational structures and aspired to social respectability, they came increasingly to perceive women's preaching as disorderly and subversive. As more churches and chapels were built, women who had preached in the informal settings of barns and cottages began to seem out of place. As formal ministerial education began to be required of men, but denied to women, the latter came to be regarded as threatening to an evolving concept of professional ministry. As ministers sought to win men for the gospel, they worried about sanctioning behavior by women that seemed to challenge patriarchal social structures, and turned rather to encouraging pious women to concentrate their attention on their own families. In the United States preaching by women virtually ceased by 1850, and it became marginal in Britain. There was also a tendency to write women preachers out of denominational records, as if their past achievements were now an embarrassment. Thus when Mary Taft died in 1851, her short obituary in the *Methodist Magazine* did not even mention her preaching activity.[19]

Female preaching had thrived in a lower-class milieu both of religious revival

---

[18]Heyrman, *Southern Cross*, pp. 161-71; Valenze, *Prophetic Sons and Daughters*, pp. 43-47; Taft, *Holy Women*, pp. 254-65.

[19]Brekus, *Strangers and Pilgrims*, pp. 270-304; Valenze, *Prophetic Sons and Daughters*, pp. 64, 274-81; Heyrman, *Southern Cross*, pp. 197-205.

and social instability, in which some fluidity in gender roles was acceptable. A similar sense of both social and gender mobility was apparent in the life and career of Hannah More, who became highly influential, both as a writer and as a role model for activist evangelical women.[20] More was the daughter of a Gloucestershire village schoolmaster in an age when that profession offered minimal social esteem and even less financial reward. Nevertheless, in her thirties she gained acceptance in leading London literary and intellectual circles, and subsequently became a friend of bishops and aristocrats. Having initially made her literary reputation as a dramatist and poet, during the 1780s she underwent a gradual evangelical conversion and turned her energies to writing with a more explicit moral or spiritual agenda. *Sacred Dramas* (1782) was followed by *Slavery: A Poem* (1788), her contribution to the campaign against the slave trade, and two books criticizing contemporary social mores, *Thoughts on the Importance of the Manners of the Great* (1788) and *An Estimate of the Religion of the Fashionable World* (1791). American editions of these four works were published in 1787, 1788, 1797 and 1793 respectively.[21]

During the next twenty years More became the childless matriarch of English evangelicalism whose impact extended across the Atlantic through her writings. In the aftermath of the French Revolution there was extensive concern in Britain about the potential for lower-class unrest. For More such political anxieties combined with distinctively evangelical aspirations for conversion and moral improvement through religious education. Thus during the 1790s she simultaneously set up and supported a network of village schools near her home in north Somerset, and turned her literary gifts to the writing of improving tracts. Both explicitly in *Village Politics* (1793) and implicitly in the series of 114 *Cheap Repository Tracts* (1795-1798), of which she was the editor and principal author, she provided a lively defense of the existing social order, undergirded by

---

[20]The definitive biography is Anne Stott, *Hannah More: The First Victorian* (Oxford: Oxford University Press, 2003), to which the brief account that follows here is much indebted. For extracts from More's writings see Robert Hole, ed., *Selected Writings of Hannah More* (London: William Pickering, 1996), and Clare Macdonald Shaw, ed., *Tales for the Common People and Other Cheap Repository Tracts* (Nottingham: Trent Editions, 2002). Her earlier career is surveyed in Mark A. Noll, *The Rise of Evangelicalism: The Age of Edwards, Whitefield and the Wesleys* (Leicester, U.K.: Inter-Varsity Press, 2004), pp. 225-27.

[21]Stott, *Hannah More*, pp. 1-102, 131-33; Harry B. Weiss, *Hannah More's Cheap Repository Tracts in America* (New York: New York Public Library, 1946), p. 5.

morality and religion. More shrewdly imitated the format of existing popular literature while replacing its often irreverent content. By March 1796 over two million tracts had already been sold, so it is likely that total circulation amounted to many millions. Both collected editions and individual tracts continued to be reprinted until well into the nineteenth century. Even if their wide circulation was direct evidence more of the enthusiasm of middle-class distributors than of lower-class readers, they were credited with giving a significant check to popular discontent. In America, too, despite differences in political and social conditions, publishers still found a market for the tracts: individual numbers were reprinted there from 1797 onward; forty-two of the series were published in Philadelphia in 1800; and the whole set was released in Boston in 1802-1803.[22]

More's success as a writer for a popular audience lay in her genuine sympathetic awareness of lower-class hardships, and in a conservatism that was balanced and compassionate rather than merely reactionary. Moreover, in her passionate denunciation of the slave trade she was a blistering critic of complacent self-interested patriotism:

> Cease, ye British Sons of murder!
> Cease from forging Afric's chain
> Mock your Saviour's name no further,
> Cease your savage lust of gain.

> Ye that boast *"Ye rule the waves,"*
> Bid no Slave Ship soil the sea,
> Ye, that *"never will be slaves"*
> Bid poor Afric's land be free.[23]

A parallel complexity was apparent in her views on the role of women in society. Although More appears an anomalous figure from the perspective of

---

[22]Stott, *Hannah More*, pp. 103-90; G. H. Spinney, "Cheap Repository Tracts: Hazard and Marshall Edition," *The Library*, 4th series (1939), p. 302; Susan Pedersen, "Hannah More Meets Simple Simon: Tracts, Chapbooks and Popular Culture in Late Eighteenth-Century England," *Journal of British Studies* 25 (1986): 84-113; Weiss, *Cheap Repository Tracts in America*, pp. 6, 9, 14-19.

[23]From "The Sorrows of Yamba," one of the *Cheap Repository Tracts*, quoted in Hole, *Hannah More*, p. 47. The allusion is to the popular song "Rule Britannia, Britannia rule the waves/ Britons never never never will be slaves."

twenty-first-century radical feminism, she insisted on the importance of educating women and encouraged them to follow her own example by efforts to improve spiritual, moral and material conditions outside as well as inside their own homes. In "The History of Hester Wilmot," one of the *Cheap Repository Tracts*, the story opens with Hester, a girl of fourteen, laboring ceaselessly at household chores under the control of her tyrannically house-proud mother Rebecca, who considers that if the girl could read she would become lazy. Hester is rescued from her enforced illiteracy and godlessness by Mrs. Jones, reminiscent of More herself, who has set up a Sunday school and persuades the reluctant Rebecca to allow Hester to attend. Hester is converted and shows herself a very dutiful daughter to her unworthy parents, nursing Rebecca in sickness, and lending her father money that she has saved up to buy a new dress for the Sunday school feast, but which he promptly gambles away. The story ends with the parents also converted through Hester's witness and Hester herself appointed an under-teacher in the school, with the prospect of becoming headmistress in due course.[24]

More's views on the education of women were more fully worked out in a two-volume work, *Strictures on the Modern System of Female Education*, published in 1799. The argument reflected her own underlying ambivalences: she saw women's primary sphere as the domestic one, and condemned women who overasserted themselves in the public arena. On the other hand, however, she insisted that women should be educated in a manner comparable to men, developing sound rational and moral understanding, rather than being immersed in mere sentimentalism. The book greatly inspired a teenage girl in Massachusetts, who read it in 1815. She perceived More's advocacy of preparing young women effectively for their crucial roles in caring for and educating children as showing that woman "bears the sway not man as he presumptuously supposes."[25] More's views were further developed in *Hints towards Forming the Character of a Young Princess* (1805), in which she offered the royal family very public advice on the upbringing of Princess Charlotte, the king's granddaughter, who

---

[24]Hannah More, *The History of Hester Wilmot or the Second Part of the Sunday School* (1796); *The History of Hester Wilmot; or the New Gown. Part II* (1796).

[25]Stott, *Hannah More*, pp. 215-28; Mehitable May Goddard, quoted by Nancy F. Cott, *The Bonds of Womanhood: "Women's Sphere" in New England 1780-1835* (New Haven, Conn.: Yale University Press, 1977), p. 99.

then seemed likely eventually to succeed to the throne.[26] She was concerned lest "the course of study will be adapted to the sex, rather than to the circumstances of the Princess."[27] More accordingly recommended extensive study of both ancient and modern history, and wide reading in literature, politics and philosophy. Above all, Charlotte must be given a firm grounding in Christian teaching and understand the place of the Church of England in the religious history of the nation. Past reigning queens offered both exemplars and cautionary tales: Queen Christina of Sweden was "born to rule a brave people, and naturally possessed of talents which might have made that people happy," but squandered it all because of "her false judgment, and perverted ambition"; Queen Elizabeth I of England, despite her personal faults, was "an instrument raised up by divine Providence to carry through the most arduous enterprises in the most difficult emergencies."[28] For More, although women were subject to the same human failings as men, there was no limit to what they could achieve if they had the requisite gifts of character, intellect and opportunity.

Her views on gender roles were further developed in her only full-length novel, *Coelebs in Search of a Wife* (1808), a bestseller in its day on both sides of the Atlantic, with an initial popularity greatly exceeding that of Jane Austen's most commercially successful novel, *Pride and Prejudice* (1813).[29] In *Coelebs* More offered not only a model bachelor, but also a heroine, Lucilla, who possesses all the domestic virtues, "enlivens without dazzling and entertains without overpowering," but also knows Latin and is dedicated to the Sunday school and to helping the poor. Lucilla's mother's view that the "care of the poor" is the "profession" of a lady was to have an enduring influence in inspiring and legitimating philanthropic activity by women.[30]

More's contribution to the advancement of women's role in society was

---

[26]Princess Charlotte was then George III's only legitimate grandchild, but she was to die in childbirth in 1817, predeceasing both her grandfather and her father, the Prince Regent and future George IV.

[27]Hannah More, *Hints Towards Forming the Character of a Young Princess*, 2 vols. (London: T. Cadell & W. Davies, 1805), I:xii–xiii.

[28]Ibid., 1:185; 2:79, 81.

[29]Karen Swallow Prior, *Hannah More's Coelebs in Search of A Wife—A Review of Criticism and New Analysis* (Lewiston: Edwin Mellon Press, 2003), pp. 31-33.

[30]Hannah More, *Coelebs in Search of a Wife*, ed. Mary Waldron (Bristol: Thoemmes Press, 1995), pp. 63, 138; Stott, *Hannah More*, pp. 274-78.

rooted in her conviction that "the Christian is Christian first and gendered second," which enabled her "to validate women's renegotiation of certain gender assumptions within her own society."[31] Indeed, in the final phase of her active life, More, writing as "a Christian who must die soon, to Christians who must die certainly,"[32] felt that she had established the right to preach in print. She abandoned the anonymity that she had earlier used to obscure her sex and turned to writing specifically religious works, beginning with *Practical Piety* (1811) and *Christian Morals* (1813). *An Essay on the Character and Practical Writings of St Paul* (1815) was an even bolder step in that she was presuming to expound the text of Scripture itself, although she covered herself with professions of inadequacy and the claim that her approach "was not of a critical but of a practical nature."[33] Now in her seventies, she continued to write, publishing *Moral Sketches* (1819), *Bible Rhymes* (1821) and *The Spirit of Prayer* (1825). Most of these works ran through several editions, and such was her prestige that these repeated incursions into the normally exclusively male territory of explicit Christian teaching appear to have found ready acceptance among evangelicals.

In 1824 Hannah More was visited by a much younger woman, Charlotte Elizabeth,[34] who was then becoming known as a writer. The daughter of a Norfolk clergyman, Charlotte Elizabeth had made an unhappy first marriage to an army officer, Captain Phelan. She accompanied him for two years on a posting to Halifax, Nova Scotia, where she struggled with domestic duties in the face of the harsh climate and took the "liveliest interest" in "the poor relics of the Indian race still dwelling in the woods." She then lived in Ireland for several years, where she experienced conversion and, remaining childless and looking for a worthwhile way to use her time, she began to write for the Dublin Tract Society. She began to correspond with More, and after she separated from her husband and moved

---

[31]Kathryn Sutherland, "Hannah More's Counter-Revolutionary Feminism," in *Revolution in Writing: British Literary Responses to the French Revolution*, ed. Kelvin Everest (Milton Keynes: Open University Press, 1991), pp. 50-51.

[32]Hannah More, *Practical Piety*, 2 vols. (London: T. Cadell & W. Davies, 1811), I:x.

[33]Hannah More, *An Essay on the Character and Practical Writings of St Paul*, 2 vols. (London: T. Cadell & W. Davies, 1815), I:iii-iv.

[34]She used her Christian names as a pen name. Her maiden name was Browne, and following Captain Phelan's death in 1837 she married Lewis Hippolytus Tonna in 1840, under which surname she is also known.

for a time to Bristol in 1834, they became personally acquainted.[35]

Charlotte Elizabeth was evidently inspired by More, and in many respects her own prolific writing, similarly blending political, moral and spiritual concerns, can be seen as a continuation of More's own endeavors. Charlotte Elizabeth, though, was, from a modern feminist perspective, an even more paradoxical and disconcerting writer than More herself in that, although she was a successful and influential woman, her views were intensely conservative, if not reactionary. Significantly, she "thought more of [More's] 'Cheap Repository Tracts' than of all her other works combined."[36] Her sense of the appropriate limits for women's intervention in spiritual matters was a finely balanced one. In the first number of her *Christian Lady's Magazine*, which began publication in 1834, she wrote:

> Few questions come under our consideration, as Christian Females, more weighty in their relative importance, or more difficult to answer by a precise definition, than the extent to which it is both lawful and expedient to us publicly to "intermeddle with all wisdom" in spiritual matters. That we are not excluded from this happy prerogative is clear from many passages in holy writ; that a boundary is assigned, beyond which it were unbecoming presumption in us to pass, is quite as evident.[37]

She disavowed coverage of topics of "a more masculine stamp," but in practice the content of the magazine was by no means limited to merely devotional and domestic matters. It included theological essays, reviews of serious books and regular articles on politics. Charlotte Elizabeth affirmed women's legitimate interest in moral questions such as the abolition of slavery and observance of the Sabbath, and even, at times of crisis, wider questions of political economy. In an early issue she urged her readers to interest themselves in the factory question, and to seek to influence both proprietors and parliamentarians. A "female demagogue" was an outrage to God, but "be it yours to plead and pray; and with modest perseverance in a sacred cause, adorn your stations without overstepping their boundary."[38]

---

[35] Charlotte Elizabeth, *Personal Recollections . . . Third edition, continued to the close of her life* (London: Seeley, Burnside & Seeley, 1847), pp. 96-100, 122-25, 135-36, 222-27.

[36] Ibid., p. 224.

[37] *The Christian Lady's Magazine* I (1834): 3.

[38] Ibid., 2:75, 158-60, 251, 350.

Subsequently Charlotte Elizabeth devoted her attention particularly to attacking the abuses of the factory system and the exploitation of women in the workplace, in a novel entitled *Helen Fleetwood* (serialized in *The Christian Lady's Magazine* in 1839-1840 and published in 1841), the anonymously published *Perils of the Nation* (1843) and a series of short novels called *The Wrongs of Woman* (1843-1844). She graphically described appalling living and working conditions, exposed their adverse effects on the health and morality of women and their children, and chronicled the degeneration of family life when cynical employers offered work to women but not to men. Her works combined firsthand knowledge and intensive use of government reports with the human interest of fictional narrative and have been credited with having a significant impact in strengthening the campaign for factory reform. While repudiating "all pretensions to equality with man," Charlotte Elizabeth believed that "it is the peculiar work of Christianity, wherever it is established, to elevate woman from the debased position in which she is elsewhere placed."[39]

Charlotte Elizabeth's works, like Hannah More's, were widely circulated in America as well as Britain, and the then little-known Harriet Beecher Stowe wrote an introduction for a collected edition first published by M. W. Dodd in New York in 1844. Although Stowe was clearly embarrassed by some of Charlotte Elizabeth's views, particularly her vehement anti-Catholicism, she was in no doubt about the overall value of her work. Another New York publisher, John S. Taylor, brought out a competing version, evidence of a strong American market for the books, and by 1850 the Dodd edition had been reprinted eight times.[40] Meanwhile, *The Ladies Repository*, a Methodist monthly which began publication in Cincinnati in 1841, emerged as something of an American parallel to the *Christian Lady's Magazine*. Although edited by men, it offered an opening for female writers and provided genuine intellectual stimulus for women, believing that they had an equal prerogative

---

[39]Charlotte Elizabeth, *The Wrongs of Woman, Part 1 Milliners and Dress Makers* (London:W. H. Dalton, 1843), pp. 1, 104; Ivanka Kovacevic and S. Barbara Kanner, "Blue Book into Novel: the Forgotten Industrial Fiction of Charlotte Elizabeth Tonna," *Nineteenth-Century Fiction* 25 (1970): 152-73; Joseph Kestner, "Charlotte Elizabeth Tonna's *The Wrongs of Woman*: Female Industrial Protest," *Tulsa Studies in Women's Literature* 2 (1983): 193-214.

[40]*The Works of Charlotte Elizabeth with an Introduction by Mrs H. B. Stowe*, 8th ed., 2 vols. (New York: M. W. Dodd, 1850); *The New York Observer*, January 25, 1845, advertisement.

"to seek and intermeddle with all wisdom."[41]

Stowe herself and her elder sister, Catharine Esther Beecher (1800-1878), both guided and constrained by their formidable father, had a pioneering role among American women in articulating an intense social concern rooted in evangelical Christianity. Whereas Harriet was to become particularly associated with the anti-slavery campaign, Catharine concentrated her energies on education and domesticity. She believed that, although females had no place in the professions of law, medicine and theology, teaching children was "the true and noble profession of a woman." Hence women themselves needed to be educated to a high standard, a task which Beecher herself undertook in running girls' schools in Hartford in the 1820s and in Cincinnati in the 1830s. For her, education was not only—in a phrase borrowed from Charlotte Elizabeth—the remedy for the "wrongs of woman," but an essential means of saving the nation itself by spreading "intelligence and virtue." Catharine Beecher was also an influential writer on domestic management, encouraging women to feel that their pivotal role in home and family was equally crucial to national welfare, by providing a basis for social stability that balanced the turbulence of public life.[42] She remained unmarried herself, however, and her career, like those of Hannah More and Charlotte Elizabeth in Britain, well illustrates the paradoxical situation of able women in early nineteenth-century evangelicalism. Female writers might often seem to endorse rather than to question the social subordination and separation of women, but they were themselves enjoying considerable success and influence and, inspired by a sense of spiritual equality, were probing the accepted limits of women's capabilities and concerns.

A parallel complexity was apparent in attitudes to the public ministry of women during the second quarter of the nineteenth century. Although, as we have seen, female preaching of the earlier unregulated kind was being "frozen out" by Methodists increasingly concerned for order and social respectability, at this very

---

[41] *The Ladies Repository* I (1841): 6; Joanna Brown Gillespie, "The Emerging Voice of the Methodist Woman: *The Ladies Repository*, 1841-1861," in *Rethinking Methodist History*, ed. Russell E. Richey and Kenneth E. Rowe (Nashville: Kingswood Books, 1985), pp. 148-58.

[42] Catharine Beecher, *American Women and American Children*, pp. 9-10; *The Duty of American Women to their Country* (New York: Harper & Bros., 1845); *The True Remedy for the Wrongs of Woman* (Boston: Phillips, Sampson & Co., 1851); Kathryn Kish Sklar, *Catharine Beecher: A Study in American Domesticity* (New Haven, Conn.: Yale University Press, 1973), pp. 151-67.

period alternative models of women's ministry were developing. Indeed, one of the features of Finneyite "new measures" revivalism that concerned critics like Lyman Beecher was the permission given to women to speak in "promiscuous" (mixed) gatherings, and the subsequent general acceptance of Finney's methods gave women enhanced roles in middle-class congregations. As in other respects, it was his genius to take a widespread feature of popular lower-class revivalism and render it more acceptable in other social contexts. Finney's first wife, Lydia, ably assisted her husband's ministry, particularly through organizing other women to carry out house-to-house visitations and promoting prayer meetings that, although initially intended solely for women, often came to be attended by both sexes. Such ministry was less conspicuous than public preaching, but it was perceived as vital to the overall success of the cause. His second wife, Elizabeth, whom he married in 1848 following Lydia's death the previous year, was to move a step further, taking a public role as a partner in his work. Lydia and Elizabeth Finney, through their marriages to the greatest evangelist of the age, were prominent exemplars of a wider shift in the role of the minister's wife from inconspicuous companion to active coworker, a trend that led numerous women consciously to seek marriage to a minister or missionary as a means of fulfilling their own sense of vocation.[43] A parallel movement in England is indicated by a volume entitled *Hints to a Clergyman's Wife*, published in London in 1832 and addressing itself to "those Christian females who are anxious to become true yokefellows to their husbands, in the faithful discharge of the high office of the Christian ministry." The book was entirely concerned with ways in which the wife could assist her husband in active ministry, and even develop "independent plans" of her own. Although the anonymous author acknowledged that young mothers would be largely confined to the home, it was still hoped that even for these women "some little time may be redeemed for the work of the Lord." Mere domestic companionship and childrearing was apparently insufficient.[44]

Meanwhile, at Oberlin College, Finney and the president Asa Mahan created an institution that pioneered higher education for women. Mahan asked

---

[43]Keith J. Hardman, *Charles Grandison Finney 1792-1875: Revivalist and Reformer* (Grand Rapids: Baker, 1987), pp. 100-103; Leonard I. Sweet, *The Minister's Wife: Her Role in Nineteenth-Century American Evangelicalism* (Philadelphia: Temple University Press, 1983).

[44]*Hints to a Clergyman's Wife; or Female Parochial Duties Practically Illustrated* (London, 1832), pp. iv-vi, 2-5, 202-3.

that his epitaph should read, "The first man, in the history of the race, who conducted women, in connection with members of the opposite sex, through a full course of liberal education."[45] Among early Oberlin graduates in the 1840s were a number of women who were subsequently to become prominent Christian feminists, notably Lucy Stone and Antoinette Brown, who in 1853 was the first American woman to be ordained to the Congregational ministry. It was no coincidence that Mahan was a leading exponent of holiness or Christian perfection, a recovery of the early Methodist idea that believers should expect a second crisis experience of sanctification, equipping them for a subsequent life of intensified commitment and witness.[46] Such a doctrine was particularly empowering for women, because when they believed themselves to have experienced sanctification they acquired new confidence and credibility in relation to men. In the late 1830s and 1840s, as Finney and Mahan were developing the college at Oberlin, in New York Phoebe Palmer (1807-1874) was beginning what was to become a highly influential transatlantic ministry disseminating holiness teaching. Eventually the later nineteenth-century holiness movement was to open new doors for women in public ministry. The further development of these trends extended beyond the period covered in this book, but there are good grounds for seeing evangelicalism in general and Finneyite revivalism in particular as an important seedbed of a later, more self-conscious, feminism.[47] It is also noteworthy, however, that some prominent women who had been profoundly shaped and empowered by evangelicalism in their early life later moved radically away from its teachings: for example, Antoinette Brown became a Unitarian and George Eliot a secular humanist. The association of evangelicalism and feminism was genuine, but never entirely comfortable.

RELATIONSHIPS, MARRIAGE AND FAMILY LIFE

While the history of the family is often studied in association with the history

---

[45] Quoted in Nancy A. Hardesty, *Your Daughters Shall Prophesy: Revivalism and Feminism in the Age of Finney* (Brooklyn: Carlson, 1991), p. 19.

[46] See above, pp. 49, 100-101.

[47] Hardesty, *Your Daughters Shall Prophesy*, especially pp. 19-21, 38-43; Anne C. Loveland, "Domesticity and Religion in the Antebellum Period: The Career of Phoebe Palmer," in *Religion*, vol. 13, History of Women in the United States, ed. Nancy F. Cott (Munich: K. G. Saur, 1993), pp. 35-51.

of women, it did, of course, also essentially and intimately involve men. Indeed, the question of whether home and family should be viewed as a predominantly female domain or rather as one in which both sexes were fully, if not equally, active goes straight to the heart of an ongoing historiographical debate, concerning the extent to which it is valid to think in this period of the reinforcement of "separate spheres" of women's activity in the home and men's activity in the workplace and the wider world. The role of women in society is also seen as centrally related to the development of a middle-class identity grounded in a "domestic ideology," elevating the home as the key symbol of respectability, presided over by the female "angel in the house." Such topics in social and cultural history extend well beyond the specific subject matter of this book, and accordingly no attempt is made here to explore them systematically.[48] Domestic ideology was a product of other religious and secular forces as well as evangelicalism; a rounded understanding of the development of class and social structure needs to consider economic and social factors as well as religious and ideological ones. Nevertheless, evangelicalism has been generally acknowledged as a central strand in these developments. In approaching them primarily from the perspective of evangelicalism rather than of the history of women, three key points are worthy of emphasis.

First, the converse of the argument that evangelicalism was important for women in this period is that the support of women was vital to the success and expansion of evangelicalism. Indeed it can be argued, especially in relation to the United States, that there was during this period an increasing "feminization" of church membership. In England, too, women were in the majority in

---

[48]Seminal works are Cott, *Bonds of Womanhood*; Barbara Leslie Epstein, *The Politics of Domesticity: Women, Evangelism and Temperance in Nineteenth Century America* (Middletown, Conn.: Wesleyan University Press, 1981); Mary P. Ryan, *Cradle of the Middle Class: The Family in Oneida County, New York, 1790-1865* (Cambridge: Cambridge University Press, 1981); and Leonore Davidoff and Catherine Hall, *Family Fortunes: Men and Women of the English Middle Class 1780-1850* (London: Hutchinson, 1987). Second editions of Cott (1997) and Davidoff and Hall (2002) include useful surveys and discussions of works published in the intervening years. A particular theme has been the questioning of the "separate spheres" model. For a further such survey assessing the application of American and British scholarship to Canada, see Nancy F. Christie, ed., *Households of Faith: Family, Gender, and Community in Canada, 1760-1969* (Montreal and Kingston: McGill-Queen's University Press, 2002), Introduction.

evangelical churches. They made up 57.2 percent of a sample of Wesleyans for the period 1751-1825, and a sample of Baptists and Congregationalists shows a rising trend during our period, from 54.8 percent in 1776-1800 to 60.7 percent in 1801-1825 and 65.2 percent in 1826-1850.[49] As Richard Johnson struggled to establish Christian worship in the convict colony of New South Wales, he noted that it was "especially the women" who attended his services.[50] There are indications that women could play an important role in leading their husbands to evangelical conversions, and their influence as mothers was certainly crucial in drawing the next generation into churches, especially when their husbands did not necessarily share their commitment. In a sample of church families at Whitestown, New York, between 1813 and 1816, in only six cases out of ninety-seven was the wife of a male church member not also a member. In a further forty cases both spouses were members; but in no less than forty-one families the wife was a member without her husband.[51] It has been argued, though, that precisely because male ministers were conscious that women made up a numerical majority of their congregations, they became more self-conscious in maintaining a patriarchal model of authority, more reluctant to concede them any role in leadership, and more fearful of the destabilizing potential of female sinfulness. There was in the early nineteenth century a tension between a view of women as assertive, dissimulating and seductive, and one of them as passionless, domestic and readily acquiescing in their subordination to men. Only when—in the 1820s and 1830s—the latter ideal seemed to gain general acceptance in the churches did it seem safe to restore to women some degree of controlled influence.[52]

Second, though, in significant respects evangelicalism operated, both ideologically and practically, to modify rather than to reinforce acceptance of "separate spheres." There was an underlying conviction of spiritual equality, as affirmed in sentiments attributed to Hannah More:

---

[49]C. D. Field, "Adam and Eve: Gender in the English Free Church Constituency," *Journal of Ecclesiastical History* 44 (1993): 66, 69.

[50]George Mackarness, ed., *Some Letters of Rev. Richard Johnson, BA, First Chaplain of New South Wales* (Sydney: D. S. Ford, 1954), p. 44; cf. Anne O'Brien, *God's Willing Workers: Women and Religion in Australia* (Sydney: UNSW Press, 2005), pp. 18-21.

[51]Wilson, *Constrained by Zeal*, pp. 82, 147-49; Ryan, *Cradle of the Middle Class*, p. 287.

[52]Susan Juster, *Disorderly Women: Sexual Politics and Evangelicalism in Revolutionary New England* (Ithaca, N.Y.: Cornell University Press, 2004), pp. 169-79.

Women . . . make up one half of the human race: equally with men redeemed by
the blood of Christ. In this their true dignity consists; here their best pretensions
rest, here their highest claims are allowed.[53]

At a more practical level, it has been argued that, in England,

The rising tide of religious Evangelicalism did not efface the woman in public,
rather it reorientated the public life of the more serious-minded away from
worldly entertainment towards good works.[54]

Conversion can also be seen as an experience common to both genders,
which had a leveling effect. Evangelical women perceived themselves as quite as
sinful and in need of redemption as men were, contrary to the secular "angel in
the house" image of inherently "good" and spiritual womanhood.[55] It has been
argued that, far from polarizing the sexes and confining women to a subordi-
nate domestic sphere, conversion brought them closer together by giving men
a new consciousness of family and social connections, and women increased
confidence and self-worth.[56] We have noted above the paradoxical impact of
writers such as Hannah More and Catharine Beecher, who, while accepting and
indeed advocating the exclusion of women from perceived male activities, nevertheless argued powerfully that women should be thoroughly well educated. In
1829 Beecher even introduced a course in moral philosophy at her school for
girls in Hartford.[57] By such means, women would be equipped to exercise
strong social, religious and even indirect political influence through the channels that were open to them. On the frontiers of European settlement, for example in New South Wales in the 1820s and 1830s, the combination of evangelical zeal and practical necessity drove women to take a formative role in the
development of new communities.[58]

Third, in the eyes of evangelicals, domestic and family responsibilities ac-

---

[53] *The Young Bride at Home* (Boston: James Loring, 1836), p. 246.

[54] Amanda Vickery, *The Gentleman's Daughter: Women's Lives in Georgian England* (New Haven,
Conn.: Yale University Press, 1998), p. 288.

[55] Wilson, *Constrained by Zeal*, pp. 94-95.

[56] Susan Juster, " 'In a Different Voice': Male and Female Narratives of Religious Conversion in Post-Revolutionary America," in *American Quarterly* 41 (1989): 34-62; cf. Epstein,
Politics of Domesticity, pp. 45-87.

[57] Cott, *Bonds of Womanhood*, p. 111.

[58] O'Brien, *God's Willing Workers*, pp. 24-25.

tively involved men as well as women.[59] It is true that such a commitment initially seemed ambivalent in respect of early Methodist itinerant preachers, often young single men who were perceived as subversive of family life, whether because they were seen as celibate misfits, or, worse, because they were believed in reality to be secret seducers of their female converts. Married itinerants often seemed neglectful of their own wives and families, in the face of the overriding imperative to preach the gospel.[60] In America the tone and standard was set by Bishop Francis Asbury, who remained single from the conviction that

> I could hardly expect to find a woman with grace enough to enable her to live but one week out of the fifty-two with her husband: besides, what right has any man to take advantage of the affections of a woman, make her his wife, and by a voluntary absence subvert the whole order and economy of the marriage state, but separating those whom neither God, nature, nor the requirements of the civil society permit long to be put asunder?[61]

Thus even in rejecting marriage for himself, Asbury upheld his sense of the responsibilities it imposed on other men. Indeed, as Methodism developed, countervailing tendencies for the assertion and celebration of domestic ties asserted themselves, and the family circle came to be perceived as an essential means for the upholding and spread of the gospel. The desire to live a more normal family life was the strongest factor driving the shift in American Methodism from an itinerant to a "settled" ministry during this period.[62]

Evangelical concepts of manliness were a challenge to contemporary secular male values, whether among those of the British gentry, landowners in the American South, or convicts forcibly resettled in Australia. Emphasis on "honor," machismo and lineage was confronted by stress on "calling," moral virtue and the family as a spiritual community of mutual affection rather than

---

[59]Secondary literature on masculinity remains sparse in comparison to that on femininity, but see particularly E. Anthony Rotundo, *American Manhood: Transformations in Masculinity from the Revolution to the Modern Era* (New York: Basic Books, 1993); and John Tosh, *A Man's Place: Masculinity and the Middle Class Home in Victorian England* (New Haven, Conn.: Yale University Press, 1999).

[60]Heyrman, *Southern Cross*, pp. 129-34.

[61]J. Manning Potts, Elmer T. Clark and Jacob S. Payton, eds., *The Letters and Journals of Francis Asbury*, 3 vols. (London: Epworth Press, 1958) 3:278.

[62]A. Gregory Schneider, *The Way of the Cross Leads Home: The Domestication of American Methodism* (Bloomington: Indiana University Press, 1993); Tosh, *Man's Place*, pp. 38-39.

merely an expression of patriarchal sovereignty.[63] Richard Johnson's address in 1792 to the predominantly male and non-churchgoing inhabitants of New South Wales and Norfolk Island can indeed be read as a particularly stark expression of that cultural clash, both in its negative condemnation of profanity, dishonesty and sexual license, and in its positive affirmation of prayer, Bible-reading, churchgoing and family life.[64] Exhortations and guidance to men dwelt particularly on the development of character and of public duties and responsibilities, and encouragement to uphold family responsibilities was by contrast relatively infrequent. Nevertheless, when such issues were discussed they were given considerable weight. Thus although Thomas Gisborne, who was associated with the Clapham Sect, spent the greater part of his *Enquiry into the Duties of Men* (1794) discussing different roles and professions, he concluded with a chapter on the duties of private gentlemen, which he urged all his readers to consider "as particularly addressed to himself." Gisborne affirmed that Scripture taught the subordination of women in marriage, but reminded his male readers that it also taught that men should love and honor their wives:

> They teach him to study every reasonable and prudent indulgence of her wishes; to accustom his thoughts to dwell rather on her merits than on her imperfections; and when he thinks on the latter to remember his own; to win her by his counsel, by his encouragement, and above all by his attractive example, to continual advances in every virtuous habit and pursuit; and if obliged to point out something reprehensible in her conduct, to avoid provoking expressions, taunts and sneers, with at least as much care as reproaches and invective.[65]

In lectures to young men delivered at the Independent Christian Church in Richmond, Virginia, and repeated in Charlestown, Massachusetts, E. H. Chapin strongly emphasized the "vital duty" of his hearers in relation to "the holy ties of family," urging them to take very seriously responsibilities as brothers and sons and, as husbands, to "truly cherish that deep and holy affection that brightens around your way."[66]

---

[63]Schneider, *Way of the Cross*, p. xxiv; Davidoff and Hall, *Family Fortunes*, p. 110.

[64]See above, p. 14.

[65]Thomas Gisborne, *An Enquiry into the Duties of Men in the Higher and Middle Classes of Society in Great Britain* (London, 1794), pp. 5, 603-4.

[66]E. H. Chapin, *Duties of Young Men* (Boston: Abel Tompkins & B. B. Mussey, 1840), pp. 61-68.

Domestic virtue was also upheld by the negative strategy of urging young men to resist sexual temptation. The American Sylvester Graham published a sustained diatribe against masturbation, "illicit commerce with the other sex," and even over-indulgence within marriage, in the belief "that the Bible doctrine of marriage and sexual continence and purity, is founded on the physiological principles established in the constitutional nature of man."[67] Graham's quasi-medical approach was complemented by preachers such as Henry Ward Beecher in Indianapolis and John Angell James in Birmingham, who were also forthright in urging men to resist sexual temptation, whether in disastrously corrupting an innocent girl or succumbing to the wiles of a prostitute.[68] Such evangelical preachers might presume a sexual double standard in respect of knowledge—being frank with men, while perpetuating women's ignorance—but in respect of actions they clearly affirmed the gravity of sexual sin for men as well as for women.

Although evidence is inevitably patchy and circumstantial, it seems that such standards were frequently honored in the breach as well as in the observance, as shown by church discipline records. Some of the most interesting evidence comes from Upper Canada.[69] More women than men were admonished or excommunicated for sexual lapses, and pleas that they had been raped or seduced were seldom taken seriously. There were obvious practical reasons why a woman was more likely to be disciplined: pregnancy "proved" her guilt, but there could be no such conclusive evidence against the man, who was also statistically less likely to be a church member and would find it easier to leave a community quietly to avoid retribution. Nevertheless, she was not necessarily seen as more sinful than him, and indeed evangelical churches were less subject

---

[67]Sylvester Graham, *A Lecture to Young Men on Chastity* (Boston, 1837), pp. 19, 62.

[68]Henry Ward Beecher, *Lectures to Young Men in Various Important Subjects* (Salem: J. P. Jewett & Co., 1846), pp. 170-214; J. A. James, *Youth Warned. A Sermon Preached in Carr's Lane Meeting House, on Sunday Evening, January 4th 1824, and Addressed Particularly to Young Men* (Birmingham: B. Hudson, 1824).

[69]Lynne Marks, "No Double Standard?: Leisure, Sex and Sin in Upper Canadian Church Discipline Records, 1800-1860," in *Gendered Pasts: Historical Essays in Femininity and Masculinity in Canada*, eds. Kathryn McPherson, Cecilia Morgan and Nancy M. Forestell (Toronto: University of Toronto Press, 2003), pp. 55-60. See also Juster, *Disorderly Women*, pp. 150-51, on New England; Michael R. Watts, *The Dissenters: Volume II: The Expansion of Evangelical Nonconformity* (Oxford: Oxford University Press, 1995), pp. 201-2, on England.

to a sexual double standard than the surrounding society. There was also a genuine readiness in due course to forgive the genuinely penitent: in 1844 an Edinburgh Free Church of Scotland Kirk Session minute concerned the case of Barbara Fechnie, who confessed that "five years ago she had brought forth a child in fornication." Now, however, she expressed her "deep sorrow and remorse" and it was accordingly agreed that she "should be rebuked and absolved."[70] For some evangelical males sexual temptation had to be resisted at all costs. The American itinerant preacher Jeremiah Minter who had himself castrated was probably a unique case, but other Methodist ministers startled eligible women by their studied indifference to their charms. The indications of sexual frustration prior to marriage of leading British evangelicals such as Henry Thornton and Lord Ashley form evidence that they were consistent to their professions of chastity.[71]

One rare glimpse of an upper-class evangelical's attitudes to a sexual lapse is found in the letters of Robert Inglis (1786-1855), a future member of Parliament, to his close friend Sir Thomas Acland. Inglis, then an undergraduate at Oxford, admitted that on January 28, 1806, he had had sexual relations with a servant girl named Sarah Lea. Although he acknowledged that this was a failure of "good Resolutions," his conscience did not seem to be unduly troubled by the incident as he "was not guilty of any predetermined seduction," he perceived her to be "willing" and "had no remote suspicion that the girl was, till then, innocent." Later in the year, however, he was horrified to receive a lawyer's letter informing him that Sarah was pregnant. Inglis came to believe her claims that he must be the father, as she asserted that "before and after her connection with me, she never knew man."

[70]National Archives of Scotland, Edinburgh, CH3/1195/23, Newington Free Church, Kirk Session Minutes, April 23, 1844.

[71]Heyrman, *Southern Cross*, pp. 129-32; Stott, *Hannah More*, pp. 192-93; Geoffrey B. A. M. Finlayson, *The Seventh Earl of Shaftesbury* (London: Eyre Methuen, 1981), pp. 41-49. The Minter case might seem at first sight to confirm Edward Thompson's view that "Methodism is permeated with teaching as to the sinfulness of sexuality" (E. P. Thompson, *The Making of the English Working Class* [Harmondsworth: Penguin, 1968], p. 407), but to evangelicals it was unregulated sexuality rather than sexuality *per se* that was sinful. The concerns of Methodists on this front need to be understood in the context of their recognition that the intensity of their meetings and the informal and domestic nature of much of their religious activity gave rise to particular temptations.

While readily accepting financial responsibility for the unborn child, he appeared more deeply troubled by the apparent revelation that he had been responsible for leading a virgin astray. However, when mid-November came and the baby had still not been born, his remorse turned to mingled relief and anger, as he decided it was a medical impossibility that it could be his. He now saw himself as victim rather than villain, as Sarah was exposed as promiscuous and dishonest. He did, though, desire that she be given an opportunity to redeem herself, as the inmate of a Magdalen asylum or as a servant in the household of "one who might perhaps be called a Methodist" and "who would glory in the conversion of a sinner." His own conduct clearly fell short of the evangelical ideal and showed double standards insofar as his view of the gravity of his own offense changed with his perceptions of the girl's sexual history, but it was also characterized by a degree of moral responsibility and spiritual concern that set it apart from the widespread secular standards of the day.[72]

The evangelical ideal of marriage was one of genuine partnership and spiritual equality, albeit one in which roles were different and the wife's fulfilment was to be found not in autonomous achievements but in raising a family and supporting her husband's endeavors. Edward Bickersteth, in a series of letters to his fiancée Sarah Bignold written in the months before their marriage in 1812, spelled out his hopes for their future together. He looked forward to their "fire-side evenings" as a time when "we shall often be brought near to God . . . while we enjoy communion with one another." He explained his views on money, in which, without inviting her comments, he was "persuaded we shall agree" and expected her also to concur in his wish to "use hospitality without grudging." He was, though, in all things ready "to bow to the authority of Scripture, and anxiously desirous of promoting your ease, comfort and happiness." He hoped they would have complete confidence in each other, never have interests or wishes that differed, and would enjoy a "perpetual friendship" that would continue even beyond death. Subsequently, looking back on the thirty-eight years of marriage that followed, Bickersteth's son-in-law and biographer believed that

---

[72]Devon Record Office, Exeter, Acland of Killerton Papers, 1148M add 36/76-80, Inglis to Acland (October 19, November 5, 16, 18, 24, 1806).

"these hopes were not disappointed."[73] Such sentiments were shared by John Dow, a Methodist minister in New Jersey, who in his obituary for his wife Anne, who died in December 1822, conveyed a vivid sense of a marriage of genuine companionship and friendship.[74] Similarly, Lord Ashley perceived his wife as an invaluable confidante and counselor, recording in his diary in October 1839 how they had taken a walk together and "had much interesting conversation." He felt that God had fully answered his prayers for "a wife for my comfort, improvement and safety."[75] It seems reasonable to infer, despite the inevitable lack of evidence, that such successful marriages were also sexually fulfilled: certainly some unusually uninhibited correspondence that has survived for a few Methodist marriages would support such a judgment.[76]

It is less easy to find evidence of the wife's perspective; even when they did feature in obituaries, these were often written by men. However, in Eliza Marsden's letters from Parramatta, New South Wales, one senses a genuine sense of sharing in the spiritual as well as the material trials of her husband's ministry.[77] Similarly, there was no doubting the intense mutual devotion in Barbara Wilberforce's marriage to William, in which, while he readily forgave her notorious deficiencies in conventional homemaking skills, they rejoiced in their emotional and spiritual companionship.[78] Moreover, although the wife's situation was normally the supportive one, it is still possible to find instances of evangelical marriages where public roles were reversed, or at least shared. Examples include, in England, Zachariah Taft's affirmation of the right of his wife Mary and of other women to preach; in America, the readiness of Abigail Roberts's husband to escort her on her preaching engagements; and Charlotte Elizabeth's happy second

---

[73]Thomas Rawson Birks, *Memoir of the Rev. Edward Bickersteth*, 2 vols. (London: Seelays, 1852), I:194-207.

[74]*Methodist Magazine* 6 (1823): 96-101.

[75]Edwin Hodder, *The Life and Work of the Seventh Earl of Shaftesbury, K. G.*, 3 vols. (London: Cassell, 1886), I:279.

[76]Tosh, *Man's Place*, pp. 58-59.

[77]George Mackarness, ed., *Some Private Correspondence of the Rev. Samuel Marsden and Family 1794-1824* (Sydney: D. S. Ford, 1942), pp. 14-15, 36-37.

[78]E. M. Forster, *Marianne Thornton. A Domestic Biography* (London: Edward Arnold, 1956), pp. 42-44; Stott, *Hannah More*, pp. 201-2.

marriage to Lewis Hippolytus Tonna, in which he devoted himself to encouraging and promoting her work.[79] Such relationships, though, depended on both partners being believers, as was apparent in the disastrous failure of Charlotte Elizabeth's first marriage to Captain Phelan. An address in 1839 to the Norfolk Association of Baptist Churches strongly affirmed the principle of believers marrying believers, while recognizing that it was widely breached in practice, a compromise that would in effect have been forced on many women given the gender imbalance in most churches.[80]

The experience of evangelical children, like that of evangelical women, has been vulnerable to stereotyping by historians, who have often concurred that the growing cultural ascendancy of evangelicalism during the early nineteenth century was associated with an ethos of harsh discipline and spiritual manipulation. Evangelical ideas and approaches, founded on a belief in original sin, are adversely contrasted with secular ones, seen as rooted in a belief in childhood innocence.[81] It is true that some evangelical parents, anxious for their children's eternal salvation and concerned to check any tendencies to moral corruption, could appear austere and heavy-handed. When closer attention is paid to the actual dynamics of family life, however, a more nuanced and varied picture emerges. Children are seen as genuinely internalizing evangelical beliefs, rather than being terrorized into conversion. They were attracted to heaven more than they feared hell. They were often willing participants in family religious observances, which they perceived as natural parts of their routine. Sunday was a day for decorous relaxation as well as for church attendance and spiritual pursuits. Above all, parents and others blended affection with discipline. Thus William Wilberforce wrote in 1806 to his eldest son, then eight, from whom he was separated for some weeks: "I feel the want of you every day, but we must both of us remember that we ought to be contented with that which is best,

---

[79] See above, p. 130; Brekus, *Strangers and Pilgrims*, p. 223; Charlotte Elizabeth, *Personal Recollections*, pp. 391-430.

[80] John Bane, *The Marriage of Believers with Unbelievers* (Norwich, 1839); cf. Watts, *Dissenters*, pp. 202-3.

[81] See the overview of the literature in Mary Clare Martin, "Children and Religion in Walthamstow and Leyton, c 1740-c 1870" (Ph.D. thesis, University of London, 2000), pp. 13-20.

though there may be things that would be more agreeable to us."[82] There
was also scope for children, notably in the fluid religious culture of the
American Second Great Awakening, to develop their own spiritual experience, unmediated by adults and blending evangelical teaching with ideas
from folklore and their own imaginations.[83]

The world of early nineteenth-century evangelical children was also shaped by
the increasing body of literature written for them. This can be read as encapsulat-
ing a rigid and frightening moral and spiritual discipline. Certainly this was a
world in which sinfulness toward God and disobedience to parents was likely to
bring harsh retribution. For example, in one of Charlotte Elizabeth's stories for
children, young Henry, who disobeys his father's instructions not to eat berries in
his uncle's garden, is taken horribly ill during a church service, fears that he is going to die and go to hell, and heartily repents of his sin.[84] To twenty-first-century
readers, the recurrent presence of death and serious illness in such literature is disconcerting, but in this respect it reflected the reality of many children's experience
and arguably helped to prepare them for real-life suffering and bereavement. To
authors, moreover, it served an essential purpose in enabling them to turn children's thoughts to spiritual matters.[85] Nevertheless, at its best such literature was
by no means narrowly didactic. Mary Sherwood, the most successful and influential evangelical writer for children in the early nineteenth century, was widely
published on both sides of the Atlantic. She was able to construct tales which,
while suffused with a strong sense of morality and spiritual priorities, had a viv-
idness and capacity for understanding the child's perspective that ensured them
an extensive influence. In her *History of the Fairchild Family*, first published in 1818,
the parents are strict and sanctimonious, but they also provide a secure and loving home. The evocations of childhood naughtiness are entertaining and true

---

[82]Ibid., pp. 132-54, 403-67; Doreen Rosman, *Evangelicals and Culture* (London: Croom
Helm, 1984), pp. 97-118; Wilberforce House, Hull, Wilberforce Letters, Box 6 No. 22,
Wilberforce to William Wilberforce Jr. (August 20, 1806). As Rosman observes, the written sources that have come down to us inadequately encapsulate the human reality of interactions between parents and children.

[83]Jacqueline S. Reinier, *From Virtue to Character: American Childhood, 1775-1850* (New York:
Twayne, 1996), pp. 76-78.

[84]Charlotte Elizabeth, *Short Stories for Children* (Edinburgh: Gall & Inglis, 1861).

[85]For example, Mrs. Sherwood, *The History of the Fairchild Family*, ed. Barry Westburg (New
York: Garland, 1977), pp. 145-53.

to life.[86] Underlying Mrs. Sherwood's stories was a consistent sense of the family as a fundamentally valuable institution, not just as a domestic idyll but as an essential channel for the spread of the Christian faith. Even when the family is dysfunctional or shattered by bereavement, it can still serve that purpose. Thus in *The Little Woodman*, young William, after the death of his parents, is abandoned in the forest by his brothers, but providentially finds his long-lost grandmother, who gives him a home and a Christian upbringing. After her death he marries, establishes his own Christian family, forgives and supports his estranged brothers, and has the pleasure of seeing his "children's children growing up in the fear of God."[87]

For British evangelicals, regular family prayers were a key means, as Edward Bickersteth put it, "of propagating piety to posterity." "Children," he reminded the readers of his widely read *Treatise on Prayer*, "are creatures of imitation" who "love to copy all that they see in others." The custom was already well established in evangelical families by the end of the eighteenth century, and it persisted through much of the nineteenth century. Statements such as "Every head of a family should consider himself as the minister or priest of his own family" convey an impression of patriarchy, but in reality, as Mary-Clare Martin has recently shown, such prayers were sometimes conducted by women.[88] Bickersteth argued that family prayers would promote domestic harmony and bring the presence and blessing of God into the family circle. He advised beginning with a Bible reading, singing a psalm or hymn when time and ability allowed, and then concluding with prayer for particular family circumstances, sins, wants, friends and mercies. He recommended extempore prayer as giving scope for response to personal circumstances, but he nonetheless also published a manual of set prayers for family devotions. Similarly, Robert Inglis posthumously published the family prayers used by Henry Thornton in the heyday of the Clapham Sect.[89]

---

[86]Ibid., pp. 53, 70-83; M. Nancy Cutt, *Mrs Sherwood and her Books for Children* (London: Oxford University Press, 1974), pp. 64-68, 112-13.

[87]Cutt, *Mrs Sherwood*, facsimile of *The Little Woodman and His Dog Caesar* (Wellington, Salop, 1828).

[88]Paul Sangster, *Pity my Simplicity: The Evangelical Revival and the Religious Education of Children 1738-1800* (London: Epworth Press, 1963), pp. 72-73; Edward Bickersteth, *A Treatise on Prayer* (London: L. B. Seeley, 1818), pp. 124-42; and *Family Prayers* (London: R. B. Seeley & W. Burnside, 1842); Martin, "Children and Religion," pp. 223-31; but cf. Wilson, *Constrained by Zeal*, pp. 150-52.

[89]Bickersteth, *Family Prayers*; *Treatise on Prayer*; *Family Prayers by the Late Henry Thornton* (London, 1834).

The very earnestness of the evangelical commitment to the family reflected their awareness that it was a fragile institution, although unlike its twenty-first-century counterpart more likely to be broken up by death than by divorce. The models advocated were, moreover, hard to detach from middle-class expectations of decorum, insofar as they tended to presuppose significant living space and privacy, the presence of servants, and mothers who did not need to work outside the home. The custom of family prayer was sometimes urged upon the lower classes, but it is uncertain how extensively it was adopted. Bickersteth, in his *Family Prayers*, provided a section of short "Cottager's family prayers," but the book as a whole was evidently designed for educated users with time on their hands. Much of the intensity of Charlotte Elizabeth's attack on women's work in *The Wrongs of Woman* derived from her perception that it undermined family life, but, as she so graphically illustrated, many working-class women had no economic option other than to take paid employment.[90] In the United States there were evangelical enthusiasts for family prayers, notably among the Methodists, but the custom does not appear to have been as widespread as in Britain.[91]

An individual's recollections of his or her childhood have a timeless quality that can betray the historian into perceiving evangelical family life as static rather than constantly changing. Such change was inevitable in the context of any particular family as children grew up, developed their own perspectives on their formative influences, and became parents themselves. There was also a wider trend, as the evangelical movement expanded, from early nineteenth-century families suddenly confronted by the zeal of newly converted members, to mid-century ones in which long-standing shared evangelical commitment was the professed bedrock of relationships. The latter context, though, could have its limitations as well as strengths in spreading evangelicalism to the rising generation, because the naïvely penetrating gaze of children ruthlessly exposed hypocrisy and legalism. An American Methodist writer observed in 1827:

---

[90]Bickersteth, *Family Prayers*, pp. 207-22; Charlotte Elizabeth, *Wrongs of Woman, Part II The Forsaken Home* (London: W. H. Dalton, 1843), pp. 1-35; Martin, "Children and Religion," p. 230.

[91]Schneider, *Way of the Cross*, pp. 138-43. Whereas the British Library catalogue lists dozens of manuals of family prayers for this period, the Library of Congress catalogue lists only three, two of which were by British authors. The one such work by an American author, the Episcopalian Bishop William Meade, was published in Alexandria, Virginia, in 1834.

How frequently have we heard the complaint made, that a majority of children composing the families of professors of religion, are worse than those of irreligious parents. And why, we ask, is this so? May not a satisfactory answer, in most cases, be found in the circumstance, that parents are not always as careful as they should be, to back and support, by the irresistible argument of holy living, the precepts they give their children?[92]

On the other hand, as Horace Bushnell, minister of the North Congregrational Church in Hartford, Connecticut, argued in 1846, a truly Christian home provided an environment in which a child, rather than being perceived as a sinner who could only become a true Christian after teenage conversion, would "grow up a Christian, and never know himself as being otherwise."[93] However, even when parents maintained lifestyles of unimpeachable integrity, there was no guarantee that they could transmit their full framework of belief to their children. Certainly some notable children of evangelical homes—such as Edward Henry Bickersteth, son of Edward; Catherine Marsh, daughter of William; and Henry Venn, son of John—continued straightforwardly to identify with their parental faith.[94] Many others, however, did not. For all the evangelical zeal and parental devotion that characterized their early years, the later lives of both the Beecher and the Wilberforce children, with moves to romantic liberalism and Roman Catholicism respectively, came to exemplify the adaptation and rejection of early nineteenth-century evangelicalism rather than its perpetuation.[95]

The impact of the expansion of evangelicalism on gender relations and family life was in many respects a history of unintended and sometimes paradoxical consequences, as the spiritual imperative to proclaim the gospel and transmit Chris-

---

[92]*Methodist Magazine* 10 (1827): 54.

[93]Horace Bushnell, *Christian Nurture* (reprinted, New Haven, Conn.: Yale University Press, 1947), pp. xxxviii-xxxix, 4. Such a perspective implied a relaxation of a traditional evangelical understanding of conversion.

[94]F. K. Aglionby, *The Life of Edward Henry Bickersteth DD Bishop and Poet* (London: Longmans, 1907); *BDEB*, pp. 743-44, 1138-40.

[95]For explorations of the spiritual dynamics of prominent evangelical families, see David Newsome, *The Parting of Friends: A Study of the Wilberforces and Henry Manning* (London: John Murray, 1966); Marie Caskey, *Chariot of Fire: Religion and the Beecher Family* (New Haven, Conn.: Yale University Press, 1978) (on the Beechers); and Christopher Tolley, *Domestic Biography: The Legacy of Evangelicalism in Four Nineteenth-Century Families* (Oxford: Oxford University Press, 1997) (on the Macaulays, Stephens, Thorntons and Wilberforces).

tianity to the rising generation interacted with other social and cultural forces. The affirmation of the spiritual equality of men and women was sincere, giving confidence to some women and laying an important seedbed for later Christian feminism. However, the simultaneous insistence that the two sexes had different—if overlapping—roles and responsibilities in society worked to limit women's fields of activity. In upholding the family as a crucial mechanism for spreading and sustaining the faith, evangelicals were swimming with the rising tide of nineteenth-century middle-class domesticity, but ultimately for them, as for their more secular contemporaries, the family tended to become an end in itself.

6

TRANSFORMING
SOCIETY

If the strange warming of John Wesley's heart at Aldersgate Street in the city of London on May 24, 1738, is to be seen as one of the defining moments in the early history of evangelicalism, a similarly symbolic significance for a later generation might be attributed to a meeting on January 2, 1786, between William Wilberforce and John Newton, in the suburb of Hoxton, a mile or so to the northeast. Wilberforce was then twenty-six years old, a rising politician who had already laid the foundations of a potentially glittering career; Newton had just turned sixty, and following his colorful early life as a slave trader and his curacy at Olney in the 1760s and 1770s, was now vicar of St. Mary Woolnoth in London, and an acknowledged patriarch in the small circle of Anglican Evangelicalism. The younger man had endured several months of emotional and spiritual anguish following his conviction of the reality of Christianity and of the sinfulness of his past life. His initial response was to contemplate withdrawal from the world to cultivate his relationship with God, but his close friend William Pitt, the prime minister, advised him strongly against a course of action that would "render your talents useless both to yourself and mankind." "Surely," Pitt wrote, "the principles as well as the practice of Christianity are simple, and lead not to meditation only but to action."[1] Pitt, though, was a merely conventional Christian and Wilberforce continued to agonize not only over his spiritual state, but over the appropriate course for his future life. In

---

[1]A. M. Wilberforce, ed., *Private Papers of William Wilberforce* (London: T. F. Unwin, 1897), p. 13, Pitt to Wilberforce, December 2, 1785.

some embarrassment, still "very unhappy," he secretly sought out Newton (whom he had met as a boy) and was "bitterly mov'd—he comforted me and [I was] much happier."[2] Newton's influence was crucial not only in counseling Wilberforce spiritually, but also in reinforcing from his very different perspective Pitt's advice to remain in public life, seeing it as a sphere for the exercise of his Christian vocation, rather than as a distraction from it. Significantly, the very next day, January 3, Wilberforce followed Newton's advice to call on John Thornton, the leading evangelical Anglican layman in London at the time,[3] a very wealthy merchant who was already using his substantial resources to support numerous religious causes. Thornton, who gave Wilberforce the use of a room in his house in Clapham as a refuge from London, was a role model for a Christian commitment that was outwardlooking rather than introverted. Moreover, Wilberforce's subsequent close friendship with Thornton's son Henry was the pivotal relationship around which the "Clapham Sect" of leading English evangelicals was to revolve. In the meantime, Wilberforce resumed his parliamentary duties "with increased diligence and conscientiousness."[4]

Just as the early evangelical revival would still have occurred, albeit in rather different forms, even if Wesley had not been converted in 1738, it is not suggested that the subsequent shift of evangelicalism to a greater degree of social and political engagement was contingent on Wilberforce's conversion in 1785-1786. Nevertheless, it was a highly significant event, not only in initiating the major direct contribution that Wilberforce himself was to make over the next four decades, but also in making it more socially respectable to be an evangelical, and in giving evangelicals a vision for transforming society as well as converting individuals. In October 1787 he wrote, "God Almighty has set before me two great objects, the suppression of the slave trade and the reformation of manners."[5] This personal agenda did not supersede the overriding evangelical imperative to preach the gospel, but was a recognition that his own gifts and opportunities gave him different and more specific tasks.

---

[2]Bodleian Library, Oxford, Wilberforce Papers, MS.Don.e.164 (Diary, January 2, 1786).
[3]Ibid., January 3, 1786.
[4]Wilberforce Papers, MS.Wilberforce.c.49, Autobiography, f. p. 14. On the Clapham Sect, see above, pp. 11-14.
[5]R. I. and S. Wilberforce, *The Life of William Wilberforce*, 5 vols. (London: John Murray, 1838), 1:149.

In 1797 Wilberforce published his first book, *A Practical View of the Prevailing Religious System of Professed Christians in the Higher and Middle Classes of this Country Contrasted with Real Christianity*. It was to be very widely read and reprinted on both sides of the Atlantic. The core of the book was an exposition of evangelical belief and a call to personal response, with Wilberforce convinced that "real Christianity" was vital to the nation on social and moral grounds, as well as for spiritual reasons. Since his conversion a decade before, the outbreak of revolution in France and indications of social and political unrest at home had stirred insecurities among the "higher and middle classes." Hence passages like the following struck a ready chord with his readers:

> Nor is it only by their personal conduct . . . that men of authority and influence may promote the cause of good morals. Let them in their several stations encourage virtue and discountenance vice in others. Let them enforce the laws by which the wisdom of our forefathers has guarded against the grosser infractions of morals. . . . Let them favour and take part in any plans which may be formed for the advancement of morality. Above all things, let them endeavour to instruct and improve the rising generation, that, if it be possible, an antidote may be provided for the malignity of that venom which is storing up in a neighbouring country [France]. . . . But fruitless will be all attempts to sustain, much more to revive, the fainting cause of morals unless you can in some degree restore the prevalence of Evangelical Christianity. It is in morals as in physics; unless the source of practical principles be elevated, it will be in vain to attempt to make them flow on a high level in their future course. . . . By all, therefore, who are studious of their country's welfare . . . every effort should be used to revive the Christianity of our better days.[6]

The book attracted wide interest: within a year of publication it had already sold out five editions in Britain. A first American edition appeared in Philadelphia in 1798 with a list of nearly 200 subscribers, and a Boston edition followed in 1799.[7] Wilberforce's arguments made evangelicalism seem attractive for patriotic as well as spiritual reasons, and help to explain its capacity in the first quarter of the nineteenth century to attract at least nominal support from illustrious indi-

---

[6]W. Wilberforce, *A Practical View of the Prevailing Religious System of Professed Christians in the Higher and Middle Classes of this Country Contrasted with Real Christianity* (London: T. Cadell and W. Davies, 1797), pp. 418-19.

[7]British Library catalogue; Wilberforce, *Practical View* (Philadelphia: John Ormrod, 1798), "Subscribers Names."

viduals such as George III's sons the Dukes of Kent and Sussex and his nephew the Duke of Gloucester. The Earl of Liverpool, prime minister from 1812 to 1827, was not himself an evangelical but supported numerous evangelical societies.[8] Similarly in North America, although the French revolutionaries were an ocean away, the turmoil in Europe still stimulated conservative anxieties. Meanwhile, in both the United States and Canada, a growing consciousness of social and moral turbulence particularly on the expanding western frontier gave added appeal to any movement likely to promote order and stability.[9]

In 1844 Sir James Stephen described the proliferation of evangelical organizations that had occurred in the half century since his father and his friends first gathered at Clapham in the 1790s:

> Ours is the age of societies. For the redress of every oppression that is done under the sun, there is a public meeting. For the cure of every sorrow by which our land or our race can be visited, there are patrons, vice-presidents and secretaries. For the diffusion of every blessing of which mankind can partake in common, there is a committee. That confederacy which, when pent up within the narrow limits of Clapham, jocose men invidiously called a "Sect," is now spreading through the habitable globe.[10]

Stephen was writing about Britain, but his observation was almost equally apposite in relation to the United States, where there had been a comparable growth of activity in support of almost every conceivable spiritual, moral and social purpose. The rationale for evangelical societies was to pursue specialized tasks that were not easily undertaken by local churches or denominational structures. Although, as Stephen's gently ironic tone indicates, formal organization in itself did not necessarily achieve anything, the societies had a role that was at least symbolic and at most highly strategic. They gave central roles to both laymen and laywomen,[11] in an era when the churches themselves were

---

[8] Ford K. Brown, *Fathers of the Victorians* (Cambridge: Cambridge University Press, 1961), pp. 248, 343, 354-57.

[9] Clifford S. Griffin, *Their Brothers' Keepers: Moral Stewardship in the United States, 1800-1865* (New Brunswick, N.J.: Rutgers University Press, 1960), p. 11.

[10] Stephen, "Clapham Sect," pp. 306-7.

[11] For specific discussion of female voluntary associations, see Anne M. Boylan, *The Origins of Women's Activism: New York and Boston, 1797-1840* (Chapel Hill: University of North Carolina Press, 2002).

dominated by clergy and ministers. There is no space here to list, let alone assess, all these myriad organizations, but the various fields of activity can be briefly described, major institutional developments identified, and some overall characteristics drawn out.[12] Footnotes will provide an indication of potential further reading. The first section will survey activity directed to the interlinked purposes of mission and Sunday schools, supported by evangelicals primarily as agencies for evangelism, and the second section will offer an overview of wider moral and social concerns. In the final section there will be an assessment of the extent to which the evangelical movement was responsible for wider social transformation in this period. In the next chapter we shall turn to consider more specifically political activity, notably the campaign against slavery and the overarching issue of relations between the churches and the state.

MISSION AND SUNDAY SCHOOLS

Among the earliest organizations—important both in its own right and as a prototype for other such activities—was the "Society established in London for the Support and Encouragement of Sunday Schools," set up in 1785 on the initiative of a Baptist merchant, William Fox. Fox had been inspired by the advocacy of Robert Raikes, a newspaper proprietor, who had helped to establish an Anglican school in Gloucester, his home town, in 1780. Raikes was particularly concerned to steer working-class children away from criminality. While a few Sunday schools had existed before the 1780s, he was significant in giving publicity to the idea, and also in Christianizing the institution, by ensuring that the scholars were given religious teaching and brought to church. Instruction in spelling and reading was a means to the end of reading the Bible rather than, as in the secular schools, an end in itself. The London society was interdenominational with its committee consisting "equally of members of the Church of England and Protestant Dissenters." Henry Thornton served as treasurer, and several Anglican bishops were supporters. The new society gave respectability to Sunday schools and also supported them by providing textbooks and occasional cash grants. The movement expanded rapidly, gaining notable inspiration from Hannah More's

---

[12]For extensive (but not necessarily comprehensive) lists of, respectively, English and American organizations, see Brown, *Fathers of the Victorians*, pp. 333-39; and Charles I. Foster, *An Errand of Mercy: The Evangelical United Front 1790-1837* (Chapel Hill: University of North Carolina Press, 1960), pp. 275-79.

well publicized schools in the Mendip Hills in the 1790s. There were already an estimated 69,000 children under instruction in Britain in 1797.[13]

In 1803 the Sunday School Union was established, with a view to facilitating communication and mutual encouragement among teachers, and to promoting the opening of new schools. A key role became the publication of textbooks. Unlike the Sunday School Society, it was an organization of the activists themselves rather than of their philanthropic patrons, and although the earlier organization continued in existence for several more decades it was gradually in effect superseded. The Sunday School Union, however, remained a predominantly Nonconformist organization, as Church of England schools normally did not join and Wesleyan ones were often reluctant to do so. Nevertheless, its activities expanded rapidly with 2,568 affiliated schools and 274,845 scholars in 1820 and 7,842 schools and 909,618 scholars in 1835. When Anglican and other non-affiliated Sunday schools are added, total enrollment has been calculated at 730,000 in 1821, 1,363,170 in 1833 and 2,099,611 in 1851. The 1851 figure amounted to 56.5 percent of the population of England and Wales aged between five and fifteen at that date.[14]

In 1805 the rising Wesleyan leader Jabez Bunting, in a powerful and influential sermon, had articulated the rationale for Sunday schools, which, in the language of his text, Nehemiah 6:3, he considered "a great work." Bunting saw their tasks as teaching children to read the Bible, instructing them in essential Christian belief and training them in "habits of piety and virtue." He believed that this was a work enjoined by biblical precept, which was essential because of the neglect or inability of parents to instruct their own children. It would guide the children toward virtuous and holy lives, which might lead to the conversion of their parents and would certainly benefit the nation as a whole by bringing them up to be moral and lawabiding members of society.[15] In view of

---

[13]BDEB, pp. 404, 913; *Plan of a Society Established in London for the Support and Encouragement of Sunday Schools* (London, 1787); William Henry Watson, *The History of the Sunday School Union* (London, 1853), p. 8; Thomas Walter Laqueur, *Religion and Respectability: Sunday Schools and Working Class Culture 1780-1850* (New Haven, Conn.: Yale University Press, 1976), pp. 35-36.

[14]Watson, *Sunday School Union*, p. 12; Laqueur, *Religion and Respectability*, pp. 35-44. See also Philip B. Cliff, *The Rise and Development of the Sunday School Movement in England 1780-1980* (Redhill: National Christian Education Council, 1986).

[15]Jabez Bunting, *A Great Work Described and Recommended, in a Sermon, Preached on Wednesday, May 15, 1805 . . . Before the Members of the Sunday School Union* (London: Richard Edwards, 1805), pp. 6-21.

the subsequent spectacular expansion of Sunday schools, there was some justi-
fication for the triumphalism of a hymn published in 1848, also affirming the
linkages of patriotism and Christianity in its appropriation of the tune and language of "Rule Britannia"

> When Sabbath Schools at Heaven's command
> Arose to swell the infant train,
> The ransomed choirs at Thy right hand,
> Enraptured sung this grateful strain—
> Hail Immanuel! Immanuel we'll adore
> For sin and error's reign is o'er.[16]

The development of Sunday schools in the United States lagged somewhat
behind that in Britain, with the earliest prototypes being set up in Philadelphia
in the 1790s. These initially reflected a rational Enlightenment view of education, but distinctively evangelical emphases came to the fore in the early years
of the nineteenth century and the number of schools grew rapidly in the 1810s
and 1820s. When the American Sunday School Union was founded in 1824
there were 48,681 children in its schools, increasing to 301,358 in 1832. Substantial though it was, however, that figure still only amounted to 7.9 percent
of the school-age population, a much lower proportion than the 45 percent of
English children attending Sunday school in 1833, although it should be borne
in mind that by no means all schools were affiliated to the ASSU. The full expansion of the American movement still lay in the future.[17] In British North
America, meanwhile, the Sunday School Union Society of Canada was in vigorous operation by 1824, with about 300 children regularly attending schools
in Montreal and dozens of other schools in operation across Upper and Lower
Canada. Here, too, the moral value of Sunday schools was emphasized: one
agent believed that their growth on both sides of the border with the United
States would reduce the need "for expending property in the erection of
FORTS and building of BATTLE SHIPS."[18]

---

[16] *Hymns Composed for . . . the Stockport Sunday School* (Manchester: J. Ambery, 1848), p. 24.

[17] Anne M. Boylan, *Sunday School: The Formation of an American Institution* (New Haven, Conn.:
Yale University Press, 1988), pp. 6-33; Laqueur, *Religion and Respectability*, p. 44. Boylan
does not offer a calculation of total American enrollments that would permit direct comparison with Laqueur's figures.

[18] *The Second Report of the Sunday School Union Society of Canada* (Montreal, 1824), pp. 5-13.

Whereas, arguably, the role of the national Sunday school societies was an ancillary one in a movement with strong roots in local churches and communities, other areas of activity were more heavily dependent on central organization. Overseas missions were important early exemplars for such evangelical organizations. Although the Society for the Propagation of the Gospel in Foreign Parts had already been in existence for nearly a century, its High Church Anglican ethos offered little scope for evangelicals, and its achievements had been limited ones. The Moravians with their own wide-ranging international networks had played an important role in pioneering the concept of overseas missions and in inspiring and facilitating the involvement of other evangelicals, but their direct organizational involvement was limited.[19] Growing awareness of wholly un-Christianized peoples overseas presented an initial stimulus to organize missions, articulated in 1792 in William Carey's *Enquiry into the Obligations of Christians, to use Means for the Conversion of the Heathen.* The publication of Carey's *Enquiry* was directly related to the formation of the Baptist Missionary Society in his own denomination in 1792, setting a trend that was followed by the London Missionary Society (1795), which was officially interdenominational but in practice became Congregational, the Edinburgh Missionary Society (1796, renamed the Scottish Missionary Society in 1819), the Glasgow Missionary Society (1796) and the Society for Missions to Africa and the East (1799), which became known as the Church Missionary Society (CMS) in 1812. The Methodist Missionary Society was not founded until 1813, but Methodists had in effect already been involved in missionary efforts in the West Indies and elsewhere for several decades. The first missionary organization in the United States, the American Board for Foreign Missions, was formed in 1810. It was intended to be interdenominational, but in practice became Congregational and Presbyterian. The Baptist Board of Foreign Missions followed in 1814, and Episcopalian and Methodist societies in 1820.

On both sides of the Atlantic activity was normally initially on a small scale and the CMS in its early years was heavily dependent on missionaries, like George Metzger, recruited in Germany and Switzerland through its collaboration with the Basel Mission. Nevertheless, it was in this period that the foun-

---

[19] J. C. S. Mason, *The Moravian Church and the Missionary Awakening in England 1760–1800* (Woodbridge: Royal Historical Society/Boydell Press, 2001), p. 180 and passim.

dations of the much larger missionary movement of the later nineteenth century were laid. Missions developed extensive networks of support at home, including numerous local auxiliary societies, which became channels for networking with a significance extending beyond the particular purposes of overseas mission. The CMS in particular gradually acquired considerable standing as a focal point for Anglican evangelicals, association with it being something of a "badge" of their party identity within the Church of England.[20]

For evangelicals the ready availability of the Bible was an essential prerequisite for mission. The British and Foreign Bible Society (BFBS) was founded in 1804, partly inspired by the legend of Mary Jones, the little Welsh girl who had saved money and walked a long distance to buy a Bible from the revivalist Thomas Charles of Bala, who then had none left to sell her. Like the CMS, it was closely linked to the Clapham circle, with Lord Teignmouth serving as its first president and Henry Thornton as the first treasurer. Wilberforce was also involved in the early arrangements. Unlike the CMS, however, the BFBS was non-denominational in character, defined by its central purpose of distributing the Scriptures "without note or comment," meaning that it was possible for its supporters to agree to disagree about matters of doctrine and interpretation. This provision did not, however, render the society immune to internal controversy. It was bitterly divided in the 1820s over the question of whether or not to meet European expectations for the inclusion of the Apocrypha in copies of the Bible circulated on the continent, and again in the early 1830s over whether Unitarians could be members, a dispute that led to the formation of the separate Trinitarian Bible Society. Partly as a result of the Apocrypha controversy, the expansion of the Bible Society's activities beyond England and Wales was constrained in the early nineteenth century, but during the Victorian era it developed into a major publishing enterprise, supporting the translation of the Bible into numerous languages.[21]

In the early nineteenth century, while the Americans led the evangelical

---

[20]For a recent overview of missions, with an extensive bibliography, see Andrew Porter, *Religion Versus Empire? British Protestant Missionaries and Overseas Expansion, 1700-1914* (Manchester: Manchester University Press, 2004). Despite the title, there is significant coverage of American dimensions.

[21]Leslie Howsam, *Cheap Bibles: Nineteenth-Century Publishing and the British and Foreign Bible Society* (Cambridge: Cambridge University Press, 1991).

world in revivals, the British usually led it in organization. American societies were in general not set up until some years after their British counterparts, and were heavily indebted to inspiration from across the Atlantic. This process is well illustrated by the early history of the American Bible Society, established in New York in 1816. Numerous local and state societies had existed for a few years before that date, but had operated technically as auxiliaries of the BFBS. Such links had continued and indeed strengthened during the War of 1812. The creation of an American national body was hampered by local rivalries and difficulties in communication, but was eventually overcome by a shared sense of the pressing need for Bible distribution on the unchurched frontier, and the determined initiative of Elias Boudinot, a New Jersey lawyer and businessman. Its early leadership, however, was dominated by New York Presbyterians, a factor that limited its appeal particularly in the South and West.[22]

The distribution of Bibles was part of wider publishing endeavors. In Britain the success of Hannah More's *Cheap Repository Tracts* helped to inspire the formation of the Religious Tract Society (RTS) in 1799, which, like the BFBS, succeeded in being genuinely interdenominational. By 1828 it had published 347 tracts, 67 broadsheets "suitable for affixing to the walls of Cottages, Factories, Workhouses, Prisons &c.," and handbills "for distribution among the thoughtless multitudes who are found profaning the Lord's Day in every populous neighbourhood." It also produced large quantities of children's literature, including the monthly *Child's Companion* which had a regular sale of 30,000. It was reported in 1849 that the society had distributed over 500 million tracts in its first half century.[23] The most successful of them, *The Dairyman's Daughter* written by Legh Richmond, one of its secretaries, initially published elsewhere but soon taken up by the RTS, was reputed already to have sold four million copies worldwide by the time of its author's death in 1827. This was an account of the life and model evangelical deathbed of Elizabeth Wallbridge, a farm worker in the Isle of Wight who had been con-

---

[22]Foster, *Errand of Mercy*, pp. 104-16; Griffin, *Their Brothers' Keepers*, pp. 27-29, 46, 81-83. Foster's and Griffin's books, although now somewhat dated, remain the only overall surveys of evangelical societies in the United States in the early nineteenth century.

[23]*A Brief View of the Plan and Operations of the Religious Tract Society* (London, 1828?), pp. 5-9; Ian Bradley, *The Call to Seriousness: The Evangelical Impact on the Victorians* (London: Jonathan Cape, 1976), pp. 42-43.

verted through a Methodist preacher and impressed Richmond with her deep faith. The tract was apparently influential in numerous conversions: a Massachusetts minister thought in 1834 that "The humble piety of the Dairyman's Daughter . . . will tell upon the destinies of immortal beings, until time shall be no more."[24] By this date the United States also had well-established organizations for tract distribution: the New York Religious Tract Society had been founded in 1812 and the New England Tract Society in 1814. In 1825 they merged to form the American Tract Society. It was calculated that by 1828 more than ten million tracts had been distributed in the United States, mostly reprinted from the publications of the London RTS.[25]

Home missions took two rather different forms. First, there was localized activity that grew naturally out of the witness of individual ministers and congregations, or was facilitated by associations of churches at a district county level. In England the 1790s saw an upsurge in itinerant evangelism in rural areas, supported in this way by Baptists and Congregationalists, alongside the expanding work of the Methodists. Two national organizations, the Congregational Society for Spreading the Gospel in England and the Baptist Society for the Encouragement and Support of Itinerant and Village Preaching, were both formed in 1797. The former folded in 1809, but was reestablished in 1819 as the Home Missionary Society; the latter became the Baptist Home Missionary Society in 1821. As the faltering of the Congregational society indicates, however, the main impetus for such activity came from numerous more local organizations such as the Essex Baptist Association (1796) and the Cheshire Congregational Union (1806).[26]

A second concept of home mission was as a specialist ministry that brought the gospel to remote and "frontier" regions where regular religious provision

---

[24] *The Dairyman's Daughter; an authentic narrative*, by a clergyman of the Church of England (London: W. Kent). The British Library catalogue dates this edition as 1810; the earliest RTS edition in its collection is dated as 1812. See also Bradley, *Call to Seriousness*, p. 43; Foster, *Errand of Mercy*, pp. 73-75; *BDEB*, pp. 936-37, 1153. Contrary to the impression given by both Bradley and Foster, Wallbridge was not a "young girl" but a grown woman, who was aged thirty at the time of her death in 1801.

[25] Griffin, *Their Brothers' Keepers*, pp. 32-35; *Brief View*, p. 20.

[26] Deryck W. Lovegrove, *Established Church, Sectarian People: Itinerancy and the Transformation of English Dissent, 1780-1830* (Cambridge: Cambridge University Press, 1980), pp. 195-96, 200, 182-83 and passim.

was lacking or deficient, or to particular social groups who for one reason or another were marginal to normal church life. Thus the brothers James Alexander and Robert Haldane formed the Society for Propagating the Gospel at Home in 1797-1798, directed particularly toward the Highlands and islands of Scotland.[27] Concern in America for the spiritual state of emigrants to the West led to the foundation of The Missionary Society of Connecticut in 1798, followed by a similar organization in Massachusetts in 1799, and a number of small bodies that combined in 1822 to form the United Domestic Missionary Society of New York City. These organizations sponsored itinerant evangelists and pastors among migrants from their respective states, and eventually in 1826 merged to form the American Home Missionary Society.[28] English evangelicals lacked comparable regions in their own country, although the anxiety of Newton, Wilberforce and others to ensure that an evangelical chaplain was sent to Australia fits into a similar framework.[29] In the first quarter of the nineteenth century, however, there was growing interest in the spiritual condition of Ireland. The Roman Catholic majority population, with whom Britain had been brought into closer political association by the union of the London and Dublin parliaments in 1800, was perceived as ripe for conversion to Protestantism. Joining with Irish Protestants, British evangelicals supported a range of societies designed to support that end through Bible and tract distribution and education, as well as direct proselytism. These included the Hibernian Bible Society (1808), the London Hibernian Society (1806), the Hibernian Sunday School Society (1809), the Irish Evangelical Society (1814) and the Irish Society (1818). The movement reached its climax and nemesis in the so-called Second Reformation of the 1820s, when hopes of large-scale conversions from Catholicism were first raised and then dashed in face of the growing political polarization leading to Catholic Emancipation in 1829.[30]

There was also a specific concern for the spiritual condition of merchant seamen, an occupational group inevitably unable to participate regularly in normal church life, but one of potential significance in contributing to the widespread

---

[27] *BDEB*, pp. 501-2.

[28] Griffin, *Their Brothers' Keepers*, pp. 24-25, 35-36.

[29] See above, p. 14.

[30] David Hempton and Myrtle Hill, *Evangelical Protestantism in Ulster Society 1740-1890*, (London: Routledge, 1992), pp. 52-55, 59.

geographical spread of evangelicalism. George Charles Smith, a Baptist minister, was particularly influential in developing a range of specialist evangelistic and pastoral ministries, beginning with the formation in 1819 of the Port of London Society, which set up a floating chapel and subsequently one on land. The idea gradually spread to other British ports and was also adopted in New York and Philadelphia. The atmosphere of a seamen's chapel in New Bedford, Massachusetts, was vividly evoked by Herman Melville in *Moby Dick*, first published in 1851.[31] Specialist ministries for other occupational groups did not develop substantially until the second half of the nineteenth century. The Naval and Military Bible Society, formed back in 1780, provided Bibles and other Christian literature for the British armed forces, and the Soldiers' Friend and Army Scripture Readers Society began work in the late 1830s, but it took the Crimean War (1854-1856) and the American Civil War (1861-1865) to make the military a central focus of organized evangelistic attention. Nevertheless, a number of evangelical officers in the British army exercised a significant influence on their men, and Methodism made some headway among the other ranks. Evangelicalism gained ground particularly among soldiers in India, where conditions of service allowed leisure for religious activity and the presence of missionaries supplemented the pastoral activity of regimental chaplains.[32]

American evangelicals also took an increasing interest in mission fields on their own doorsteps, constituted for them by native peoples and black slaves. Missions to "Indian" tribes were undertaken by both the domestic and the foreign missionary societies and had a checkered record, with genuine evangelistic successes tarnished by cultural assumptions inextricably associating white "civilization" with Christianization. Thus native American converts were either obliged to dissociate themselves decisively from their own cultural traditions, or regarded as still inferior "savages" if their acceptance of white people's ways of life appeared less wholehearted than their acceptance of Christ. The perception that evangelical commitment to the "Indians" was at best conditional was

[31] Kathleen Heasman, *Evangelicals in Action: An Appraisal of their Social Work in the Victorian Era* (London: Geoffrey Bles, 1962), pp. 247-51 and passim; Herman Melville, *Moby Dick*, ed. Patrick McGrath (Oxford: Oxford University Press, 1999), pp. 35-51.

[32] Michael Snape, *The Redcoat and Religion: The Forgotten History of the British Soldier from the Age of Marlborough to the Eve of the First World War* (London: Routledge, 2005), pp. 94, 99, 120-31, 138-59.

reinforced when, particularly during the presidency of Andrew Jackson (1828-1836), the land-hunger of whites led to the natives' forced removal from ancestral territories and their resettlement in reservations or in new land to the west. The deportation of the Christianized Cherokees from Georgia to Oklahoma was a particularly notorious instance of this policy. While some individual missionaries protested heroically, the missionary societies, fearful that they would otherwise be charged with acting politically, accepted the policy.[33] In Canada the relative absence of such population pressures meant that tensions were less acute and missions to native peoples had a more positive record. By 1824 the Sunday School Union of Canada was supporting a class among the Abenaki Indians at the mouth of the St. Francis River in Quebec, and the CMS was promoting schools along the Red River (in modern Manitoba), also from the 1820s. A Society for Converting and Civilizing the Indians was established in Upper Canada in 1830. The Methodists were particularly energetic and in 1836 claimed to have converted "several" tribes to Christianity, settling them in villages and teaching between 300 and 500 children in their schools. During the 1840s their missions penetrated as far as the Rockies and British Columbia.[34] Something of a parallel comparison to that between the United States and Canada in respect of the evangelical impact on indigenous peoples can be made between Australia and New Zealand. Early nineteenth-century missions to the Australian Aborigines were ineffective and rapidly curtailed, with a faint-heartedness founded in a widespread perception that they were a particularly degenerate race, but in New Zealand the CMS early secured the conversion and assistance of Maori evangelists, who during the mid-nineteenth century proved

---

[33]Robert F. Berkhofer, *Salvation and the Savage: An Analysis of Protestant Missions and American Indian Response, 1787-1862* (Lexington: University of Kentucky Press, 1965); Robert T. Handy, *A History of the Churches in the United States and Canada* (Oxford: Clarendon Press, 1976), pp. 157-58, 177-78; Mark A. Noll, *A History of Christianity in the United States and Canada* (Grand Rapids: Eerdmans, 1992), pp. 187-89.

[34]Handy, *History of the Churches in the United States and Canada*, pp. 254-56; *Second Report of the Sunday School Union Society of Canada*, pp. 10-11; *Institution for the Education of the Youth of Canada Generally, and the Most Promising Youth of the Recently Converted Indian Tribes and Teachers to their Aboriginal Countrymen* (flysheet, 1836); John Webster Grant, *A Profusion of Spires: Religion in Nineteenth-Century Ontario* (University of Toronto Press, 1988), p. 110. Cf. Terrence Murphy and Roberto Perin, eds., *A Concise History of Christianity in Canada* (Toronto: Oxford University Press, 1996), pp. 153-55.

effective in taking the gospel to their own people.[35]

Missions to slaves in the American South involved their own tensions and complexities. The prior conversions of significant numbers of black people in the late eighteenth and early nineteenth centuries meant that Christianity could already be perceived as a religion that was part of their culture rather than at odds with it. From the perspective of Southern evangelicals supportive of slavery, such indigenization was at best a mixed blessing. Black preachers were thought likely to stimulate unrest and religion was indeed a factor in several early nineteenth-century slave revolts. From the 1820s onward white Southern evangelicals promoted their own missions to the slaves, intended to Christianize them without rendering them discontented with their lot. Hence genuine evangelistic zeal combined with social and political self-interest. The most substantial initiatives were naturally taken by the two denominations most strongly represented in the South: the Baptists, who operated through numerous small-scale missions based on local churches, and the Methodists, who in 1829 began a more organized mission which eventually came to employ over 300 workers across the South. During the early 1830s Episcopalians and Presbyterians also joined in the effort.[36] Such activity ensured that Christianity continued to make headway among the slave population, but its impact was often limited by the indifference of slave-owners and understandable suspicion of the motives of white missionaries among the slaves themselves. Claims that there was a mass conversion of the "vast majority" of slaves need therefore to be treated with caution.[37] The most effective outreach to black people continued to come from African Americans themselves

---

[35]J. D. Bollen, "English Missionary Societies and the Australian Aborigine," *Journal of Religious History* 9 (1977): 263-91; Raeburn Lange, "Indigenous Agents of Religious Change in New Zealand, 1830-1860," *Journal of Religious History* 24 (2000): 279-95.

[36]Janet Duitsman Cornelius, *Slave Missions and the Black Church in the Antebellum South* (Columbia: University of South Carolina Press, 1999), pp. 28, 47-48, 88-102 and passim; Anne C. Loveland, *Southern Evangelicals and the Social Order 1800-1860* (Baton Rouge: Louisiana State University Press, 1980), pp. 219-56; Noll, *History of Christianity in the United States and Canada*, pp. 204-5; Milton C. Sernett, *Black Religion and American Evangelicalism: White Protestants, Plantation Missions and the Flowering of Negro Christianity, 1787-1865* (Metuchen, N.J.: Scarecrow Press, 1975).

[37]William Courtland Johnson, " 'A Delusive Clothing': Christian Conversion in the Antebellum Slave Community," *The Journal of Negro History* 82 (1997): 295-311.

Meanwhile, there was a gradual recognition that there were large unchurched populations in recent industrial settlements and major cities. This problem was greatest and most widespread in Britain, but America's largest cities, above all New York and Philadelphia, were beginning to present comparable challenges. The New York City Tract Society was founded in 1827 to restore the local focus lost when the New York Religious Tract Society had merged into the American Tract Society. It initially followed the rather haphazard approach to tract distribution that had characterized the earlier societies, but in 1829 adopted a proposal from the philanthropist Arthur Tappan systematically to divide the city into districts with a view to regular visitation of every family. This was a radical new departure, both in bringing tract distributors into regular contact with the poor rather than merely the ungodly of their own class, and also in expanding their role from one of simply handing out literature to specific endeavors to secure conversions. The shift from tract society to mission was encouraged by Charles Finney's ministry in New York in the early 1830s.[38]

The next step was a movement spearheaded by a Scot, David Nasmith (1799-1839), to set up organizations explicitly committed to evangelism in cities. Nasmith began by establishing the Glasgow City Mission in 1826, then moved to Ireland, where he founded the Dublin City Mission in 1828. The Belfast Town Mission had already been founded in 1827, by a local Presbyterian minister, John Bryce. Nasmith visited North America in 1830-1831, where he was reportedly instrumental in forming 16 City Missions, although many of these were short-lived, and his flagship New York City Mission, formed in September 1830, built upon the existing work of the Tract Society.[39] Nasmith's greatest and most lasting achievement was the London City Mission, founded in 1835, which was notable for its interdenominational character in a period of particularly tense relations between Anglicans and Nonconformists. After a slight setback in the late 1830s it grew steadily, employing 40 agents in 1836, 58 in 1840, 121 in 1845 and 242 in 1850. From 1844 its work was supplemented by the exclusively Anglican Scripture Readers' Association, which employed 33 agents in 1845

---

[38] Carroll Smith Rosenberg, *Religion and the Rise of the American City: The New York City Mission Movement 1812-1870* (Ithaca, N.Y.: Cornell University Press, 1971), pp. 70-96.

[39] John Campbell, *Memoirs of David Nasmith* (London: John Snow, 1844), pp. 209-10, 260; Hempton and Hill, *Evangelical Protestantism in Ulster Society*, p. 115.

and 98 in 1850. Regular visits from lay evangelists working for such organizations were to punctuate the lives of the poor in Victorian London. The concept, promoted by the City and Town Mission Society, also rapidly expanded in other parts of Britain, with 53 missions established between 1837 and 1844, such as that in Manchester, which in 1844 was employing 35 agents.[40] A related initiative among Anglican Evangelicals was the formation in 1836 of the Church Pastoral Aid Society, which raised money to give grants to support curates and lay workers in needy parishes.

Evangelical efforts to promote education were initially primarily focused on Sunday schools. Neither of the two major English organizations supporting day schools, the National Society for Promoting the Education of the Poor in the Principles of the Established Church (founded in 1811) and the British and Foreign Schools Society (1814), was distinctively evangelical. The former was dominated by High Church Anglicans and the latter, although actively supported by evangelical Nonconformists, also drew support from those with more liberal or secular views on education. Evangelicals, though, could take important local initiatives in day education, for example in Nottingham where they were the dominant religious force in the town, and where between 1785 and 1835 both Nonconformists and Anglicans worked hard to build schools and promote working-class literacy. Nevertheless, in 1834 the town's Sunday schools were attended by 7,636 pupils, whereas its working-class day schools only had 2,794, an indication of their relative growth.[41] North of the border Evangelicals such as Andrew Thomson of St. George's, Edinburgh, were instrumental in the 1820s in stimulating revival and expansion in the Church of Scotland's long-standing network of parochial schools. Here too, though, local initiatives were crucial. For example, David Stow, an elder in Thomas Chalmers's congregation, took a pioneering role in Glasgow, leading to the formation in 1826 of the Glasgow Infant School Society, which became the Glasgow Educational Society in 1834.[42]

Evangelical interest in day schooling was driven primarily by religious con-

---

[40]Campbell, *David Nasmith*, pp. 465-67.

[41]S. D. Chapman, "The Evangelical Revival and Education in Nottingham," *Transactions of the Thoroton Society of Nottinghamshire* 66 (1962): 35-66.

[42]Stewart Mechie, *The Church and Scottish Social Development 1780-1870* (London: Oxford University Press, 1960), pp. 139-46.

viction, above all an insistence that children must be taught to read the Bible, without any restrictions. The impetus was strongest in situations where evangelicals perceived themselves to be in competition with Roman Catholics for the souls of the rising generation. Thus education was a prominent feature of the "Second Reformation" movement in Ireland: in 1830 the London Hibernian Society was operating 1,373 schools with 80,513 scholars, and the Irish Society was running a further 491 schools. When, starting in 1831, the British government tried to establish a non-denominational national educational system in Ireland, Presbyterians eventually negotiated successfully to secure government support for what were, in effect, their own schools. Meanwhile, Anglicans in 1839 founded their own Church Education Society, which a decade later claimed to be educating over 100,000 children outside the national system.[43] In Liverpool, with its growing Roman Catholic population, the town council's attempt in the later 1830s to introduce a non-denominational system on the Irish model stirred heated political controversy and a similar movement by local Anglican Evangelicals to establish their own independent schools.[44]

In the United States national voluntary organization for educational purposes was limited in scope: the American Education Society, founded in 1815, concentrated on ministerial rather than general education. Nevertheless, evangelicals exercised a considerable influence at a local level on the development of common schools. Their efforts were given a further stimulus when, in 1835, Lyman Beecher, now president of Lane Seminary in Cincinnati, published *A Plea for the West*, arguing passionately for the vital importance of providing effective education in the recently settled states. "The sun and the rain of heaven," he wrote, "are not more sure to call forth a bounteous vegetation, than Bibles, and Sabbaths, and schools and seminaries, are to diffuse intellectual light and warmth for the bounteous fruits of righteousness and peace." His efforts were ably supported by his eldest daughter Catharine, whose advocacy "legitimatized the common school movement as an aspect

---

[43]Hempton and Hill, *Evangelical Protestantism in Ulster Society*, p. 56; Donald H. Akenson, *The Irish Education Experiment: The National System of Education in the Nineteenth Century* (London: Routledge & Kegan Paul, 1970), pp. 157-224.

[44]James Murphy, *The Religious Problem in English Education: The Crucial Experiment* (Liverpool: Liverpool University Press, 1959).

of the evangelical crusade."[45] As in Ireland, a sense of conflict with Roman Catholicism was a powerful motivating force. In the later pages of *A Plea for the West*, Lyman Beecher turned to a sustained polemic against the Roman Catholic Church, which he believed was now flooding the United States with its ignorant votaries. Meanwhile, in New York City, as in Liverpool, strong local competition between evangelicals and Catholics made education a central issue in local politics.[46] A similar dynamic was apparent in Canada, where the numerical dominance of evangelicals over Catholics, except in the French-speaking regions, meant that they were able in effect to determine the religious tone of the emerging common school system. Hence they had little need to resort to voluntary action.[47] In the 1840s, however, a powerful Canadian evangelical voice was lifted in favor of non-denominational education: when the leading Methodist Egerton Ryerson (1803-1882) became superintendent of schools in Upper Canada in 1844, he decided that "all that is essential to the moral interests of youth may be taught in what are termed mixed schools."[48]

Toward the end of the period, British evangelicals undertook a further significant educational initiative, the "ragged school" movement, to provide rudimentary instruction for destitute children. The idea crystallized in London in the early 1840s, developing earlier work by the London City Mission, Sunday schools and others. The primary commitment of the Ragged School Union, formed in 1844, was to bring "neglected and ignorant children within the reach of the doctrine of Christ," with other aspects of elementary education ancillary to that end. The ragged schools were supported by the effective advocacy of Lord Ashley, and in Scotland by the Free Church leader and social reformer Thomas Guthrie, who established schools in Edinburgh in 1847. In that year there were already eighty schools in London, some op-

---

[45]Lyman Beecher, *A Plea for the West* (Cincinnati: Truman & Smith, 1835), p. 37; Lawrence A. Cremin, *American Education: The National Experience 1783-1876* (New York: Harper Row, 1980), pp. 36-38, 58, 66-67, 145. On Catharine Beecher's views of education see further above, p. 141.

[46]Beecher, *Plea for the West*, p. 55ff.; R. A. Billington, *The Protestant Crusade 1800-1860* (New York: Macmillan, 1938), pp. 142-65.

[47]Murphy, *Christianity in Canada*, p. 183.

[48]C. B. Sissons, *Egerton Ryerson: His Life and Letters*, 2 vols. (Toronto: Clark, Irwin & Co., 1937, 1947), 2:95-96.

erating during the day, others in the evening and some on Sundays, and during the next decade the idea was also taken up in Liverpool and Manchester. In 1848 the Ragged School Union began an emigration scheme, with some initial assistance from the government, to support the passage of successful pupils to Australia, Canada, New Zealand and the United States.[49]

The evangelical contribution to higher education was also notable. A number of prominent figures in the movement held influential positions at major universities: for example, Isaac Milner, Charles Simeon and James Scholefield at Cambridge, John Hill and John MacBride at Oxford, Thomas Chalmers at St Andrews and at Edinburgh, and Timothy Dwight and Nathaniel Taylor at Yale. Also important, however, was the energy and commitment of evangelicals in founding and sustaining numerous smaller institutions. Such activity was driven particularly by growing demands for well-educated ministers, but also served to stimulate theological reflection and broader intellectual life. In 1838 there were twenty-one Nonconformist academies in England and Wales, the majority of them serving evangelical denominations; by 1860 there were more than fifty seminaries in the United States.[50] Many of these colleges were quite small and fragile institutions, but some of them, such as Andover (Massachusetts) and Oberlin (Ohio), led by Charles Finney and Asa Mahan, exercised significant influence. Evangelicals such as Thomas McCulloch, first principal both of Pictou Academy and of Dalhousie University (Halifax, Nova Scotia), and Egerton Ryerson as principal of Victoria College in Cobourg on Lake Ontario, also played a major role in the early development of higher education in British North America.[51]

MORAL AND SOCIAL REFORM

The initial impetus for evangelical efforts to promote moral reformation came from a royal proclamation issued by George III in 1787, at Wilberforce's instigation, transmitted through William Pitt and John Moore, the Archbishop of

---

[49]Claire Seymour, *Ragged Schools, Ragged Children* (London: Ragged School Museum Trust, 1995), pp. 1-7, 35-36; Geoffrey B. A. M. Finlayson, *The Seventh Earl of Shaftsbury* (London: Eyre Methuen, 1981), pp. 251-52; Thomas Guthrie, *A Plea for Ragged Schools* (Edinburgh, 1847); *BDEB*, pp. 493-94.

[50]Watts, *Dissenters*, p. 273; Noll, *America's God*, p. 254.

[51]Gauvreau, "Protestantism Transformed," pp. 68-85.

Canterbury. It was customary for sovereigns on their accession to issue procla-
mations "for the Encouragement of Piety and Virtue." The king was persuaded
to reissue the one used when he had come to the throne in 1760 with a new
preamble observing "with inexpressible concern, the rapid progress of impiety
and licentiousness, and that deluge of profaneness, immorality and every kind
of vice, which . . . have broken upon this nation." Wilberforce then proceeded
to set up "The Society for Carrying into Effect His Majesty's Proclamation
Against Vice and Immorality," known as the Proclamation Society.[52] The Proclamation Society's membership, like that of the Sunday School Society set up
two years earlier, was not exclusively evangelical, but rather comprised a broader
coalition of morally concerned laymen and senior clergy. The president was the
Bishop of London, Beilby Porteus, and Wilberforce was vice-president. It
launched prosecutions of offenders, circulated tracts and tried to encourage
Sunday observance.[53] By 1799, however, it was losing momentum, and in 1802
the Society for the Suppression of Vice was set up to supplement its efforts and
eventually superseded it.[54] Sustained efforts were made to check a range of activities seen as subversive of public morality, including nude bathing, gambling
and the sale of obscene articles and publications. Blasphemy also fell within the
remit of the society, which concerned itself both with profane swearing and
with atheistic publications. Prostitution could not be suppressed, but it was
obliged to make itself less conspicuous.[55]

An important specific offshoot of the Vice Society's work was the sabbatar-
ian movement, which reflected the conviction that failure to observe Sunday
properly was indicative of social disorder as well as spiritual disobedience. The
Vice Society claimed in 1825 that

> It is, in fact, the unanimous opinion of all our ablest moralists, that, on the de-
> cent and orderly, though not austere and pharisaical, observance of the Lord's
> Day, the preservation of the religion of the bulk of our people must depend.[56]

Wilberforce himself, while committed to the distinctiveness of Sunday, was

---

[52]Pollock, *Wilberforce*, pp. 59-66.

[53]*Report of the Committee of the Society for Carrying into Effect his Majesty's Proclamation against Vice and Immorality for the Year 1799 together with a list of the Members* (London: J. Hatchard, 1799).

[54]Ibid., pp. 22-23; *Society for the Suppression of Vice* (London, 1825), pp. 5-6.

[55]Ibid., passim; Bradley, *Call to Seriousness*, pp. 97-100.

[56]*Society for the Suppression of Vice*, p. 7.

not a rigid legalist in this matter, commenting in 1821 that some laid "more stress on the strictness of the Sunday than on its spirituality."[57] Nevertheless, the dominant trend in British evangelicalism was toward tighter regulation of Sunday behavior, leading to the formation in 1809 of the Society for Promoting the Observance of the Christian Sabbath, and in 1831 to the Society for Promoting the Due Observance of the Lord's Day, better known as the Lord's Day Observance Society. During the 1830s the LDOS unsuccessfully attempted to secure comprehensive Sunday observance legislation, but subsequently achieved many of its objectives in a more piecemeal manner, creating the austere Sundays of Victorian Britain.[58]

In the United States there could, of course, be no royal proclamation, and distaste for legal regulation of private behavior meant that initially movements for moral reform and Sunday observance were weaker than their British counterparts. Although in the early nineteenth century Lyman Beecher and others advocated and formed societies for the suppression of vice and reformation of manners, their impact was localized and limited.[59] The New York Society for the Suppression of Vice, the first major body explicitly directed to that purpose, was not to be established until 1873, nearly three quarters of a century after its London counterpart.[60] In 1828 the General Union for Promoting the Observance of the Christian Sabbath was set up in New York and in an address to the American people commended its objective not only for spiritual reasons but as "the great moral conservator of nations." Its promoters were, however, sensitive to the charge of unconstitutional interference with the liberties of the individual, and emphasized that they intended to proceed by means of persuasion rather than coercion, albeit defending the boycotting of Sabbath-breakers as a legitimate "persuasive" tactic. A particular issue was a campaign for the abolition of Sunday mails,

---

[57] Quoted in John Wigley, *The Rise and Fall of the Victorian Sunday* (Manchester: Manchester University Press, 1980), p. 29.

[58] Ibid., passim; Bradley, *Call to Seriousness*, pp. 104-6.

[59] Robert Abzug, *Cosmos Crumbling: American Reform and the Religious Imagination* (New York: Oxford University Press, 1994), pp. 40-48; Jonathan D. Sassi, *A Republic of Righteousness: The Public Christianity of the Post-Revolutionary New England Clergy* (New York: Oxford University Press, 2001), pp. 140-42.

[60] Paul S. Boyer, *Purity in Print: The Vice-Society Movement and Book Censorship in America* (New York: Charles Scribner's Sons, 1968), pp. 3-5.

but it failed to make political headway and the organization declined in the mid-1830s.[61] Some of the most effective efforts at moral reform were led by women, who had the advantages of appearing apolitical and of being well placed to operate informally in communities through such tactics as the "naming and shaming" of seducers and adulterers. The New York Female Moral Reform Society was formed in 1834, aiming to reclaim prostitutes and generally to advocate "moral perfection." By 1837 it was already having a significant impact at Utica, in upstate New York. An American Female Moral Reform Society was set up in 1839.[62]

In one specific moral matter, however, Americans did lead the way. During the early decades of the republic, it became very much apparent that abuse of alcohol was having serious consequences for both the health and social fabric of the nation. In the 1790s the prominent Philadelphia physician and philanthropist Dr. Benjamin Rush was already urging restraint, a call that was taken up in a more explicitly evangelical framework by Lyman Beecher in an extensively reprinted and influential series of sermons first published in 1825. "Intemperance," Beecher asserted, "is a national sin, carrying destruction from the centre to every extremity of the empire, and calling upon the nation to array itself, *en masse*, against it."[63] The American Society for the Promotion of Temperance was formed in 1826. Despite its name, its operations were largely confined to Massachusetts, but numerous parallel organizations came into existence in other parts of the country. In May 1833 delegates from twenty-one states met in Philadelphia and agreed to form the United States Temperance Union. In 1836 it extended its activities to Canada and was accordingly re-

---

[61] *Proceedings in Relation to the Formation of the Auxiliary Union of the City of Boston, for Promoting the Observance of the Christian Sabbath, with Address of the General Union to the People of the United States* (Boston, 1828), pp. 9, 11-13; Griffin, *Their Brothers' Keepers*, pp. 119-23; Richard R. John, *Spreading the News: The American Postal System from Franklin to Morse* (Cambridge, Mass.: Harvard University Press, 1995), pp. 169-205.

[62] Rosenberg, *Religion and the Rise of the American City*, p. 97; Mary P. Ryan, *Cradle of the Middle Class: The Family in Oneida County, New York, 1790-1865* (Cambridge: Cambridge University Press, 1981), pp. 116-23; Foster, *Errand of Mercy*, p. 275.

[63] Benjamin Rush, *An Enquiry into the effects of Spirituous Liquors upon the Human Body, and Their Influence on the Happiness of Society* (Edinburgh, 1791; originally published in Philadelphia); Lyman Beecher, *Six Sermons on the Nature, Occasions, Signs, Evils, and Remedy of Intemperance* (Boston: Perkins and Marvin, 1829), p. 60.

named as the American Temperance Union.[64] The organized movement in the
United Kingdom was relatively slow to develop and in its early years owed much
to American guidance and inspiration. The earliest local societies were formed
in Ireland and Scotland in 1829, and the British and Foreign Temperance Society (BFTS) was established in London in 1831. The British movement also
had a more limited impact than its American counterpart: whereas in the
United States alcohol consumption per capita fell by more than two thirds between 1830 and 1845, in Britain, although a sharp rise in spirit drinking in the
1820s halted in the 1830s, there was no such dramatic reversal of the trend.[65]

While there were strong links between evangelicalism and the temperance
movement, the connection was not a straightforward one. For all its passion,
Beecher's condemnation was directed specifically against "the daily use of ardent spirits"[66] rather than the consumption of alcohol in general, and numerous evangelicals continued to drink beer and wine in moderation. Some, such
as the Buxtons in England and the Guinnesses in Ireland, were themselves brew-
ers. Meanwhile, the temperance movement had from the outset a secular as well
as religious dimension. The consequent tensions increased from the mid-1830s
onward, as on both sides of the Atlantic the "moderationists" such as Beecher
were outflanked by teetotalers who called for complete abstinence from all alcoholic beverages. The United States Temperance Union was divided by the
controversy, and in Britain the teetotalers formed rival organizations in competition with the moderationist BFTS.[67] Although teetotalism was advocated by
some prominent evangelicals such as George Barrell Cheever, a New England
Congregational minister, and John Hope, an Edinburgh solicitor, many others
were ambivalent or hostile toward it. The state of evangelical opinion in the late
1830s was well illustrated by the experience of George Cheever, who himself
believed intemperance the "grand cause of all the wretchedness that exists on

---

[64]Griffin, *Their Brothers' Keepers*, pp. 69-72.

[65]Brian Harrison, *Drink and the Victorians: The Temperance Question in England 1815-1872* (Keele:
   Keele University Press, 1994), pp. 65, 71, 98-102; Thomas R. Pegram, *Battling Demon
   Rum: The Struggle for a Dry America, 1800-1933* (Chicago: Ivan R. Dee, 1998), p. 31. See also
   Ian R. Tyrrell, *Sobering Up: From Temperance to Prohibition in America* (Westport, Conn.: Green-
   wood Press, 1979).

[66]Beecher, *Intemperance*, p. 11.

[67]For details see Griffin, *Their Brothers' Keepers*, pp. 70-72; Harrison, *Drink and the Victorians*, pp.
   121-38.

earth." Having been publicly horsewhipped and imprisoned in Salem, Massachusetts, for his alleged libel on a local distiller, in 1837 Cheever sought recreation in a visit to Europe. At a dinner party in Edinburgh he

> got into quite an argument with Mr Brown[68] on the cause of Temperance, as to the propriety of including wine in the Temperance pledge. It is something when the cause has so far advanced in Scotland that an argument of this nature will be patiently listened to with the decanters on the table.

Cheever, though, regarded it as "disgusting irreverence" when another guest started talking about the operation of the Holy Spirit on the heart with his wine glass in his hand.[69] Other middle- and upper-class evangelicals, however, were disconcerted by the radical zeal of working-class teetotalers that seemed to challenge social mores in a way they felt went beyond Scripture. Moreover, while the decisiveness of a clear-cut pledge to abstain from all alcohol was to prove a most effective psychological tool, it rapidly became something of a secular substitute for evangelical conversion. Such considerations meant that until the 1860s only a minority of British evangelicals—primarily Baptists, Congregationalists and non-Wesleyan Methodists—actively supported teetotalism, and in 1841 the Wesleyan Conference even condemned it. Furthermore, the growth of teetotalism undermined the moderationists and the BFTS, in striking contrast to other evangelical societies, went into terminal decline in the 1840s.[70] In the United States, the "Maine Law" of 1851 marked a significant transition from voluntary moral argument against drink to state-by-state legislation and from a specifically evangelical reform to a broad social program.

Much financial and practical assistance to the poor and destitute was still given in the personal, unsystematic and hence unrecorded manner characteristic of paternalist pre-industrial communities. However, the expansion of evangelicalism concurrently with the development of larger, more anonymous urban communities helped to stimulate more organized philanthropy. In 1796 Sir

---

[68]Probably John Brown (1784-1858), minister of Broughton Place Church and one of the most influential Edinburgh Presbyterian dissenters of his day (*BDEB*, pp. 150-51).

[69]Robert M. York, *George B. Cheever: Religious and Social Reformer 1807-1890* (Orono: University of Maine Press, 1955), pp. 70-78; American Antiquarian Society, Worcester, Mass., Cheever Family Papers, Box 27, Vol. 3 (Diary for July 18, 1837).

[70]Heasman, *Evangelicals in Action*, p. 128; Harrison, *Drink and the Victorians*, pp. 124-31, 138, 168-71.

Thomas Bernard and William Wilberforce were instrumental in setting up the Society for Bettering the Condition and Increasing the Comforts of the Poor, aiming to stimulate good practice while leaving actual relief to local societies.[71] Such a local body was formed on Wilberforce's own doorstep in Clapham in 1799 under the leadership of the vicar, John Venn. It particularly deployed the energies of women. The parish, which was already too large for there to be close personal links between rich and poor, was divided into nine districts for systematic visitation organized by a group of "upwards of 30 Ladies and Gentlemen" who met monthly to review progress. They aimed to supplement the official work of the parish overseers by "the moral improvement of the poor—their more complete relief in distress—and their permanent benefit by the encouragement of habits of industry."[72] Organizations of this kind proliferated in both Britain and America in the late eighteenth and early nineteenth centuries, operating either on a specific local basis or by targeting a particular disadvantaged group. Examples include the Edinburgh Society for the Relief of the Destitute Sick (1785), the London Association for the Relief and Benefit of the Manufacturing and Labouring Poor (1816), the Female Society of Philadelphia for the Relief and Employment of the Poor (1817), the Halifax (Nova Scotia) Poor Man's Friend Society (1820), the Society for the Relief of Distressed Widows (London, 1823) and the Society for the Relief of Half Orphan and Destitute Children (New York, 1836).[73]

From the 1820s onward the evangelical response to urban social deprivation was strongly influenced by the ideas of Thomas Chalmers, developed in his own parochial work in Glasgow between 1815 and 1823, and publicized in his three-volume work, *The Christian and Civic Economy of Large Towns*, which appeared between 1819 and 1826. Chalmers had been shaped intellectually by political economy and pastorally by his previous ministry at Kilmany in

---

[71]Pollock, *Wilberforce*, pp. 140-42.

[72]*Rules and Regulations of the Society for Bettering the Condition of the Poor, at Clapham, Surrey . . . To which is prefixed, An Account of the Origins and Designs of the Society* (London, 1805).

[73]Olive Checkland, *Philanthropy in Victorian Scotland* (Edinburgh: John Donald, 1980), p. 22; Allen B. Robertson, " 'Give All You Can' Methodists and Charitable Causes in Nineteenth-Century Nova Scotia," in *The Contribution of Methodism to Atlantic Canada*, ed. Charles H. H. Scobie and John Webster Grant (Montreal and Kingston: McGill-Queen's University Press, 1992), pp. 93-95; Brown, *Fathers of the Victorians*, pp. 336-37; Foster, *Errand of Mercy*, pp. 277, 279.

the Fife countryside between 1802 and 1815. His consequent key convictions were a belief in the moral and spiritual efficacy of the free market, and an admiration for the mutual support in hardship that he saw in rural communities, and which he thought could be recreated in cities, given effective parochial organization and the transforming influence of the Christian gospel. In 1819 Chalmers began an experiment in the new, predominantly working-class parish of St. John's, which he divided into small districts, each under the oversight of an elder, deacon and Sunday school teachers. His vision was that these districts, each comprising a few hundred souls, should develop into supportive self-contained communities analogous to small rural villages, with mutual self-help eliminating the need for legal poor relief or significant charitable support. According to Chalmers, such external assistance to the poor was positively injurious to them because it led to demoralization and dependency, and encouraged profligacy and large families.[74]

The success of the St. John's experiment was open to serious question: parish expenditure on poor relief was reduced, but it was likely that this saving was as much due to tight financial control by officials (and their readiness to add to funds from their own pockets) as to the genuine Christian good-neighborliness among the poor that Chalmers sought to inspire. Nevertheless, Chalmers's ideas had considerable appeal, especially in Britain,[75] and their impact helps to explain why evangelical organization to assist the destitute remained limited and fragmentary in nature. Mission rather than material support remained the priority, because unless the souls of the poor were saved, efforts to improve the welfare of their bodies were perceived by many as at best useless and at worst counterproductive. Such thinking led to widespread evangelical acquiescence in the harsh provisions of the English New Poor Law of 1834, which discouraged paupers from seeking public assistance by concentrating support for them in unattractive institutional workhouses. Attitudes, though, remained ambivalent.

---

[74] On Chalmers and his influence, see Brown, *Thomas Chalmers*; John Roxborogh, *Thomas Chalmers: Enthusiast for Mission* (Carlisle: Paternoster, 1999); Boyd Hilton, *The Age of Atonement: The Influence of Evangelicalism on Social and Economic Thought 1785-1865* (Oxford: Clarendon Press, 1988), pp. 81-89.

[75] Mark Noll, "Thomas Chalmers (1780-1847) in North America (ca. 1830-1917)," *Church History* 66 (1997): 762-77, concludes that, during his lifetime, although Chalmers stirred considerable admiration in North America, actual assimilation of his ideas was limited.

Ironically, Chalmers himself criticized the New Poor Law, because although he was all in favor of ensuring the undeserving would not exploit the system, he believed that those genuinely in need of help should be supported within their home communities rather than lifted out of them.[76] Moreover, in practice the growth of the urban missionary movement also tended in the 1830s and 1840s to make evangelicals more ready to give practical charitable assistance, as they were brought into immediate encounter with harsh material and human realities. Thus, for example, the New York Association for Improving the Condition of the Poor was founded by the New York City Tract Society in 1843.[77]

THE AGE OF SOCIETIES

To what extent did the evangelical societies and the movement they represented stimulate social change? Certainly they became increasingly visible and institutionalized. In Britain they gained a new physical focus in London in 1831, when Exeter Hall was opened in The Strand, providing large and small halls, committee rooms and offices. It became a focal point for the annual "May Meetings" of the societies, which extended over several weeks in the late spring and drew supporters from the provinces, and indeed from America and overseas, to participate in an intensive season of speech-making and networking between their overlapping memberships and leaderships.[78] Similar seasons of meetings developed in other major centers, notably New York, where by the 1830s an "anniversary week" involving more than a dozen societies was taking place in early May.[79] Such gatherings were symptomatic of a mood of postmillennial optimism in which the progress of Christianity was believed to be inexorable, preparing the way for an era of universal peace and knowledge of the Lord. More prosaically, they expressed the growing visibility and self-confidence of middle- and upper-class evangelicals.

In many ways the most eloquent and penetrating statement of the thesis that the broader evangelical movement was responsible for major social change re-

---

[76]Hilton, *Age of Atonement*, p. 242.

[77]Rosenberg, *Religion and the Rise of the American* City, pp. 245-73; Donald M. Lewis, *Lighten Their Darkness: The Evangelical Mission to Working Class London, 1828-1860* (Westport, Conn.: Greenwood Press, 1986), pp. 164-69.

[78]Leonard W. Cowie, "Exeter Hall," *History Today* 18, no. 6 (June 1968): 390-97.

[79]*New York Observer*, May 4, 1833.

mains the one penned by George Eliot in her early short novel "Janet's Repentance," first published in 1857. She described the transformation of life in Milby, based on the small town of Nuneaton in Warwickshire, between the 1820s and the 1850s:

> Evangelicalism was making its way in Milby, and gradually diffusing its subtle odour into chambers that were bolted and barred against it. The movement, like all other religious "revivals," had a mixed effect. Religious ideas have the fate of melodies, which, once set afloat in the world, are taken up by all sorts of instruments, some of them woefully coarse, feeble, or out of tune, until people are in danger of crying out that the melody itself is detestable.... Nevertheless, Evangelicalism had brought into palpable existence and operation in Milby society that idea of duty, that recognition of something to be lived for beyond the mere satisfaction of self, which is to moral life what the addition of a great central ganglion is to animal life.[80]

The view that evangelicalism had a profound formative influence on Victorian Britain was restated in successive generations of twentieth-century historical scholarship, not only by those sympathetic to the movement, but also by those neutral or hostile toward it.[81] The most substantial such book to be published in the last twenty years is Boyd Hilton's *Age of Atonement* (1988), in which it is argued that the ethos of evangelicalism was dominant in shaping the attitudes of the upper and middle classes during the first half of the nineteenth century. Hilton approaches the subject primarily through the history of ideas, emphasizing particularly how the concept of atonement permeated social and economic thought. It is a treatment that complements a focus on the evangelical societies, such as that adopted in this chapter, which highlights other key aspects of evangelicalism, its

---

[80]George Eliot, *Scenes of Clerical Life* (London: Penguin, 1998), pp. 264-65.

[81]Treatments sympathetic to evangelicalism include John Wesley Bready's two books *Lord Shaftesbury and Socio-Economic Progress* (London: Allen and Unwin, 1926), and *England Before and after Wesley* (London: Hodder and Stoughton, 1938); Bradley, *Call to Seriousness*; Herbert Schlossberg, *The Silent Revolution and the Making of Victorian England* (Columbus: Ohio State University Press, 2000); and Clifford Hill, *The Wilberforce Connection* (Oxford: Monarch, 2004). For more detached treatments by major historians, see G. M. Young, *Victorian England: Portrait of an Age* (London: Oxford University Press, 1936); and G. Kitson Clark, *The Making of Victorian England* (London: Methuen, 1965). John Wolffe, ed., *Evangelical Faith and Public Zeal: Evangelicals and Society in Britain 1780-1980* (London: SPCK, 1995) attempts a sympathetic but not uncritical evaluation.

conversionist and biblicist zeal, and above all its restless, relentless activism.

In relation to the United States, both contemporaries and subsequent historians saw the proliferation of societies as a dynamic mechanism of social reform. Such a perception was not limited to evangelicals themselves. At a meeting in the Capitol in 1833 to promote the cause of temperance, Lewis Cass, the secretary of war, reflected on this burgeoning activity:

> And it is one of the great characteristics of the age in which we live, that men are now uniting for the accomplishment of objects, upon which the peace and welfare of society must rest, with a firmness of resolution, a contempt of danger, a sacrifice of personal considerations, and a spirit of active benevolence, which offer the fairest prospects of success.[82]

For Cass, responsible for Jackson's controversial "Indian" resettlement policy, "the propagation of the gospel" was but one "great object" among many, but even if some of his own priorities were different from those of the evangelicals, his tribute to their energy and impact was a telling one. Similarly, the Frenchman Alexis de Tocqueville, who visited the United States in 1831-1832, was struck by the formative influence of religion in society, which although exercising little immediate political influence, "directs the customs of the community, and, by regulating domestic life, regulates the state."[83] During the last two generations these contemporary perceptions have been developed and reinforced in a substantial body of scholarship that has rendered the importance of evangelicals in transforming American society during the early republican period something of a commonplace of both religious and secular historiography.[84]

The key to evaluation of such claims is to resist overgeneralization. It is salutary to note George Metzger's assessment of the impact of evangelical Chris-

---

[82] *Proceedings and Speeches at A Meeting for the Promotion of the Cause of Temperance in the United States, held in the Capitol, in Washington City, February 24, 1833* (Washington: Way & Gideon, 1833), pp. 4-5. For Cass's relationship to evangelicalism, see Richard J. Carwardine, *Evangelicals and Politics in Antebellum America* (New Haven, Conn.: Yale University Press, 1993), p. 91.

[83] Alexis de Tocqueville, *Democracy in America*, 2 vols. (London: Everyman's Library, 1994), 1:304.

[84] For an authoritative overview of the literature, see Daniel Walker Howe, "Religion and Politics in the Antebellum North," in *Religion and American Politics From the Colonial Period to the 1980s*, ed. Mark A. Noll (New York: Oxford University Press, 1990), pp. 121-45. Subsequent contributions include Abzug, *Cosmos Crumbling*; and Steven Mintz, *Moralists and Modernizers: America's Pre-Civil War Reformers* (Baltimore: Johns Hopkins University Press, 1995).

tianity in America, made as he traveled west along the Erie Canal in 1834, when other more privileged observers were hailing its ascendancy:

> As yet I have nowhere found that religious appearance which is so much spoke [sic] of in other countries much less any vital religion with the exception of a few I had the opportunity of becoming acquainted with whilst at New York.[85]

Metzger acknowledged that he was as yet "but a traveller," but his perceptions are no less valid than those of other travelers such as Tocqueville and Fanny Trollope. They imply that the religiosity apparent in certain social circles, church communities and public occasions could be much less evident in the casual encounters of everyday life.

There was also an important difference of perspective in the American South from that operative in New England and New York. From Maryland southward the appeal of the evangelical societies was limited by their close association with Yankee "Presbygationalism," and by suspicions that their agents were sympathizers with the anti-slavery movement. Among Baptists in the South there was also a significant strain of anti-mission opinion, which rejected organized evangelistic and socially reforming endeavors on the basis of an enduring hyper-Calvinism that discounted human efforts as impious. Hence, although Southern evangelicals espoused some causes, notably temperance, sabbatarianism and opposition to duelling, their active identification with national movements was limited. Their impact, too, was constrained by the continuing influence of social mores founded in codes of honor rather than piety: although values inspired by evangelicalism made significant headway from the late eighteenth century onward, a sense of competing "ethical systems" persisted at least until the Civil War. A particular consequence was a preference for focusing on individual behavior rather than on wider social issues that could also raise uncomfortable questions in a slave-holding society.[86]

---

[85] CMS Archives, G/AC 15/111/4, August 26, 1834. On Metzger, see above, pp. 17-18.
[86] Loveland, *Southern Evangelicals*; John W. Kuykendall, *Southern Enterprise: The Work of National Evangelical Societies in the Antebellum South* (Westport, Conn.: Greenwood Press, 1982); Bertram Wyatt-Brown, "The Antimission Movement in the Jacksonian South: A Study in Regional Folk Culture," *The Journal of Southern History* 36 (1970): 501-29; and "Religion and the 'Civilizing Process' in the Early American South, 1600-1860," in *Religion and American Politics from the Colonial Period to the 1980s*, ed. Mark A. Noll (New York: Oxford University Press, 1990), pp. 172-95.

In Britain, too, regional and indeed local differences were important. London-based societies were by no means automatically popular in the English provinces, and seldom made much headway at all in Scotland or Wales. Much depended on existing contacts and so their activities were likely to reinforce prior areas of evangelical strength without having much impact on other districts. It was certainly possible for an energetic evangelical ministry, such as that in Nuneaton in the 1820s of John Edmund Jones, the real-life model for Eliot's reforming curate Mr. Tryan in "Janet's Repentance," to transform the moral as well as religious life of a small town. Another good example is Francis Close's incumbency at Cheltenham from 1826 to 1856.[87] Larger towns, though, whether Thomas Chalmers's Glasgow or John Angell James's Birmingham, were not so easily changed, and the social and spiritual needs of metropolitan London remained to challenge successive generations of evangelicals.

It was indeed apparent that, taking the English-speaking world as a whole, the impact of evangelicals on working-class life was less than on that of the middle class. This generalization must itself immediately be qualified by the recognition that there were substantial lower-class communities profoundly shaped by evangelicalism, for example through Primitive Methodism in England, the chapels of the Welsh valleys, and revivalism among the "plain folk" of the American South and West. On the other hand, evidence of working-class resistance to evangelicalism is also substantial, especially in urban areas, and the city mission movement of the 1820s and 1830s can be interpreted as a belated recognition of the extent of earlier evangelistic failure. Even in Belfast, where Protestant communal solidarity in the face of Roman Catholic resurgence might have been expected to work to the advantage of evangelicalism, the Town Mission, "a moral engine for the benefit of the poor," found that it faced an uphill struggle.[88] In such contexts, however, there could be a selective and distorted working-class assimilation of evangelical values, for example in the adoption of anti-Catholic attitudes—in Glasgow, Liverpool and Philadelphia as well as in Belfast—or in commitment to teetotalism.

A further dimension to consider is the chronological one. In the United States, the activity of the evangelical societies rose rapidly to an initial peak in

---

[87]On Close see A. F. Munden, *A Cheltenham Gemaliel: Dean Close of Cheltenham* (Cheltenham: Dean Close School, 1997).

[88]Hempton and Hill, *Evangelical Protestantism in Ulster Society,* p. 113.

the early 1830s, but then suffered a substantial setback in 1837, under the combined impact of an economic crisis that bankrupted some key supporters and the split of the Presbyterian Church into New and Old School groupings. In Britain there was no such single enforced contraction of activity, but the movement was, of course, equally vulnerable to the fluctuations of economic cycles as well as spiritual ones. Personal factors ensured that such fluctuations operated on very different timescales in different localities: thus the deaths and departures of the original Clapham Sect members meant that the period of greatest evangelical influence in south London was already coming to an end by 1815, the year in which Thomas Chalmers moved to Glasgow.

The complexities inherent in assessing the social impact of evangelicalism in Britain and the United States are pointed out by comparisons with smaller English-speaking societies, where differing local circumstances produced diverse patterns of influence. In Australia, while the convicts in New South Wales continued to present stony ground for evangelicalism, the free settlers in Adelaide and Melbourne showed strong support for the churches. South Australia in particular, founded in the 1830s on principles of religious liberty, was in its early decades a society very much shaped by evangelical influence. Moreover, by the 1840s the outward ethos at least of Sydney society was changing under the influence of free settlers, many of them evangelicals: an Anglican clergyman wrote in 1846 that "the public feeling is all on the side of the form of religion, how much of the power exists among us, the searcher of hearts alone can tell."[89] The situation in Upper Canada was quite similar, with evangelical influence strong, but working mainly through the denominations and hence rather less visibly active than in the northern United States, and awareness that less respectable elements of society remained largely untouched.[90] In the West Indies, on the other hand, there was a reversal of the otherwise widespread pattern of evangelical values strongly influencing the middle and upper classes while having a patchier and limited impact on the lower orders. In early nineteenth-century Jamaica the slaves converted to evangelicalism in increasing numbers,

---

[89] Allan M. Grocott, *Convicts, Clergyman and Churches: Attitudes of Convicts and Ex-Convicts Toward the Churches and Clergy in New South Wales from 1788-1851* (Sydney: Sydney University Press, 1980), pp. 99-103; Douglas Pike, *Paradise of Dissent: South Australia 1829-1857* (Carlton: Melbourne University Press, 1957), pp. 70-71, 249-50.

[90] Grant, *Profusion of Spires*, pp. 112-17.

while the planters looked on with mixed feelings. Evangelicalism was in the medium term to become a significant factor contributing to the undermining of
West Indian slave society, by inviting the slaves "to make a radical break from
the traditional moral, sexual and social mores of plantation life," giving them
an enhanced sense of self-worth and an opportunity to develop community life
and organizational experience in their churches.[91]

In the first volume of this series Mark Noll observed in relation to the eighteenth century that "for the evangelical movement in general, approaches to society tended to be tactical, personal and *ad hoc* rather than strategic, structural
and systematic."[92] As we have seen in this chapter, from the 1780s and 1790s
onward sustained organizational responses developed and there was a growing
sense of what has been termed an "interdenominational evangelical united
front."[93] Nevertheless, despite superficial coherence, there remained a lack of
articulated general strategy, little aspiration for structural social change this
side of the millennium, and a preoccupation with particular causes rather than
any systematic overall plan or vision. As we shall see in chapter eight, efforts in
the 1840s to organize an umbrella Evangelical Alliance were to prove frustrat-
ing and disappointing. Historians indeed have attributed an overarching agenda
to evangelicals, whether for conservative "social control" or, less commonly, for
radical democratization and liberation. Both such tendencies can certainly be
discerned in their attitudes and actions. However, the debate as to which agenda
was dominant is an ultimately sterile one that risks missing the point that for
early nineteenth-century evangelicals themselves commitment to Christ was
paramount and for them a voluntarily adopted Christian discipline was "at one
and the same time liberating and restrictive."[94] Their agendas could accordingly,
from a more secular perspective, appear variegated and sometimes misdirected.
They achieved much, but there could be no easy or uncontested victories in
their continual struggle against the sinfulness of humanity and the moral and
social challenges of the early industrial age.

---

[91]Mary Turner, *Slaves and Missionaries: The Disintegration of Jamaican Slave Society 1787-1834* (Urbana: University of Illinois Press, 1957), pp. 198-99 and passim.
[92]Noll, *Rise of Evangelicalism*, p. 241.
[93]Sassi, *Republic of Righteousness*, p. 185.
[94]Howe, "Religion and Politics," p. 128.

7

POLITICS

Freeing Slaves, Saving Nations

Policy . . . Sir, is not my principle and I am not ashamed to say it. There is a principle above everything that is political; and when I reflect on the command which says "Thou shalt do no murder," believing the authority to be divine, how can I dare to set up any reasonings of my own against it? And Sir, when we think of eternity, and of the future consequences of all human conduct, what is there in this life that should make any man contradict the dictates of his conscience, the principles of justice, the laws of religion, and of God.[1]

William Wilberforce's words, from the peroration of his first great speech against the slave trade delivered in the House of Commons on May 12, 1789, powerfully articulated his specific motivation for launching this parliamentary campaign. They also effectively introduce wider discussion of evangelical political activities. They came at the end of a speech in which Wilberforce had for three hours carefully accumulated rational arguments, supported by extensive evidence. For him an appeal to divine authority was not a substitute for human intellectual effort, but rather its culmination. Herein lies one key to understanding his own effectiveness as an evangelical in politics, in that for him Christian faith went hand in hand with political professionalism, in an age of much political amateurism. Nevertheless, in the closing minutes of his speech he disarmingly admitted that "I have urged many things that are not

---

[1] *The Parliamentary History of England from the Earliest Period to the Year 1803* (London: Longman & Co., 1816), pp. xviii, 62-63.

my own leading motives" and turned to a ringing affirmation of the moral and spiritual principles that lay behind his actions.

In this chapter the contribution of evangelicals to national politics is assessed. The work of the numerous societies surveyed in the previous chapter, much of which might well be regarded as "political" in a broad sense of the word, provided an important context for such activity, in that they offered both important networks of connection and influence, and sometimes agendas for potential legislation or executive action. Their essential character, however, was that of religious and social organizations rather than political pressure groups. They might want governments to assist their activities, for example by facilitating missionary access to new territories, or by legislating to promote Sunday observance, but their primary strategy was to achieve their ends through their own efforts rather than looking toward the agency of the state. In this respect the anti-slavery campaign, which is the point of departure for this chapter, was fundamentally different. While voluntary action might help to mitigate the worst excesses of slavery, the abolition of the legally sanctioned institutions of the slave trade and eventually of slavery itself necessarily required legislation.

Evangelical involvement in politics stemmed from a zeal to develop and sustain the Christian character of the state itself, or in the United States, with the division of church and state, more generally to promote a Christian social order. The campaign against slavery was central to this task because of the conviction that such heinous oppression of fellow human beings was inconsistent with allegiance to the teaching of the gospel. However, the aspiration to uphold national Christianity also raised major questions about relationships between the institutional churches and the state, issues on which evangelical opinion was itself divided. Whereas Anglican Evangelicals emerged as some of the most convinced defenders of the establishment of the Church of England, many of their Nonconformist counterparts believed that a state church was at best superfluous and at worst counterproductive to sustaining the Christian character of the nation. In Scotland the growing perception of evangelicals, led by Thomas Chalmers, that the current basis of connection with the state hampered the integrity and effectiveness of Christian witness led to the Disruption of 1843 and the subsequent formation of the Free Church. This development had significant repercussions in Canada, with its strong Scottish Presbyterian connections. Meanwhile, in the United States this period saw the development of what was to become an enduring formative paradox of American history. The separation of church and state—articulated for the federal government in the First Amendment of 1791—was finalized for the states in Connecticut in 1818 and in Massachusetts in 1833, the last establishments to fall. It also became a constitutional axiom, shared by evangelicals themselves, that there should be no formal connections between organized religion and civil government. At the very same time, however, evangelicals emerged as a major political force as they sought to shape America into a genuinely Christian nation.

ABOLISHING THE ATLANTIC SLAVE TRADE, 1780S-1807

The campaign against slavery falls into two distinct chronological phases: the efforts to end the Atlantic slave trade, which eventually met with success in 1807 in both Britain and—with much less fanfare—the United States, and the movement to secure the freedom of existing slaves, which culminated with the British emancipation act of 1833. In the United States, though, slaves in the Southern states had to wait another three decades, as arguments over their future sharply divided both evangelicals and the nation as a whole, only to be resolved in the cataclysm of the Civil War. This pronounced transatlantic divergence in the later history of the slavery question should not, however, obscure the extent to which in the earlier part of the period public opinion and the law had appeared to be moving in similar directions on both sides of the Atlantic.

Historical assessments of the contribution of evangelicals to the wider campaign have varied. There is no space here to survey adequately the vast and rich historical literature, but some different perspectives can be highlighted. A central debate over the last half century was initiated by Eric Williams in *Capitalism and Slavery*,[2] in which he argued that slavery ended in the British West Indies primarily because economic conditions became less favorable. According to this view, the anti-slavery agitation was coincidental rather than the main cause of the demise of the slave system. More recently, though, the economic argument has been turned on its head, as it has been shown that the slave trade was becoming increasingly profitable in the last years before its abolition.[3] Hence the

---

[2]Eric Williams, *Capitalism and Slavery* (Chapel Hill: University of North Carolina Press, 1944).

[3]Seymour Drescher, *Econocide: British Slavery in the Era of Abolition* (Pittsburgh: University of Pittsburgh Press, 1977).

historiographical pendulum has swung back toward emphasizing the significance of an ideological and cultural movement against slavery from the 1780s
onward. Some scholars, notably Roger Anstey in *The Atlantic Slave Trade and British
Abolition 1760-1810*,[4] gave pride of place to evangelicals in this movement, but
others have presented evangelicalism as but one strand in a complex tapestry of
anti-slavery ideas, also encompassing other Christians, notably Quakers, and
secular thinkers inspired by the Enlightenment. In this context evangelicalism
as such was subsumed in a wider ideological movement of progress or patriotism, with abolition a symbol of humanity's moral and social advance, or a
means of asserting national moral integrity against the backdrop of the French
wars.[5] The debate about the inspiration for anti-slavery relates to one about political process: should the abolition of the slave trade be seen primarily as the
achievement of the small elite evangelical circle around Wilberforce and the
Clapham Sect, or was it more the consequence of agitation among a larger and
more ideologically variegated constituency in the country as a whole, that
brought pressure to bear on parliament through petitioning and elections?[6]
Nor was evangelical influence exerted solely, or even predominantly, on the
anti-slavery side. The caution of evangelicals who believed that the conversion
of the slaves was a more pressing need than their emancipation was a significant
brake on the anti-slavery movement in both Britain and the Northern United
States. In the Southern United States, almost all white evangelicals believed
that slavery was sanctioned in Scripture and came to perceive abolitionism as
subversive of the authority of the Bible as well as of the order of society as they
knew it. This view was also well represented among Northern evangelicals.[7]

---

[4]Roger Anstey, *The Atlantic Slave Trade and British Abolition 1760-1810* (London: Macmillan,
1975).

[5]David Brion Davis, *Slavery and Human Progress* (New York: Oxford University Press, 1984);
Linda Colley, *Britons: Forging the Nation 1707-1837* (London: Pimlico, 1994), pp. 350-60.

[6]Seymour Drescher, "Whose Abolition? Popular Pressure and the Ending of the British
Slave Trade," *Past and Present* 143 (May 1994): 136-66; J. R. Oldfield, *Popular Politics and Brit-
ish Anti-Slavery: The mobilisation of public opinion against the slave trade 1787-1807* (Manchester:
Manchester University Press, 1994).

[7]Davis, *Slavery and Human Progress*; Kenneth P. Minkema and Harry S. Stout, "The Edwardsean Traditon and the Antislavery Debate, 1740-1865," *Journal of American History* 92
(2005): 47-74; Mark A. Noll, *America's God from Jonathan Edwards to Abraham Lincoln* (New
York: Oxford University Press, 2002), pp. 386-401.

In this historiographical framework, it is essential to be specific about the ways in which evangelicalism contributed to the cause of anti-slavery. Mark Noll, in the first volume of this series, has noted the important early advocacy of John Wesley in England and Samuel Hopkins in America.[8] As the British movement gathered momentum in the 1780s, its propaganda resources were strengthened by several significant evangelical publications, notably John Newton's *Thoughts Upon the African Slave Trade*, drawing on his first-hand experience, and Hannah More's *Slavery: A Poem*, both published in 1788. Perhaps most effective of all publications in that year was "The Negro's Complaint" by William Cowper, co-author of the *Olney Hymns* and one of the foremost poets of the age. In words put into the mouths of a slave, Cowper affirmed that "affection dwells in white and black the same," attacked the shallowness of a Christianity that sanctioned slavery, and saw it as condemned by divine providence:

Is there—as ye sometimes tell us—
Is there One who reigns on high?
Has He bid you buy and sell us,
Speaking from his throne, the sky?
Ask Him, if your knotted scourges,
Matches, blood-extorting screws,
Are the means that duty urges
Agents of His will to use?

Hark! He answers—Wild tornadoes
Strewing yonder sea with wrecks,
Wasting towns, plantations, meadows,
Are the voice with which He speaks.
He, forseeing what vexations
Afric's sons should undergo,
Fixed their tyrants' habitations
Where his whirlwinds answer—"No."[9]

During the 1790s and early 1800s the framework of evangelical theology

---

[8]Mark A. Noll, *The Rise of Evangelicalism: The Age of Edwards, Whitefield and the Wesleys* (Leicester, U.K.: Inter-Varsity Press, 2004), pp. 235-37.
[9]William Benham, ed., *The Poetical Works of William Cowper* (London: Macmillan, 1874), p. 361.

and spirituality gave a significant ideological impetus to anti-slavery on both sides of the Atlantic. In particular, the very language of conversion as liberation from the metaphorical slavery of sin inspired evangelicals to work for the liberation of Africans from the literal slavery of the plantations. In America the worldly turmoil of the Revolution and the early republic caused an initially embattled evangelical minority to strive for greater spiritual integrity and to renounce slave-holding as a characteristic of a godless lifestyle. The Methodist leader Francis Asbury, for example, was a staunch opponent of slavery. Such convictions also developed an explicitly political dimension. Newton felt that it was inappropriate for him as a clergyman to interfere directly in politics, but he still affirmed that "it is Righteousness that exalteth a nation; and Wickedness is the present reproach, and will sooner or later, unless repentance intervene, prove the ruin of any people."[10] In America slavery was presented as a stain on the moral purity of the young republic. In Britain in 1807, as prospects for abolition at last brightened, anti-slavery leaders expressed their fears that continuing defiance of the will of the Almighty on this matter could lead to retributive divine judgments on the nation. James Stephen, Wilberforce's brother-in-law and close friend, dwelt on the horrors that would arise from a French invasion of England, recalled the plagues of Egypt and the destruction of Jerusalem after the Jews rejected the Messiah, and then warned ominously that "severe chastisements for the guilt of the Slave Trade, have already been felt, and that still severer are approaching."[11]

When one looks, however, at the specific organizational and political activity working toward the abolition of the slave trade, evangelical involvement was initially limited. In Britain it was the Quakers who, in 1783, first set up a committee to consider the slave trade. When the more broadly based London Abolition Committee began work in 1787, nine out of its twelve initial members were Quakers, who were in general associated more with the liberal wing of the Society of Friends than with its emerging evangelical ten-

---

[10]John Newton, *Thoughts Upon the African Slave Trade* (London: J. Buckland, J. Johnson, 1788), p. 6.
[11]James Stephen, *The Dangers of the Country* (London: J. Butterworth, J. Hatchard, 1807), p. 198; Anstey, *Atlantic Slave Trade*, pp. 184-99; James Essig, *The Bonds of Wickedness: American Evangelicals Against Slavery, 1770-1808* (Philadelphia: Temple University Press, 1982), pp. 26-72, 94-95.

dency.[12] The three Anglicans included two of the key figures in British slave
trade abolition, Thomas Clarkson and Granville Sharp, but although both
these men were certainly strongly influenced by evangelicalism, neither of
them can be unambiguously identified with the movement. The activities of
abolition committees, in London and elsewhere, were vital in rousing public
opinion and coordinating its expression through petitions. Clarkson did essential work as a traveling agent, gathering information on the slave trade
and mobilizing anti-slavery forces in the provinces. In parliament, although
Wilberforce had decided in 1787 to commit himself to the cause, he was
prevented by illness from taking an active part in 1788 and so the first moves
were made by the prime minister, William Pitt, and Sir William Dolben,
who successfully promoted a bill to regulate the capacity of slave ships and
thereby improve conditions.[13] A parallel point can be made about the early
provincial supporters of the movement: the Manchester Abolition Committee has been characterized as "led by political radicals who had closer ties
with Paine and the Enlightenment than with evangelical religion."[14] Although a few evangelicals, such as Caleb Evans, minister of Broadmead Baptist Church, participated in the Bristol committee, it also included Quakers,
prominent non-evangelical Anglicans and a Unitarian minister.[15] Similarly
in the United States, Quakers rather than evangelicals were the main driving
force in the most important early abolition societies, such as those in New
York and Pennsylvania, and the more evangelical Connecticut Society for
the Promotion of Freedom and the Relief of Persons Unlawfully Holden in
Bondage, founded in 1790, was relatively ineffective politically.[16]

Nevertheless, the contribution of evangelicals—Wilberforce and the
Clapham Sect above all—to the abolition of the British slave trade was a crucial

---

[12]Judith Jennings, *The Business of Abolishing the Atlantic Slave Trade 1783-1807* (London: Frank
Cass, 1997), p. 35. Only two of the nine Quakers listed by Jennings, Samuel Hoare and
Richard Philips, are included in the *BDEB*.

[13]Dolben is included in the *BDEB* (p. 316), but no specific evidence is offered for his evangelicalism, other than his support for the abolition of the slave trade.

[14]Davis, *Slavery and Human Progress*, p. 138.

[15]Madge Dresser, *Slavery Obscured: The Social History of the Slave Trade in An English Provincial Port*
(London: Continuum, 2001), p. 139.

[16]Arthur Zilversmit, *The First Emancipation: The Abolition of Slavery in the North* (Chicago: University of Chicago Press, 1967), pp. 166-67.

one.[17] Sentiment in the country needed to be convincingly communicated to parliament, and the eloquent, well-connected and politically astute young member from Yorkshire was the ideal person to carry out that task. In 1790 he obtained a select committee to gather evidence on the trade and worked extremely hard to gather and condense material. In April 1791 he moved for permission to bring in an abolition bill, but was defeated in the vote. He tried again in April 1792. This time the House of Commons agreed a compromise proposal for gradual abolition, but this apparent partial victory was stalemated by the delaying tactics of his opponents and the obstruction of the House of Lords. Cowper nevertheless hailed Wilberforce's achievement:

> Thou has achieved a part; has gained the ear
> Of Britain's senate to thy glorious cause.
> Hope smiles, joy springs, and though cold caution pause
> And weave delay, the better hour is near
> That shall remunerate thy toils severe
> By peace for Afric, fenced with British laws.[18]

Thereafter, however, the war with France and fear of revolution in Britain made it impossible for Wilberforce to make further progress, because of fears that abolition would destabilize society and the economy in the West Indies, compromise British strategic interests and open the way to further radical measures. It is possible, with the luxury of hindsight, to argue that Wilberforce had made some tactical misjudgments in the early years of the campaign, when success before the outbreak of war in 1793 might have been possible. Subsequently, however, he ensured that the issue remained firmly on the political agenda for the next decade, by raising it in Parliament nearly every year.[19]

---

[17] After Wilberforce's death there was an unedifying controversy between his sons, who had minimized Clarkson's role in their biography of their father, and Clarkson himself, who felt he had to give his side of the story. See R. and S. Wilberforce, *Life of William Wilberforce*, 1:146-54; and Thomas Clarkson, *Strictures on a Life of William Wilberforce* (London: Longman & Co., 1838). In reality both men played vital but different and complementary roles.

[18] Benham, *Cowper*, p. 384.

[19] For a short account of Wilberforce's parliamentary campaign against the slave trade summarized in this and following paragraphs, see John Wolffe, "William Wilberforce," in *The Oxford Dictionary of National Biography*, ed. H. C. G. Matthew and Brian Harrison (Oxford: Oxford University Press, 2004); and for more detail Pollock, *Wilberforce*. Jennings, *Atlantic Slave Trade*, offers a more critical perspective.

From 1804 onward Wilberforce's dogged persistence began at last to bear fruit. Although the war with France continued, suspicion of radicalism in Britain had receded and it became possible to argue that abolition, far from being a dangerously destabilizing change in wartime, was a patriotic measure that would enhance the nation's moral authority and ensure it continuing divine favor in the ongoing conflict. It was in this final phase of Wilberforce's efforts against the slave trade that the Clapham network was particularly important, both in providing a nucleus of committed evangelical supporters in Parliament and as a source of vital advice and encouragement. Wilberforce managed to get an abolition bill through the House of Commons in May and June 1804, only to have to abandon it as there was no time that year to get it through the House of Lords. After he was again disappointed in 1805, the death early in 1806 of Wilberforce's old friend, the prime minister William Pitt, was followed by the formation of a new government under two firm supporters of abolition, Lord Grenville and Charles James Fox. They were willing to promote abolition as a government measure in a way that Pitt had never been, despite his personal sympathy, and Wilberforce, always ready to cooperate with nonevangelicals for the sake of a common cause, was happy to join forces with them. Legislation for abolition at last passed through parliament and became law on March 25, 1807. The bill was actually moved on behalf of the government by Viscount Howick (later Earl Grey), a future Whig prime minister, but the credit was given to Wilberforce and his supporters. It must be emphasized, however, that this great achievement of evangelicals in politics was not achieved in isolation, but was possible only because evangelicals were prepared to work as part of a wider coalition of forces opposed to the slave trade.

The epic quality of Wilberforce's parliamentary campaign in Britain for the abolition of the slave trade tends to obscure the significant progress made against slavery in the United States during the same period. Many of the Northern states had moved during the late eighteenth century to abolish not only the slave trade but slavery itself, albeit only through the long-term process of declaring the children of slaves born after a stated date to be free. The final Northern states to take this step were New York in 1799 and New Jersey in 1803.[20] Thereafter slavery literally began to die out in the North, although

---

[20]Zilversmit, *First Emancipation*.

black people remained for many years very much second-class citizens, as Mrs. Metzger and her family were to find in the 1830s.[21] Meanwhile, most states, both North and South, had suspended involvement in the Atlantic slave trade, and although South Carolina reopened it for a few years after 1803, in 1807 Congress passed legislation to prohibit American participation. This measure was acceptable to the slave-holders because in the American South, unlike the West Indies, the existing slave population was growing fast, by 27 percent in the single decade of the 1790s. A large-scale internal slave trade, within the Southern states, continued until the Civil War.[22] Nevertheless, qualified though these steps were, it still seemed in the early nineteenth century that the United States was moving in parallel with Britain, or was even somewhat in advance.

In America, however, political and legal gains for anti-slavery in this phase were made without significant direct evangelical involvement. Evangelicals were more important at the ideological level, notably in New England through the preaching and writing of Samuel Hopkins (1721-1803) and Jonathan Edwards Jr. (1745-1801), both of whom were radical opponents of slavery. The Methodists, led by Asbury, initially committed themselves strongly against slavery and their direct influence led a few slave-holders to free their slaves, but they had no direct impact on state policy and legislation. Nevertheless, in spite of, or perhaps because of, the legislative progress made by the early nineteenth century, evangelical commitment to the cause then seemed to waver and decline. Hopkins and Edwards were both dead by 1807 and a younger generation of New England evangelicals appeared more ready to countenance the continuance of slavery in the South now that it was disappearing from their own neighborhoods. For example, Lyman Beecher, although sympathetic to emancipation, was publicly noncommittal, in striking contrast to his energetic and vocal support of many other reforming causes. During the 1790s and early 1800s the very evangelistic successes of the Methodists in the slave-holding states obliged them to retreat from their earlier explicit opposition to slavery in order to avoid alienating their own converts. The Baptists and Presbyterians followed a similar pattern, making firm pronouncements which they subsequently felt obliged to soften. Lemuel Haynes (1753-1833), a black Congregationalist

---

[21]See above, p. 17.
[22]Michael Tadman, *Speculators and Slaves: Masters, Traders and Slaves in the Old South* (Madison: University of Wisconsin Press, 1989), pp. 12, 19.

minister in Vermont, remained a vigorous opponent of slavery, but by the time he faded from the scene in the 1820s he had become a lonely voice.[23]

In both Britain and America, the ending of the Atlantic slave trade was followed by a significant lull in anti-slavery activity. Wilberforce's long-term aspiration remained for the abolition of slavery, but his hope was that in the medium term the consequence of cutting off the supply of new stock from Africa would be to force the West Indian planters to improve conditions for their existing slaves. In the meantime, he turned his attention to ensuring that the 1807 legislation was being enforced, and to pressing for the adoption of similar measures by other countries. He tried unsuccessfully in 1814-1815 to get an agreement for general abolition incorporated into the peace settlement following the end of the Napoleonic Wars. Evangelical concern for black people also translated itself into support for the colonization movement, returning Christian freed slaves to settle in Africa, promoted in Britain through the African Institution, set up in 1807, and by the American Colonization Society, formed in 1816. This activity was significant in establishing an evangelical presence in Liberia and Sierra Leone, which it was hoped would become bridgeheads for missionary advance in Africa, but controversial in that it implied acceptance rather than challenge to the continuance of slavery in America. The scheme was generally unattractive to free blacks and offered no direct assistance to slaves.

THE CAMPAIGN FOR SLAVE EMANCIPATION, 1823-1840S

By the early 1820s it was becoming apparent that the abolition of the slave trade had not led to a significant improvement in conditions in the West Indies, and the opponents of slavery in Britain hence decided to launch a campaign to obtain freedom for the slaves. The intervening years had seen significant expansion in evangelical Nonconformity, which was to provide a powerful network for the agitation of the question. Wilberforce, now too old and frail to provide effective parliamentary leadership, nevertheless gave an important ideological

---

[23]Essig, *Bonds of Wickedness*, pp. 159-62; Minkema and Stout, "Edwardsean Tradition"; Donald G. Mathews, *Slavery and Methodism: A Chapter in American Morality 1780-1845* (Princeton, N.J.: Princeton University Press, 1965), pp. 3-29; David Brion Davis, *The Problem of Slavery in the Age of Revolution 1780-1823* (New York: Oxford University Press, 1999), pp. 204-5; John Saillant, *Black Puritan, Black Republican: The Life and Thought of Lemuel Haynes 1753-1833* (New York: Oxford University Press, 2003).

and propaganda impetus through publishing *An Appeal to the Religion, Justice and Humanity of the Inhabitants of the British Empire, in Behalf of the Negro Slaves in the West Indies* (London, 1823). While delineating the various evils of slavery, his over-riding argument for emancipation was a spiritual one, as "the almost universal destitution of religious and moral instruction among the slaves is the most se-rious of all the vices of the West Indian system." Moreover, he urged his com-patriots not to "presume too far on the forbearance of the Almighty": the in-justice to the slaves needed to be remedied, and in a political system where "the popular voice" had a powerful influence on government, it was incumbent on all to call for the reform of such abuses, lest they share in guilt for them.[24] As his successor in leading the anti-slavery forces in the Commons, Wilberforce re-cruited a fellow evangelical, Thomas Fowell Buxton (1786-1845). Buxton was an Anglican himself, but his wife and mother were Quakers and he had at-tended a Friends' Meeting House when first married, and he thus illustrated in his own person the close links of both evangelicals and Quakers to the anti-slavery cause.[25] While Buxton's leadership ensured that anti-slavery continued to be strongly associated with evangelicalism, his efforts also received impor-tant parliamentary support from more secularly minded reformers, notably Henry (later Lord) Brougham and Stephen Lushington.

The new campaign was decisively launched in 1823, when Zachary Macaulay organized the London Anti-Slavery Society to coordinate the agita-tion in the country. Thomas Clarkson, another veteran of the anti-slave trade campaign, resumed his old role as a traveling agent, and although now aged over sixty, energetically toured England promoting local committees and petitions. James Stephen gave intellectual and legal ballast to the cause, complementing Wilberforce's short *Appeal* by a substantial work, *The Slavery in the West Indies De-lineated*, which appeared in two volumes in 1824 and 1830. Meanwhile, Wilber-force and Buxton raised the matter in the Commons, with mixed success. Bux-ton's motion submitted on May 15, 1823, was passed, but only after it had been heavily amended at the instigation of George Canning, leader of the Tory government in the Commons. Canning was sympathetic to the abolitionists, but also anxious not to antagonize the West Indian planters and concerned to

---

[24]Wilberforce, *Appeal*, pp. 24, 73-74.

[25]On Buxton, see Oliver Barclay, *Thomas Fowell Buxton and the Liberation of the Slaves* (York: Wil-liam Sessions, 2001).

maintain property rights. The result of his intervention was to change Buxton's original call for slavery to be "gradually abolished" into merely a commitment to "adopt effectual and decisive measures for ameliorating the condition of the slave population." Canning offered some specific reforms to the practice of slavery, which Wilberforce decided to accept, but at the price of stalling progress toward abolition.[26]

Moderate though Canning's reforms were, when news of them reached the West Indies, the planters tried to avoid implementing them. In Demerara (part of Guyana) their inaction sparked protests among slaves, who demanded liberation. This unrest was then suppressed with brutal and disproportionate force, and a London Missionary Society missionary named John Smith was imprisoned and sentenced to death for alleged complicity with the protesters. Smith died in prison before the sentence could be carried out. Smith's case was symptomatic of growing tensions between missionaries and planters in the West Indies, as the former were perceived as stirring aspirations for liberation and the latter obstructed the development of church life among the slaves. In Barbados, white people attacked the Methodist Chapel, and the missionary William Shrewsbury had to be transferred to Cape Colony for his own safety. Smith came to be perceived as a martyr for the cause, and his case received full publicity when Brougham, Wilberforce and others drew attention to it in parliament in June 1824. Buxton then raised the Shrewsbury case in 1825. The effect of these and other attacks on missionaries was to galvanize evangelical public opinion in Britain in support of the slaves. Nevertheless, while Tory governments continued in the late 1820s, there was no realistic prospect of making headway in parliament. Buxton bided his time, while also giving some attention to other humanitarian causes, notably in 1828 when his advocacy assisted John Philip, director of the London Missionary Society's work in South Africa, in securing a government commitment to equitable treatment of the Khoi native people in Cape Colony.[27]

---

[26]Ernest Marshall Howse, *Saints in Politics: The "Clapham Sect" and the Growth of Freedom* (London: Allen and Unwin, 1971), pp. 154-56; Edith F. Hurwitz, *Politics and the Public Conscience: Slave Emancipation and the Abolitionist Movement in Britain* (London: Allen and Unwin, 1973), p. 36; Barclay, *Buxton*, p. 67.

[27]Andrew Porter, *Religion Versus Empire? British Protestant Missionaries and Overseas Expansion, 1700-1914* (Manchester: Manchester University Press, 2004), pp. 81-82, 88-89; Barclay, *Thomas Fowell Buxton*, pp. 68-77; Howse, *Saints in Politics*, pp. 157-60.

By 1830 it was clear that Canning's 1823 reforms would not be implemented, and anti-slavery opinion in Britain shifted to demand immediate
emancipation as the only solution, given that experience suggested it was impossible to improve the slave system gradually. This ideological shift was in part
a response to practical disappointment and frustration, but it also reflected the
influence of evangelical conviction: the institutionalized sin of slavery had to be
rooted out by radical change, just as individuals needed to confront the sinfulness of their own lives in the radical change of personal conversion. At the annual meeting of the Anti-Slavery Society in May 1830, Clarkson and Wilberforce, the two grand old men of the cause, both appeared to lend their support
to a new phase of intensive activity. An Agency Committee was formed and set
new standards for effective mobilization of public opinion. Later that year the
medium-term prospects for emancipation were substantially improved when
the Tory government fell and was succeeded by a reforming Whig administration, in which Brougham was Lord Chancellor. In the short term, however, the
government was preoccupied with securing parliamentary reform at home and,
facing a major struggle with the House of Lords on this matter, was anxious to
avoid controversy on other fronts. Hence the abolitionists were obliged to bide
their time in Parliament, while building up support in the country that expressed itself in ongoing petitioning campaigns.[28]

Matters came to a head in the summer of 1832. On June 6, at Buxton's instigation, a House of Commons committee was appointed to report on the best
means "of effecting the extinction of slavery throughout the British dominions at
the earliest period compatible with the interests of all classes in the colonies."
Meanwhile, at the end of 1831, there had been a further slave revolt, this time in
Jamaica, and again missionaries were blamed. It was indeed apparent that evangelical convictions, especially among Baptists, had helped to inspire slaves to resist
the oppression of their masters, but there was no evidence that missionaries had
directly incited violence.[29] Some of them returned to England in September 1832
and had graphic tales to tell of persecution and destruction of chapels, received
by the evangelical public as further evidence of the inherently anti-Christian char-

---

[28]For accounts of developments from 1830 to 1833, see Hurwitz, *Politics and the Public Conscience*, pp. 48-72; Barclay, *Thomas Fowell Buxton*, pp. 81-99.

[29]Mary Turner, *Slaves and Missionaries: The Disintegration of Jamaican Slave Society 1787-1834* (Urbana: University of Illinois Press, 1982), pp. 148-73.

acter of the slave system. William Knibb, the most prominent of the missionaries, linked patriotism and faith in urging, "Britons, patriots, fathers, females, join me in my endeavours to rid my country of this Moloch of iniquity!"[30] In the general election that December, the first under the newly reformed electoral system, many candidates were pressed to commit themselves against slavery. The revised franchise and constituency structure disenfranchised the so-called rotten boroughs that had provided parliamentary spokesmen for the planters, and gave seats to the growing industrial towns where evangelical Nonconformity was generally strong. Hence the balance of the new House of Commons was more supportive of emancipation than had been the case in the unreformed parliament.

The Colonial Secretary Lord Stanley eventually announced his proposals on May 14, 1833. In the meantime, the abolitionists had organized a convention which met in London from April 18 to 29 and included a march to Downing Street to impress their views on the government. It was attended by many Dissenting ministers, although Anglican evangelicals outside Buxton's immediate circle were more cautious, being inclined to suspicion of a measure they now associated with the liberalism of the Whig administration. There was also a concerted petitioning campaign, which built up during April to reach a climax on the day of Stanley's speech, when over 500 petitions were presented to the House of Commons and over 600 to the House of Lords. The strength of popular evangelical support at this juncture is illustrated by the case of the Wesleyans, 229,426 of whom signed petitions, a figure corresponding to 95.2 percent of the current denominational membership of 241,000.[31] A further notable feature of the petitioning was the extensive involvement of women, who had been mobilized particularly by their identification with the sufferings of female slaves, vulnerable to physical and sexual exploitation and denied responsibility for their own children. Women were statistically more likely than men to be evangelicals and for them "the intertwining of their religious selves with their identity as women was . . . complete." In all, 178,000 of them signed a petition that Buxton presented on May 14, with the assistance of the three men needed to carry it into the House.[32]

---

[30]Quoted in Hurwitz, *Politics and the Public Conscience*, p. 137.

[31]Clare Midgley, *Women Against Slavery: The British Campaigns 1780-1870* (London: Routledge, 1992), p. 65. It should not be assumed that all those who signed Wesleyan petitions were necessarily members, but the extent of signing was still very impressive.

[32]Hurwitz, *Politics and the Public Conscience*, p. 89; Thomas Fowell Barclay, *Thomas Fowell Buxton*, p. 97.

The specific terms of the slave emancipation were a disappointment at least to the more radical abolitionists, as they included a period of six years' "apprenticeship" to their existing owners, who also received twenty million pounds in compensation from the government. This was viewed by some as tainted money, rewarding people who had done terrible evil. Others, though, accepted that the nation itself had a responsibility in the matter, in view of the past sanction given to slavery, and noted that the slaves themselves lost nothing by the money given to the planters. Such was the view of William Wilberforce, who in a fitting close to his earthly labors died while the bill was going through parliament—but not before he had heard that the crucial second reading had been passed through the Commons. He responded to the news, "Thank God, that I should have lived to witness a day in which England is willing to give twenty millions sterling for the Abolition of Slavery."[33]

Despite its perceived flaws, the "Act for the Abolition of Slavery throughout the British Colonies," which became law on August 28, 1833, was well received in the West Indies. When emancipation became effective on August 1, 1834, the transition was a peaceful one, with slaves gathering in churches and chapels to give thanks and celebrate.[34] It was also a culminating political achievement of British evangelicals. As with the abolition of the slave trade a quarter of a century before, evangelicals must, however, be seen in the context of a broader coalition of progressive forces, with their success contingent on their willingness to cooperate, and indeed at times to compromise, with proponents of different beliefs and agendas.

In the United States, in contrast with Britain, abolitionism continued dormant in the 1820s. Evangelical efforts were directed rather toward mitigating the condition of the slaves by spreading Christianity among them and their masters. The very success of this strategy made slavery appear more morally and religiously acceptable in the American South than it had been in the West Indies, and led to the emergence of a generation of Southern evangelical apologists for slavery. Their arguments appeared well grounded in Scripture, as slavery was tolerated in both the Old and New Testaments. At its most assertive, the pro-slavery argument was that slavery was divinely ordained, a secure basis

---

[33]Hurwitz, *Politics and the Public Conscience*, pp. 154-55; *Life of Wilberforce*, v. p. 370.
[34]Turner, *Slaves and Missionaries*, p. 202.

for social stability and "a positive blessing ordained to be permanent in America." By no means all Southern evangelicals went that far, but many accepted slavery fatalistically as an inevitable evil, analogous to poverty or sickness, which might be alleviated by human compassion but could not be removed, at least not in the foreseeable future. Hence the object was to save the slaves' souls and moralize their lives rather than change their legal status. It followed, crucially, that slave-holding as such was not sinful, provided the slaves were well treated.[35]

Such acceptance of the moral legitimacy of slavery also had significant currency in the North. Other Northern evangelicals, though opposed to slavery in principle, advocated merely a gradualist approach, favoring the eventual freeing of the slaves but without any preconceived timetable, and not if doing so hindered the proclamation of the gospel or fractured national and denominational unity.[36] Anxiety over the divisive potential of the slavery issue had been heightened by the controversy in 1819-1821 over the admission of Missouri to the Union as a slave-holding state, which revealed the depth of the political conflicts that could be stirred. In the 1830s, however, in the aftermath of Nat Turner's slave revolt in Virginia, opinion became more polarized, with Southern defenders of slavery becoming more numerous and articulate, and abolitionism increasing in the North.

In December 1833, encouraged by the abolition of slavery by Britain, the New York evangelical philanthropists Arthur and Lewis Tappan launched the American Anti-Slavery Society (AASS) to campaign for immediate emancipation.[37] During the remainder of the decade this organization, emulating its London counterpart, established a network of support across the Northern states. Its expansion was fueled by the Finneyite revivalism of these years. Finney himself, although giving primacy to the task of saving souls from sin, was unequivocal in his denunciation of slavery, which he described in his *Lectures on Revivals* as "a great national sin," sustained with the connivance of the churches.[38] Oberlin College in Ohio, where Finney subsequently settled, had

---

[35]Carwardine, *Evangelicals and Politics*, pp. 53-59; John Patrick Daly, *When Slavery was Called Freedom: Evangelicalism, Proslavery, and the Causes of the Civil War* (Lexington: University Press of Kentucky, 2002).

[36]Stout and Minkema, "Edwardsean Tradition," pp. 63-70.

[37]Bertram Wyatt-Brown, *Lewis Tappan and the Evangelical War Against Slavery* (Cleveland: Press of Case Western University, 1969), pp. 107-9 and passim.

[38]Keith J. Hardman, *Charles Grandison Finney 1792-1875: Revivalist and Reformer* (Grand Rapids: Baker, 1987), p. 273.

been founded by abolitionists driven out of Lane Seminary in Cincinnati and was a center of evangelical abolitionist activity. It was, though, Finney's religious style—as much as his specific words—that inspired the abolitionists, with a sense that radical rejection of sin in national as in personal life was both essential and possible. Some of his converts and pupils, for example Theodore Dwight, were to become leaders of the anti-slavery movement. The AASS nevertheless faced difficulties on two fronts. On the one hand there was its own radical wing, led by William Lloyd Garrison, which held more liberal theological views and was inclined to espouse other progressive causes. The Garrisonians were absolutely uncompromising in their insistence on immediate emancipation, and hostile to the churches themselves because of their at best lukewarm and divided attitude to abolitionism. On the other hand there was substantial continuing caution toward abolition in all the major churches, with the Methodists facing a particularly painful tension between the recollection of their early commitment to abolition under Wesley and Asbury, and the current constraints placed upon them by their large Southern membership.[39]

The 1840s saw the development of more firmly entrenched positions, with anti-slavery opinions firmly repressed in the South, but advocated with greater vigor in the North, where, however, numerous shades of opinion remained. Slavery had already been a secondary factor in the Presbyterian schism of 1837-1838, with the New School associated with abolitionism, and now it became primary when schisms in two other major evangelical denominations ensued. First, however, in 1840 the anti-slavery movement itself split when the Garrisonians gained control of the AASS and the more conservative evangelical membership seceded to form the American and Foreign Anti-Slavery Society. In the same year the World Anti-Slavery Convention in London in June 1840 encouraged the Americans to take a firm stance against slaveholders in their churches.[40] In 1843 some committed abolitionists seceded from the Methodist Episcopal Church (MEC) to form the Wesleyan Methodist Church (WMC). Their departure did not, however, prevent a fullscale split in the MEC itself in the following year. The specific question that divided the church was whether Bishop James Andrew of Georgia, whose wife owned slaves, should be sus-

---

[39]John R. McKivigan, *The War Against Proslavery Religion: Abolitionism and the Northern Churches* (Ithaca, N.Y.: Cornell University Press, 1984), pp. 36-61.
[40]Ibid., pp. 43, 63-64.

pended from office. Andrew considered resigning in order to preserve unity, but Southerners forced the issue by persuading him not to do so. Northerners, for their part, felt a need to take a stand rather than risk further losses to the WMC. When the General Conference in May 1844 voted against Andrew, it proceeded to agree to a Plan of Separation, whereby Methodists in the slave states formed the independent Methodist Episcopal Church, South. Later in 1844, as embittered Methodists worked through the consequences of their division, the Baptists too reached a crisis point because of refusals to appoint slave-holders as missionaries. Southerners renounced connection with the existing Northern-dominated denominational societies and at Augusta, Georgia, in May 1845 formed the separate Southern Baptist Convention.[41]

Another noteworthy trend in American anti-slavery in the 1840s was a turn to third-party political activity. Initially abolitionists had attempted to make headway by influencing candidates for the Whig and Democratic parties, but the impact of this strategy was disappointing and in the 1840 presidential election neither of the main candidates, Harrison and Van Buren, then appeared ready to confront slavery. Hence the Liberty party was organized and in April 1840 nominated for the presidency James G. Birney, a Presbyterian from Kentucky who had freed his own inherited slaves and emerged as a forceful critic of fellow evangelicals who compromised with slavery. Although some evangelical abolitionists, notably Lewis Tappan, perceived direct political action as corrupting, others, notably Charles Finney, gave active support to the Liberty party. In general it was a movement permeated with the ethos of evangelicalism, which found its natural supporters among ministers and their congregations. It failed, however, to make significant electoral headway, gaining only 0.29 percent of the popular vote in 1840, and only 2.31 percent in 1844, when Birney stood again.[42] Nevertheless, its intervention in the 1844 campaign was significant because in New York the 15,000 votes Birney took from Henry Clay, the Whig candidate, gave the state and —through its large electoral college vote—the presidency to the pro-slavery Democrat James Polk.[43] The 1848 election saw a rather more successful antislavery third party, the Free Soilers. They campaigned for firm implementation of the so-called Wilmot Proviso that would

---

[41]Carwardine, *Evangelicals and Politics*, pp. 159-69.

[42]McKivigan, *War Against Proslavery Religion*, p. 148.

[43]Carwardine, *Evangelicals and Politics*, p. 89.

exclude slavery from any territory to be acquired from Mexico, thus containing it within the existing Southern states. Like the Liberty party, Free Soil was supported by numerous evangelicals and its convention at Buffalo in August 1848 had a revivalistic atmosphere. The Free Soil candidate, Martin Van Buren, a former president, was not an evangelical, but he gained over 14 percent of the vote in the Northern states.[44] Many Northern evangelicals, though, remained loyal to the Whigs in this election, despite the fact that their candidate, the eventual victor Zachary Taylor, was a Louisiana slave-holder.

The further development of the American anti-slavery campaign, up to its culmination in the crucible of the Civil War, falls outside the chronological range of this book. By 1850, however, some of the contours of future conflict were becoming clear. In the United States, as in Britain, the evangelical contribution was but part, albeit a prominent and central part, of a broader alignment of anti-slavery forces. In both countries, too, the conviction of many evangelicals that slave-holding was a national sin gave fervor to anti-slavery forces and meant that compromise appeared unpatriotic as well as immoral. On the other hand, the American situation differed fundamentally from the British in respect of diversity of opinion on slavery among evangelicals. In Britain evangelical zeal and energy weighed in very predominantly on the abolitionist side of the scale; in America, as evangelicals pursued their own radical differences over slavery, they contributed substantially to the ongoing ominous polarization in the nation.

SAVING NATIONS

There were numerous other political issues in addition to slavery that concerned evangelicals, reflecting their underlying vision of Christian nations that honored God in public life and facilitated the practice of evangelical piety in private life. In the 1830s and early 1840s the pivotal question in Britain was the ongoing relationship between church and state. Although this matter had in formal constitutional terms been settled by disestablishment in the United States, evangelicals remained concerned to Christianize national life. Meanwhile, on both sides of the Atlantic, the growth of Roman Catholicism was

---

[44]Ibid., p. 152. Some Free Soilers combined racism with anti-slavery in wanting all black Americans excluded from the territories.

viewed with alarm by evangelicals who saw their national identities in essentially Protestant terms. William Wilberforce was the most prominent figure in
a significant group[45] of evangelicals, sometimes known as "Saints," in the British Parliament in the late eighteenth and early nineteenth centuries, who actively
involved themselves in a wide range of matters. For the core of the group religious commitment meant that they showed no consistent adherence to secular
party ties; there was a larger group of evangelicals who sometimes voted with
them but generally remained loyal to either the Whigs or, more usually, the Tories. In part their concerns were specifically religious ones: in particular at re-
newals of the East India Company's charter, they pressed hard for the admission of missionaries to India. They were unsuccessful in 1793, but successful
in 1813, when the bishopric of Calcutta was established, subsequently occupied from 1834 to 1858 by Daniel Wilson, a prominent evangelical. They also
took an active interest in more secular issues. Sometimes these were matters of
public morality. For example, Wilberforce played a key role in the 1805 im-
peachment of Lord Melville, who had allegedly condoned the misappropria-
tion of naval funds. In 1820 he worked hard to try to mediate a settlement in
the case of George IV's estranged wife Caroline of Brunswick, who was de-
manding her rights as queen and was tried by the House of Lords on account
of her alleged infidelities. Evangelicals also actively supported moderate, or so-
called economical, reform, believing that this would purify the state of abuses
and corruption. Thus they hoped to encourage the reform of parliament itself.
Henry Thornton was a leading authority on the currency, who believed that
rigorous financial probity must undergird public policy. Wilberforce and Buxton also found time to be active supporters of penal reform to limit excessive
use of capital punishment.[46]

Questions of church and state inexorably gave rise to tension and division
among British evangelicals. On the one hand the great expansion of evangelical

---

[45]Ian Bradley, in "The Politics of Godliness: Evangelicals in Parliament 1784-1832,"
(D.Phil. thesis, Oxford University, 1974), p. 7, calculates that there were a total of 112
evangelical MPs between 1784 and 1832, although of course the number active at any
one time was significantly smaller.

[46]For further detail, see Bradley, "Politics of Godliness"; Pollock, *Wilberforce*; Howse, *Saints
in Politics*; and Richard R. Follett, *Evangelicalism, Penal Theory and the Politics of Criminal Law Reform in England, 1808-30* (Basingstoke: Palgrave, 2001).

Nonconformity from the 1790s onward generated increasing political pressure to reform and curtail the privileges of the established churches of England and Scotland. There was similar pressure for reform in Ireland, although here the impetus in numerical terms came more from Roman Catholics than from Protestant Dissenters. On the other hand there was a substantial evangelical presence within the established churches themselves. Such Anglican and Church of Scotland Evangelicals in general saw the church-state connection not as a shackle to be abandoned, but rather as a providential association that furthered the spread of the gospel and must be maintained and indeed strengthened. They differed, however, from Anglican High Churchmen in that their defense of religious establishments was normally on the basis that they were an effective means to pastoral and spiritual ends, rather than because they were specifically divinely ordained. Moreover, they were also often prepared to respect the ministries of evangelical Nonconformists.[47] Wesleyan Methodists occupied something of a middle position, in that their own rapid growth was perceived as a challenge to the establishment, but they continued to profess underlying loyalty to the Church of England. In general there were numerous shades of opinion within British evangelicalism. In this respect the church-state controversy in Britain merits comparison with the slavery question in the United States, with its similar capacity to divide evangelicals from each other.

In a further analogy with slavery in the United States, political agitation of church-state issues in Britain was muted in the first half of the period, before breaking out into vigorous and divisive controversy around 1830. In a context of war and some domestic unrest, Nonconformists were initially more concerned to be allowed to worship without interference than to risk provoking the authorities by political self-assertion. The danger was a real one, as became apparent in May 1811 when the Tory home secretary Lord Sidmouth proposed legislation which would have meant that Dissenting ministers could only be licensed if they were attached to a specified congregation and had been recommended by "substantial and reputable householders belonging to the said congregation." The effect would have been severely to limit the freedom of Methodist and other itinerants to operate, especially among poorer people.

---

[47]Cf. G. F. A. Best, "The Evangelicals and the Established Church in the Early Nineteenth Century," *Journal of Theological Studies* 10 (1959): 63-78.

The Methodists, however, mobilized effective opposition and the legislation was dropped. Following up on this success, Thomas Allan, legal adviser to the Wesleyans, negotiated with the government to secure a Toleration Act, passed in July 1812, which repealed offensive, albeit disused, seventeenth-century legislation against Dissenters. These modest successes, though, were contingent on the Methodists and Nonconformists effectively representing themselves as loyal subjects who did not present any serious challenge to the constitution in church and state.[48] Such sentiments were reaffirmed as opportunity arose: for example, John Morison, a Congregational minister and future editor of the *Evangelical Magazine,* preaching at Trevor Chapel, Brompton, on the death of George III in 1820, claimed that the late king had "no better or more loyal subjects" than Protestant Dissenters. He urged his congregation to maintain a steady patriotism, which implied attachment to the constitution and to the new king, George IV.[49]

In the meantime, evangelical Anglicans in Parliament were instrumental in securing some significant improvements in the situation of the Church of England. In 1809 the prime minister, Spencer Perceval (1762-1812), himself an evangelical, proposed, with strong support from Wilberforce and the Saints, the first of a series of annual parliamentary grants of £100,000 to improve the endowments of poorer livings, thus enhancing the incomes of the local Church of England clergy. These grants were continued regularly until 1821. In 1812, following Perceval's assassination, his evangelical friend the Earl of Harrowby, the lord president of the council, successfully promoted the Stipendiary Curates Act that, when incumbents were non-resident, empowered bishops to appoint a curate and fix a fair stipend. Then in 1818, a third evangelical in high office, Nicholas Vansittart, the chancellor of the exchequer, proposed a grant of £1,000,000 for church extension, which was agreed by Parliament and used to build the so-called "Waterloo churches." A further grant of £500,000 was made in 1824. Meanwhile, substantial public funds—of the order of £1,000,000 and £350,000 respectively—were also given to the Church of Ireland and the Church of Scotland to build new churches, glebe houses and schools, and to improve the stipends of the clergy. Evangelicals, growing in

---

[48]Hempton, *Methodism and Politics,* pp. 99-103.

[49]John Morison, *Patriotic Regrets for the Loss of a Good King* (London, 1820), pp. 20, 25. On Morison, see *BDEB,* p. 793.

strength in both the Irish and Scottish establishments at this period, benefited from these improved conditions and opportunities.[50]

In the late 1820s the atmosphere of compliant Nonconformity, gentle parliamentary encouragement of state churches and denominational non-confrontation changed quite suddenly. The causes of this change were both spiritual and political. Spiritually, a younger generation of Anglican and Church of Scotland evangelicals, inspired in particular by Edward Irving, some adopting a premillennialist eschatology, developed a radically conservative vision for the role of the state churches in national life. They perceived the older generation of Wilberforce and the Clapham Sect as too inclined to political compromise and believed that they were called to give uncompromising testimony in the public arena to the righteousness of God and the prospect of imminent divine judgment of national sins. This group was particularly associated with *The Record* newspaper, a bi-weekly (later triweekly) evangelical Anglican publication, which began publication in 1828 and was owned and edited from soon after its commencement by Alexander Haldane (1800-1882), son of James Alexander Haldane, whose 1797 tour had helped to stir revival in northern Scotland. The younger Haldane was to become a powerful *éminence grise* in setting the political and cultural tone of early Victorian evangelical Anglicanism. A small but vociferous group of "Recordite" MPs, including James Edward Gordon, Andrew Johnston, Viscount Mandeville and Spencer Perceval the younger (son of the prime minister) were prominent in the Commons in the early 1830s.[51]

The political climate after 1828 made the "Recordites" feel their hour had come. Early in 1827 the Earl of Liverpool, prime minister since 1812, suffered an incapacitating stroke and had to leave office, to be succeeded by a succession of unstable Tory administrations. In February 1828 the Whigs proposed the repeal of the Test and Corporation Acts, which had restricted conscientious Nonconformists from holding public office, and when the government abandoned its initial opposition to repeal, it was duly enacted. Then, in the summer of 1828, the Irish Roman Catholic leader Daniel O'Connell won a byelection

---

[50]Stewart J. Brown, *The National Churches of England, Ireland and Scotland 1801-46* (Oxford: Oxford University Press, 2001), pp. 62-74.

[51]I. S. Rennie, "Evangelicalism and English Public Life" (Ph.D. thesis, University of Toronto, 1962); J. L. Altholz, "Alexander Haldane, the *Record* and Religious Journalism," *Victorian Periodicals Review* 20 (1987): 23-31; on James Alexander Haldane, see above, pp. 52-53.

in County Clare. This victory served notice to the Duke of Wellington's government that if the result were to be replicated across Catholic Ireland at a general election, there would be a serious risk of civil war or secession led by the Catholic MPs who had a popular mandate but were not entitled to sit in Parliament. Hence the government concluded that Catholic Emancipation had to be conceded.

The government's change of heart sharply divided evangelicals. On earlier occasions when Catholic Emancipation had been discussed in Parliament, Wilberforce and the Claphamites had been generally in favor of it, believing that even though they might dislike the Catholic religion, it was wrong and impolitic to deny civil equality to its adherents. Such views were still very much apparent in 1828-1829, and were eloquently stated by Thomas Chalmers on March 14, 1829, at a public meeting in Edinburgh. Chalmers argued that the exclusion of Irish Catholics from Parliament confirmed their alienation from the British state and weakened Protestantism by allowing it to rely on political privilege rather than spiritual force.[52] On the other side of the argument was a concept of the British state as essentially defined by its Protestantism, which would be disastrously compromised by the admission of Roman Catholics to Parliament. This view was generally more characteristic of Tory High Churchmen, but it was also shared by some Anglican Evangelical opponents of emancipation, notably some but not all of the Recordites. *The Record* itself recognized the divided views of its readers, publishing letters on both sides of the question, but not taking sides itself.[53] Catholic Emancipation became law in April 1829.

The advent of the Whig government in late 1830 gave an opening to critics of the church, just as it gave fresh hope to the opponents of slavery. During the struggle for parliamentary and electoral reform in 1831 and 1832 political pressure on the church increased, especially when in October 1831 the votes of the bishops in the House of Lords were seen as determining the initial rejection of the reform bill. Although the initial running in agitation against the church was made by secular radicals such as John Wade, the author of *The Extraordinary Black Book* which attacked sinecures and abuses, Dissenters increasingly became

---

[52]Stewart J. Brown, *Thomas Chalmers and the Godly Commonwealth in Scotland*, (Oxford: Oxford University Press, 2001), pp. 187-88.

[53]John Wolffe, *The Protestant Crusade in Great Britain 1829-1860* (Oxford: Clarendon Press, 1991), pp. 43-44.

involved, albeit generally at this stage pressing for moderate reform and the removal of their residual civil disabilities rather than for disestablishment. Others, though, notably Wesleyans, remained supportive of the Church of England,
seeing it as an essential bulwark of Protestantism. The Recordites, too, played
the Protestant card in the House of Commons in 1831, launching a series of
attacks on the newly admitted Roman Catholic members under the guise of
discussion of Irish education policy.[54]

There is no space here to give a full account of the evangelical role in the
turbulent and complex British politics of the 1830s and 1840s, but four key
trends can be identified.[55] First, Nonconformists became more politically conscious and well organized. In some respects the anti-slavery campaign can be
seen as a political apprenticeship which equipped them to advance their own
interests more effectively in matters such as education and the compulsory pay-
ment of church rates to support the Church of England. Eventually in 1844 an
explicit organization to campaign for disestablishment was formed, in the
shape of the Anti-State Church Association, later the Liberation Society. Their
natural political affinities were in general with the Whigs, who were in government from 1830 to 1841, except for a brief period in 1834-1835, and again
from 1846 to 1852. The Wesleyans, though, continued to hold something of
a middle position, more sympathetic to the Tories and to the Church of England, although in 1843 they joined with other Nonconformists to ensure the
defeat of government education proposals that were perceived as giving too
much influence to the established church.

Second, continuing political pressure on the Church of Ireland and the
Church of England caused Anglican Evangelicals to identify more predominantly and exclusively with the Conservative/Tory party than they had done
hitherto. In 1833, at the very time that the slavery bill was also passing through
parliament, the government brought forward legislation for a major reorganiza-
tion and streamlining of the Church of Ireland, including the amalgamation of
numerous bishoprics. This measure, which John Keble condemned as "national
apostasy," triggering the High Church Oxford Movement, was barely more

---

[54]Ibid., pp. 68-71.

[55]For a detailed account of religious issues in the politics of these years, see G. I. T. Machin,
    Politics and the Churches in Great Britain 1832 to 1868 (Oxford: Oxford University Press,
    1977).

popular with Evangelicals, who saw it as a betrayal of their vision of the Church
of Ireland as a means for effective evangelization of the Catholic population
rather than merely serving the Protestant minority. Continuing concern about
government policy toward the Irish Church led in May 1834 to the resignation
of two cabinet ministers, Sir James Graham and Lord Stanley, and several Evangelical MPs followed them into the Conservative party. After the mid-1830s
Whig Evangelical Anglicans were a rarity.[56] The gradual recovery in Conservative political fortunes, to which both Anglican Evangelicals and Wesleyans contributed, helped to ensure that when reform of the Church of England came,
from 1835 onward, the measures adopted were much less drastic than had
seemed likely in the fevered atmosphere of the early 1830s.

Third, the consolidation of party ties after the 1832 Reform Act meant that
there was now little scope for a semi-independent grouping of MPs defined by
its evangelicalism, such as had existed under Wilberforce's leadership in the early
part of the century, and again, albeit in a more short-lived and embattled manner,
with the Recordites of the years around 1830. There remained distinguished individuals who, motivated by evangelical commitment, resisted party ties in order
to secure specific political ends. In 1832 Lord Ashley (later Earl of Shaftesbury)
took over parliamentary leadership of the campaign for factory reform from
Michael Sadler, a fellow evangelical who had lost his seat in the general election.
He eventually achieved partial success with the passing of the Ten Hours Act of
1847. Ashley's sympathies were with the Tories, but after 1835 he refused government office in order to preserve his own freedom of action.[57] There was also
Sir Robert Inglis, a younger associate of the Clapham Sect, who saw himself as a
particular advocate of the interests of the Church of England, and in June 1840
came within a few votes of securing public money to revive the church extension
grants of the 1820s.[58] Both men, though, operated as individuals rather than as
part of even an informal grouping. Nevertheless, the aspiration for an evangelical

---

[56]Wolffe, *Protestant Crusade*, p. 76.

[57]For details, see Geoffrey B. A. M. Finlayson, *The Seventh Earl of Shaftesbury* (London: Eyre
Methuen, 1981), passim. The factory reform campaign, like the anti-slavery movement,
brought evangelicals like Ashley, Sadler (*BDEB*, p. 968), Richard Oastler (*BDEB*, pp. 839-
40) and George Stringer Bull (*BDEB*, pp. 162-63) into association with nonevangelicals
in pursuit of a common cause.

[58]Brown, *National Churches*, pp. 236-38.

party did not wholly die. In 1841, Thomas Chalmers wrote of his longing for "a Wilberforce party in Parliament, consisting of men who would make it the polar star of their public and parliamentary conduct, to adopt such measures as were best for the moral and religious well-being of the population." He told Henrietta Maria Colquhoun, wife of the evangelical Conservative MP John Campbell Colquhoun, that he would "rejoice" to see her husband leading such a party, provided he was prepared "to relinquish all common-place politics" in favor of more "imperishable distinction" than could be obtained from "secular partisanship."[59] Colquhoun, though, failed to fulfill Chalmers's expectations, although in 1845 he was a key promoter of the National Club, which sought to provide a political focus for those with firm Protestant convictions, but operated as a pressure group rather than as a parliamentary party.[60]

Finally, anti-Catholicism was an important feature of evangelical attitudes toward politics in the 1830s and 1840s, a consistent undercurrent that sometimes rose strongly to the surface. Such attitudes were stirred in part by the passing of Emancipation, which left a feeling that national Protestantism now had to be asserted rather than just assumed; in part by resurgence in the Roman Catholic Church itself, both in Britain and Ireland; and in part by the growing influence of premillennialist eschatologies in which Rome was equated with cosmic forces of evil. A further stimulus, from 1833 onward, was the Oxford Movement led by John Henry Newman (a former evangelical), John Keble and others, which aspired to shift the Church of England to a more Catholic identity and which, by the early 1840s, was perceived as setting a clear Romeward course. This development was viewed with increasing alarm by many Anglican Evangelicals, and divisions within the Church of England therefore became more pronounced. The Protestant Association was formed in 1835-1836 in order to promote political anti-Catholicism. While its core membership was small, it had a significant impact on the tone of Sir Robert Peel's Conservative opposition in the later 1830s. Peel found anti-Catholicism a politically useful tool with which to attack the Whigs, because of their alleged favor toward the Irish Catholics. This movement in Britain was closely linked to a consolidation of evangelical forces in the north of Ireland on anti-Catholic lines, as during

---

[59]Colquhoun Papers, Cultybraggan Estates Office, Comrie, Perthshire, Chalmers to H. M. Colquhoun, June 26, 1841.
[60]Wolffe, *Protestant Crusade*, pp. 210-19.

the mid-1830s the Presbyterian leader Henry Cooke shared Protestant platforms with Anglican Evangelicals. In Australia, too, a political anti-Catholicism
that owed much to evangelicalism emerged in 1843 in the first elections for the
New South Wales Legislative Council, when the leading Presbyterian minister
John Dunmore Lang successfully stood on an openly sectarian platform.[61]

When Peel became prime minister in 1841, his political calculations changed
and in 1845, to the outrage of many evangelicals, he secured legislation to increase and make permanent the state subsidy to the Irish Roman Catholic seminary at Maynooth near Dublin. In such a context anti-Catholicism had the potential both to divide and to unite evangelical political action. The more common
pattern was one of division, because Anglican Evangelicals were apt to perceive
Nonconformists as doing the Pope's work for him by attacking the Church of
England, which they held to be the most secure bulwark of Protestantism in the
nation. Nonconformists, for their part, were liable to see the Church of England
as a Roman Trojan horse, given its residual Catholic characteristics which the Oxford Movement was currently seeking to revive. On the other hand, the Maynooth crisis brought Anglicans and Nonconformists together in common opposition to state financial support being given to a Roman Catholic institution.[62]

Developments in Scotland were important and distinctive. In 1834 the
Evangelicals, led by Thomas Chalmers, gained control of the General Assembly of the Church of Scotland and took two immediate steps. First, they
passed the so-called veto act, which gave heads of households in a congregation the right to veto the appointment of a patron's nominated minister for
a vacant parish. The measure thus asserted the principle known as non-intrusionism, the local church's right to ensure the spiritual integrity of its own
ministry, rather than being subject to the whims of lay patrons, who might
be absentees and were unlikely to be evangelicals. Second, they began a vigorous church extension campaign, raising money to build new churches and
creating new *quoad sacra* (ecclesiastical) parishes. The urgency with which they
pursued these initiatives reflected the pressure the Church of Scotland was already under from evangelical voluntaryists in the dissenting Presbyterian

---

[61]Ibid., pp. 98-106; Hempton and Hill, *Evangelical Protestantism in Ulster Society*, pp. 98-99;
  D. W. A. Baker, *Days of Wrath: A Life of John Dunmore Lang* (Carlton: Melbourne University
  Press, 1985), pp. 193-201.
[62]Ibid., pp. 134-37, 198-205.

churches, who argued, on the American model, for the severing of ties between church and state.

During the later 1830s the consequences of these two policies set the Church of Scotland on a collision course with the civil courts.[63] In 1838 the government rebuffed requests for state financial assistance for the church extension campaign. Chalmers responded with a series of "lectures on the establishment and extension of national churches," delivered in London where they would have the maximum political impact.[64] He argued that, as awareness of spiritual need, unlike more basic instincts, is not spontaneous and has to be awakened, a voluntary system for the support of Christianity would never on its own be sufficient to ensure that the gospel would be preached to every human being. His lectures were a compelling statement of the Evangelical case for national churches, but although enthusiastically received, they did nothing to change the current political and legal situation of the Church of Scotland. Meanwhile, non-intrusionism was being held to be inconsistent with the civil law, but the church refused to back down. Hence a series of local disputes became deadlocked, with, eventually, presbyteries responsible for the institution of new ministers facing an unenviable choice between the possibility of imprisonment if they obeyed the church, and suspension from office if they obeyed the civil courts. In 1840 in the presbytery of Strathbogie (Aberdeenshire), seven ministers who proposed to ordain a patron's nominee were suspended by the General Assembly, which appointed replacements. These men were promptly interdicted by the (civil) Court of Session from entering the churches and hence preached in the open air, in defiance of a subsequent extended interdict which prohibited them from even doing that. The political shock waves from the conflict were now substantial, both in influencing elections in Scotland and in the discussion of Scottish affairs at Westminster.[65]

The final straw for the Evangelicals came in 1842, when the Court of Session ruled that the *quoad sacra* parishes had no legal status and that their minis-

---

[63]For a recent detailed account of the developments summarized here, see Brown, *National Churches*, pp. 176-80, 190-97, 217-27, 292-312.

[64]Published in W. Hanna, ed., *Select Works of Thomas Chalmers* (Edinburgh: Constable, 1857), vol. II.

[65]I. G. C. Hutchison, *A Political History of Scotland 1832-1924: Parties, Elections and Issues* (Edinburgh: John Donald, 1986), pp. 20-22, 45-48.

ters and elders accordingly could not sit in the church courts. Hence the non-intrusionist majority in the General Assembly was wiped out and the legitimacy of all its proceedings since 1834 could be called into question. Frustrated in further negotiations with the government, they now decided that secession was their only option and in May 1843, in a carefully stage-managed demonstration in the streets of Edinburgh, literally walked out of the General Assembly and gathered again as the first General Assembly of the Free Church of Scotland. Over one-third of the Church of Scotland's ministers left. Although technically a dissenting body, the Free Church emphatically saw itself as still a national church, with a presence in every part of the country: its quarrel was not with the principle of state support for religion, but with the unacceptable terms on which such support was then being given to the Church of Scotland.[66] Events in Scotland had a significant impact elsewhere in the United Kingdom, particularly in encouraging English Nonconformists by prompting hopes of a similar disruption of the Church of England by discontented Evangelicals. Anglican secessions, though, were relatively very small in number. In 1843 James Shore, a Devon clergyman in dispute with the High Church Bishop of Exeter, Henry Phillpotts, left to form the Free Church of England, but it remained a tiny denomination. A prominent London evangelical clergyman, the appropriately named Baptist Noel, joined the Baptists in 1848, but his secession was also an isolated incident.[67] The position of the Evangelicals in the Church of England was then secured by the Gorham Judgment in 1850, in which the Judicial Committee of the Privy Council upheld the position of George Gorham, whom Bishop Phillpotts had refused to institute to a living because, consistently with evangelical convictions, he had denied that an infant was unconditionally spiritually regenerated in baptism.[68]

Events in Scotland were also watched with keen interest in North America, especially, but not only, by Presbyterians. While awaiting news of developments in

---

[66] Brown, *National Churches*, pp. 348-62.

[67] Grayson Carter, *Anglican Evangelicals: Protestant Secessions from the Via Media c. 1800-1850* (Oxford: Oxford University Press, 2001); David W. Bebbington, "The Life of Baptist Noel: Its Setting and Significance," *Baptist Quarterly* 24 (1972): 389-411.

[68] For a full account, see Owen Chadwick, *The Victorian Church Part 1 1829-1859* (London: SCM, 1987), pp. 250-71. Chadwick dwells on the anguish of High Churchmen at the Judicial Committee's decision; Evangelicals would have faced a converse dilemma had it gone the other way.

Edinburgh, William Sprague wrote from Albany, New York, to assure Chalmers of his sympathy and support, and his belief "that the great principle for which you contend is destined to stand forth as a leading element in the world's renovation."[69] John Spratt, who had been a student with Chalmers in Edinburgh forty years before and was now ministering in obscurity at Musquidaboit, Nova Scotia, assured him that "we read the Scottish papers, we see all your movements and mingle our prayers with our wishes for success in a great and good cause."[70] A Free Church delegation, led by William Cunningham, visited the United States in late 1843 and early 1844, and although they only raised limited funds, they were warmly received. Sprague judged that they exerted "a powerful influence in attracting different evangelical denominations . . . more towards each other, and especially in healing the divisions [between Old and New School Presbyterians] that have for some time existed in our own church."[71]

In the United States, with churches already separated from the state, sympathy for the Free Church was unproblematic. In Canada, on the other hand, British ecclesiastical conflicts were replicated as Anglicans and Presbyterians both claimed a privileged constitutional status and the right to a share in the income from the clergy reserves, lands set aside in 1791 to support the Protestant clergy. The War of 1812 created a good deal of alienation from American denominations, to which Canadian Methodists in particular had once been very close. As a consequence, almost all Canadian Protestants grew closer to their respective denominations in Britain. Tensions between church and state were symbolized when in May 1826 Egerton Ryerson, an ardent young Methodist revivalist, made his name by making a spirited published attack on the Anglican Rector of York (Toronto), John Strachan, who had recently asserted the Church of England's claim to a fully established status in Upper Canada. Ryerson argued that religious establishments were inherently Romish in tendency, and they were in any case unnecessary in Canada.[72] During the ensuing years, however, Ryerson, who became the dominant figure in Canadian Methodism, moderated his antagonism to state in-

---

[69]Chalmers Papers, CHA 4.311.33 (June 3, 1843).

[70]Ibid., CHA 4.311.37 (July 14, 1843).

[71]Ibid., CHA 4.315.68, Sprague to Chalmers (April 24, 1844); Thomas Brown, *Annals of the Disruption* (Edinburgh: MacNiven and Wallace, 1892), pp. 545-50.

[72]William Westfall, *Two Worlds: The Protestant Culture of Nineteenth Century Ontario* (Kingston and Montreal: McGill-Queens University Press, 1989), pp. 21-27.

tervention in religion and from 1844 as superintendent of the public educational system in Upper Canada he worked more in the British manner than the American for state support of non-denominational Protestant teaching. In 1840 the government had attempted a compromise resolution of the clergy reserves question by sharing the income between the Anglicans and the Presbyterians, and any other denomination that wished to claim a proportion of it. This settlement, however, was weakened by the Scottish Disruption, which provoked a split among Presbyterians in Upper Canada in 1844 and the wholesale identification of Presbyterians in Nova Scotia and Prince Edward Island with the Free Church. The Disruption also inspired the Scottish emigrant journalists Peter and George Brown to become vigorous critics of the Anglican establishment. Nevertheless, when in 1854 the clergy reserves were eventually secularized, the outcome was not a strict separation of church and state on the American pattern, but continuing informal recognition of the Protestant churches as essential for the public well-being of Canada.[73]

From one perspective the American political experience in the 1830s and 1840s was totally different from the British one, in that whereas in Britain explicitly religious issues took up a very substantial share of parliamentary time, in the United States the separation of church and state meant that religious issues as such did not enter into the political arena. Viewed in other ways, however, evangelicalism had a substantial impact. In terms of political culture it was significant in providing a theological and moral basis for the political thought of the young republic, in developing models of organization that gave coherence to civil society and examples for politicians to emulate, and even, it has been argued, in providing revivalism as a technique that could be appropriated to electoral as well as evangelistic purposes.[74]

In this era of the so-called second party system, Northern evangelicals usually aligned themselves with the Whigs, although groups such as the Old

---

[73] Goldwin French, *Parsons and Politics: The role of the Wesleyan Methodists in Upper Canada and the Maritimes from 1780 to 1855* (Toronto: Ryerson Press, 1962); John S. Moir, *Enduring Witness: A History of the Presbyterian Church in Canada* (Toronto: Presbyterian Church in Canada, 1987), pp. 94, 104-6; Michael Gauvreau, "Reluctant Voluntaries: Peter and George Brown; The Scottish Disruption and the Politics of Church and State in Canada," *Journal of Religious History* 25 (2001): 134-57. I am also grateful to Mark Noll for particular guidance on this paragraph.

[74] Howe, "Religion and Politics in the Antebellum North"; Noll, *America's God*.

School Presbyterians and the Antimission Baptists inclined more to the Democrats, and the Methodists took little interest in politics. Such predominantly Southern evangelicals distrusted broad national programs of reform and believed that the spiritual witness of the church should not be diluted by political dabbling. For more politically activist evangelicals, however, the Whigs were seen as offering a rather higher standard of political morality than the unscrupulous, if popular, Andrew Jackson, and also as more sympathetic to the blacks and "Indians," who were potential targets for evangelism. The Whigs also shared evangelical suspicion of large-scale immigration, which was already threatening to subvert the predominant Protestant identity of the United States. As in other parts of the English-speaking world, evangelicals were alarmed by increasing numbers of Roman Catholics, who were courted politically by the Democrats. Concerns were focused particularly when from 1839 onward Catholics in New York started successfully to challenge the reading of the King James Bible in the public schools. Evangelicals were not actively involved in the subsequent upsurge of organized political nativism, expressed in the American Republican Party formed in 1843, nor in the sectarian Philadelphia Riots of 1844, but they were strongly supportive of the more moderate anti-Catholicism represented by the Whigs.[75]

The presidential campaigns of the 1840s revealed the extent to which the Whigs valued the evangelical vote.[76] In each contest an initially unpromising candidate was packaged as a paragon of Christian principle, who would be God's instrument in reclaiming a corrupt nation. The tactic was at least plausible in the case of William Harrison in 1840 and Zachary Taylor in 1848, both of whom showed some outward attributes of conformity to evangelical ideals, but wholly unconvincing in the case of Henry Clay in 1844, who was a gambler, duelist and womanizer who made no convincing professions of personal piety. Realizing this problem, Clay chose as his vice-presidential running mate Theodore Frelinghuysen, perhaps the leading lay evangelical of his day, a former at-

[75]Daniel Walker Howe, *The Political Culture of the American Whigs* (Chicago: University of Chicago Press, 1979), pp. 150-80; John Wolffe, "Anti-Catholicism and Evangelical Identity in Britain and the United States 1830-1860," in *Evangelicalism: Comparative Studies of Popular Protestantism in North America, the British Isles and Beyond, 1700-1990*, ed. Mark A. Noll, David W. Bebbington and George A. Rawlyk (New York: Oxford University Press, 1994), pp. 186-87.
[76]For detailed discussion, see Carwardine, *Evangelicals and Politics*, pp. 50-96.

torney general of New Jersey and an active supporter of numerous religious organizations. As a U.S. senator in the early 1830s he had been a prominent opponent both of Sunday mails and of the resettlement of the Cherokees. In 1838 Frelinghuysen had published anonymously *An Enquiry into the Moral and Religious Character of the American Government,* in which he argued that the separation of church and state did not justify "political railing against religion" and that public men should set "a positive Christian example."[77] Nevertheless, even with Frelinghuysen sanctifying his ticket, Clay lost to James Polk, who had the asset of a staunchly Presbyterian wife. Harrison and Taylor both enjoyed electoral success, only subsequently to die in office, Harrison barely a month after his inauguration. The rather spurious hopes pinned on them by evangelicals perished with them.

CONCLUSION

The 1840s were in many respects a decade in which the political limitations of evangelicalism became apparent. Evangelicals were unsuccessful in securing their vision of an effective man of God in the White House who would lead national spiritual regeneration; they were unable to win a political battle to reform the Church of Scotland and accordingly the majority of them seceded from it; in 1845, even when they found a rare unity in opposing Peel's Maynooth measure, their protests were still ineffective. Their own divisions also became painfully apparent, on church-state matters in Britain and on slavery in the United States. Such a negative assessment should not, however, obscure the substantial achievements of earlier years—above all their crucial role in Britain in the abolition of the slave trade and, eventually, of slavery itself. Their influence was also very significant in shaping the underlying political landscape of the early nineteenth century, in maintaining a moral and spiritual dimension in secular politics, in energizing political parties even as they sought to transcend their limitations, and in stimulating widespread popular engagement in political life. Even if they could not have freed the slaves without assistance from others, and the state of their respective nations tended to fill them more with foreboding than with exultation, they still proved an effective leaven in the dough of political life.

---

[77] *An Enquiry into the Moral and Religious Character of the American Government* (New York, 1838), pp. 199, 201; Talbot W. Chambers, *Memoir of the Life and Character of the Late Hon. Theo. Frelinghuysen, LLD* (New York: Harper and Bros., 1863), pp. 59-83.

8

DIVERSITY AND UNITY IN THE EXPANSION OF EVANGELICALISM

All true believers are the ransomed church,
Children of God by Jesus owned and loved . . .[1]

In these lines, published in 1844 Baptist Noel, then minister of the Anglican chapel of St. John's, Bedford Row in London, articulated a deep-rooted sense in which evangelicals believed that, underlying all their institutional, theological and geographical diversity, they had as "true believers" a fundamental spiritual unity in Christ. Leonard Bacon, minister of the First Congregrational Church in New Haven, Connecticut, preaching in 1845, found the Atlantic Ocean itself to offer an appropriate metaphor for the shared spiritual consciousness of the seemingly divided churches that bordered it. Common influences operated "like the tide raised from the bosom of the vast Atlantic . . . [which] swells into every estuary and every bay and sound, and every quiet cove and sheltered haven, and is felt far inland where mighty streams rise in their channels and pause on their journey to the sea."[2] The specific expressions of evangelicalism on the banks of the Clyde, Foyle and Connecticut, let alone the Mississippi, St. Lawrence and Murray, differed from those alongside the Thames. Moreover, close geographical proximity was quite as likely in practice

---

[1]B. W. Noel, *Protestant Thoughts in Rhyme* (London, 1844), p. 73.
[2]Leonard Bacon, *Christian Unity* (New Haven, Conn.: Foreign Evangelical Society, 1845), p. 25.

to divide evangelicals as to bind them together. Nevertheless, despite all their visible disunity, evangelicals could still be powerfully inspired by their consciousness of themselves as an invisibly united movement.

In this final chapter this paradox will be explored, particularly in relation to the efforts culminating in 1847 to establish the Evangelical Alliance as a focal point for the evangelical movement throughout the world. First, however, in order to provide a more specific impression of both the strength and diversity of evangelicalism at the middle of the nineteenth century, we shall look at the evidence provided by two key contemporary documents, Robert Baird's book *Religion in the United States of America*, first published in 1843, and the 1851 Census of Religious Worship, conducted in Britain.

Robert Baird (1798-1863), a Presbyterian minister originally from Pennsylvania, was one of the most cosmopolitan of nineteenth-century evangelicals. He crossed the Atlantic eighteen times, spent much of his working life in Europe, and wrote *Religion in America*, the most impressive early work of its kind, in the hope of diffusing accurate information regarding his native country.[3] After surveying the various denominations, he attempted calculations and estimates of their respective numerical strengths, which are summarized in table 4.

Baird considered all the denominations listed in the table to be primarily evangelical. He included the Lutheran Church on the basis that it "has become much more [doctrinally] sound than it once was, and than some of its branches in Europe are."[4] Baird acknowledged that the Episcopalians were internally diverse, but included all of them in his statistics, while estimating that only about two-thirds of them were evangelicals.[5] On the other hand, he did not include the Disciples of Christ, partly because he could not find any statistics for them, but partly because he thought "that all they consider necessary to salvation is a cold, speculative, philosophical faith" that did not require genuine repentance and conversion.[6] By "population," Baird meant the number of people attending church occasionally or in some way influenced by a denomination without being regular communicants. His estimates here are very much open to debate

---

[3]On Baird, see *BDEB*, p. 49.
[4]Ibid., p. 588.
[5]Ibid., p. 506.
[6]Ibid., pp. 573-75.

Table 4: Evangelical Denominations in the United States, 1844[a]

	Churches	Ministers	Communicants	Population
Episcopalians	1,140	1,000	100,000	700,000[c]
Moravians	24	33	5,745	12,000
Congregationalists	1,500	1,250	160,000	1,000,000
"Regular" Presbyterians— Old and New School	3,400	2,551	243,000	
Cumberland Presbyterians	550	550	70,000	
Dutch Reformed Church	253	234	26,000	
Associate Synod	183	87	16,000	
Associate Reformed	214	116	12,000	
Lutherans	1,371	423	146,303	
German Reformed	600	180	75,000	
TOTAL: Congregational, Presbyterian, Lutheran, Reformed	4,350,000			
Regular Baptists	7,766	3,717	570,758	
Free Will Baptists	753	612	47,217	
Seventh Day Baptists	42	46	4,503	
TOTAL: Baptists				3,423,000
Methodist Episcopal Church	25,109	3,587[b]	852,918	5,000,000
Protestant Methodists		400	60,000	300,000
United German Brethren		100	20,000	100,000
Welsh Calvinistic Methodists	25	25	2,500	12,500

[a]Robert Baird, *Religion in the United States of America* (Glasgow and Edinburgh: Blackie and Son, 1844), pp. 600-601.

[b]This was the number of itinerant ministers; Baird stated that there were also 6,393 local preachers.

and probably too high,[7] but if they were to be accepted they would suggest that up to 13 million people, out of the total population of the United States at the 1841 Census of just over 17 million, were at least loosely linked to evangelicalism. Whatever the exact count, Richard Carwardine is certainly correct when he asserts that the network of evangelical churches constituted "the largest and

---

[7]Robert Baird, *Religion in America: A Critical Abridgement,* ed. Henry Warner Bowden (New York: Harper and Row, 1970), pp. xxii-xxiii.

most formidable subculture in American society" at the time.[8] Baird's list of denominations was also striking testimony to the institutional diversity of mid-
century American evangelicalism. In some respects, indeed, it understates it, as
the justice of his exclusion of the Disciples of Christ is debatable, he bracketed
Old and New School Presbyterians together, he did not list the separate African Methodist Episcopal Church, nor some other small Methodist secessions,
and he published his book before the 1844 schisms over slavery among the
Methodists and the Baptists.

The 1851 Census of Religious Worship in Britain was a unique survey undertaken by the government, but without legal compulsion, of church accommodation and attendances on Sunday, March 30, 1851. Historians continue to
debate its reliability and interpretation, and it must be used with caution, particularly because there is no way of confidently translating the figures for atten-
d*ances* into ones for attend*ers*, as many people would have gone to church more
than once, at the same or a different place of worship. There were also omis-
sions where churches failed to make a return.[9] These were especially substantial
in Scotland, where returns for 32 percent of Church of Scotland churches, 12
percent of Free Churches and 10 percent of United Presbyterians were lacking.[10] Nevertheless, although the apparent precision of the figures is misleading,
the census still provides a valuable general indication of levels of attendance and
enables denominations and localities to be compared with each other. It is also
useful in showing the existence not only of churches and chapels but also of numerous small cottage meetings. Tables 5 and 6 summarize the results for the
great majority of evangelical groups, alongside membership figures, where these
are available.

It is impossible to provide accurate figures for the strength of evangelicalism
in the Church of England and the Church of Scotland. There are, however,

---

[8]Carwardine, *Evangelicals and Politics*, pp. 44, 343 n. 114, 344 n. 115.

[9]Starting points for the voluminous literature on the census are Clive D. Field, "The 1851
Census of Religious Worship: A Bibliographical Guide for Local and Regional Histori-
ans," *The Local Historian* 27 (1997): 194-217; K. D. M. Snell and Paul Ell, *Rival Jerusalems:
The Geography of Victorian Religion* (Cambridge: Cambridge University Press, 2000); and John
Wolffe, *The Religious Census of 1851 in Yorkshire*, Borthwick Paper 108 (York: University of
York, 2005).

[10]Callum G. Brown, *Religion and Society in Scotland since 1707* (Edinburgh: Edinburgh University Press, 1997), pp. 43-44.

plausible contemporary estimates. In 1853 the journalist and educationalist
W. J. Conybeare estimated that 5,800 of the Church of England 18,300 clergy
were Evangelicals, a proportion of 31.7 percent.[11] In 1843, shortly after the
Disruption, James MacCosh, a Free Church minister and editor of the *Dundee
Warder,* carried out a similar calculation for the Church of Scotland. Of the 741
ministers who remained in the Church of Scotland, he classified 260 (35.1 percent) as Evangelicals, the remainder being "of the old Moderate type." It seems
reasonable to suppose that Evangelical churches were in roughly similar proportion and that Evangelicals made up at least as large a proportion of attendances.
Hence in Tables 5 and 6 the figures given for Church of England and Church
of Scotland Evangelicals are 31.7 percent and 35.1 percent of the respective
overall figures for these churches contained in the census report.[12] The small
Scottish Episcopal Church was predominantly non-evangelical and so is not included.[13]

The sum of all the attendances in the tables corresponds in England and
Wales to 35.66 percent of the population and 61.35 percent of all recorded
attendances at religious worship on the census Sunday and in Scotland to
36.21 percent of the population and 74.94 percent of attendances. It must be

---

[11]W. J. Conybeare, "Church Parties," ed. Arthur Burns, in *From Cranmer to Davidson A Church
of England Miscellany,* ed. Stephen Taylor (Woodbridge: Boydell/Church of England Record
Society, 1999), pp. 356-57.

[12]James MacCosh, *The Wheat and the Chaff Gathered Into Bundles: A Statistical Contribution Towards
the History of the Great Disruption of the Scottish Establishment* (Perth: James Dewar, 1843), pp. 6,
12. The consequent estimates in the tables should be regarded as rough indicators only.
Both Conybeare's and MacCosh's calculations might well be debated, but in the absence
of systematic modern research on party identifications, they are the best available. Conybeare's figure was based on a sample. MacCosh's 1843 figure included some men whose
evangelicalism was uncertain, but as the evangelicals were generally the younger men (14),
it seems probable that they were an increasing proportion of the total between 1843 and
1851, and it accordingly appears a reasonable estimate of the proportions at the time of
the Religious Census. I am much indebted to David Bebbington and Stewart J. Brown for
advice on the Scottish figures.

[13]It has, however, been calculated that in the period 1842-1854, 13 percent of Episcopal
congregrations were served by Evangelical clergy (Patricia Meldrum, "Evangelical Epis-
copalism in Nineteenth-Century Scotland," [Ph.D. thesis, University of Stirling, 2004],
p. 27). If this percentage is applied to the total Episcopal census figures of 112 churches
and 34,402 attendances, it would give estimates for Evangelical Episcopalians of 15
churches and 4,472 attendances.

reiterated that these are figures for attend*ances* rather than attend*ers*, but they are nevertheless important evidence of the strength of evangelicalism in the British churches. No direct comparison with the United States is possible, as attendances are an intermediate measure of commitment falling between Baird's figures for communicants and his estimates of "population," but the religious cen-

Table 5: Evangelical Denominations in England and Wales, 1851[a]

	Places of Worship	Attendances	Membership
Church of England Evangelicals (estimates)	4,462	1,565,826	
Congregationalists	3,244	1,191,978	
Presbyterians [b]	84	41,928	
General Baptist New Connexion[c]	182	63,614	18,277
Particular Baptists	1,947	726,294	
Scotch Baptists	15	1,947	
Baptists (not otherwise defined)	550	96,768	
Moravians	32	10,195	4,955
Wesleyan Methodists	6,579	1,513,304	298,406
Methodist New Connexion	297	98,041	16,962
Primitive Methodists	2,871	500,331	106,074
Bible Chistians	482	72,705	13,324
Wesleyan Methodist Association	419	92,980	20,557
Independent Methodists	20	2,964	
Wesleyan Reformers	339	90, 145	
Welsh Calvinistic Methodists	828	264,112	52,600 (1848 figure)
Countess of Huntingdon's Connexion	109	41,994	
Brethren[d]	132	17,326	
TOTAL		6,392,452	

[a] *Census of Great Britain, 1851: Religious Worship, England and Wales—Report and Tables* (London, 1853), House of Commons Sessional Papers, 1852-1853, Vol. 89, pp. clxxviii–clxxix. Membership figures are from Currie, Gilbert and Horsley, *Churches and Churchgoers*.

[b] Includes Church of Scotland and United Presbyterian congregations in England, but not the Presbyterian Church in England which was, by this date, predominantly Unitarian in its teaching.

[c] The small General Baptist Old Connection inclined to Unitarianism, so is not included here.

[d] These figures may somewhat overstate Brethren strength, because they probably include some congregations cen of the distinct Christian Brethren, a heterodox secession from the Methodist New Connexion.

sus conveys a similarly striking impression of the extent of evangelical expansion by the middle of the nineteenth century.

The available statistics for Ireland and British North America are different in nature from those for Britain and the United States, in that they relate to religious profession rather than communicants or attendances. They therefore include some whose active religious practice is likely to have been minimal or nonexistent. In Ireland the continuing overwhelming numerical dominance of Roman Catholicism limited the (Anglican) Church of Ireland to 10.7 percent and Presbyterians to 8.1 percent in 1834. Other denominations, among which the Methodists were the largest, amounted to just 0.3 percent in total.[14] The next available statistics, collected in the census of 1861, showed the Anglicans at 12 percent, the Presbyterians at 9 percent and the Methodists at 0.8 percent.[15] These modest proportional increases are mainly attributable to the negative factor that the decline in population consequent on emigration and the Great Famine of 1847 fell most heavily on the Roman Catholics; nevertheless, evangelical influence was advancing within the Anglican and Presbyterian churches.[16] In relation to British North America, too, it must be borne in mind that there was a large Roman Catholic presence—40.4 percent of the total population, predominantly French-speakers—but in the census of 1851, 10.6 percent of the population professed to be Methodists, 12.7 percent to be Presbyterians and 3.8 percent Baptists. Anglicans, among whom evangelical influence was growing, made up a further 12.5 percent and the proportion of people professing no religious allegiance was rapidly declining.[17] Evangelicalism had established itself as a major religious force among Protestants. While systematic statistics are not available for the small European populations of Australia, New Zealand and South Africa, it is probable that the evangelical presence there was at least as strong as in Britain.

---

[14]Sean Connolly, *Religion and Society in Nineteenth-Century Ireland* (Dundalk: Dundalgan Press, 1985), p. 3.

[15]*Enumeration Abstracts of Numbers of Inhabitants in Ireland, Religious Profession* (London, 1861), House of Commons Sessional Papers, 1861, 2854, pp. 10-11.

[16]David Hempton and Myrtle Hill, *Evangelical Protestantism in Ulster Society 1740-1890* (London: Routledge, 1992), pp. 63-76.

[17]Brian Clarke, "English Speaking Canada from 1854," in *A Concise History of Christianity in Canada*, ed. Terrence Murphy and Roberto Perin (Toronto: Oxford University Press, 1996), p. 262.

Table 6: Evangelical Denominations in Scotland, 1851[a]

	Places of Worship	Attendances
Church of Scotland Evangelicals (estimates)	317	129,402
Free Church of Scotland	824	485,693
United Presbyterian Church	427	303,132
Original Seccession Church	30	11,209
Reformed Presbyterian Church	37	13,609
Congregationalists	168	57,466
Baptists	100	16,379
Methodists	73	18,019
Evangelical Union[b]	27	10,192
TOTAL		1,044,101

[a] *Census of Great Britain, 1851: Religious Worship and Education, Scotland* (London, 1854), House of Commons Sessional Papers, 1854, Vol. 59, pp. 2-3. The census report also included (5) estimated overall totals based on the assumption that attendances at churches for which there were no returns corresponded to the average of those returns that were made. These enhanced figures would make evangelical attendances 43.1 percent of the total Scottish population, and 71 percent of overall attendances.
[b] The Evangelical Union was formed in 1843 by Presbyterian seceders. It was characterized by Arminian theology and Congregational church polity.

Robert Baird implied that great denominational diversity was a distinctive feature of American evangelicalism, but tables 5 and 6 indicate that it was almost equally prevalent in Britain, especially in England. There were some amalgamations, notably in Scotland in 1847 between the United Secession Church and the Relief Church to form the United Presbyterian Church, but the overall trend was for the number of different evangelical denominations to increase. English Methodism was experiencing yet another schism at the very time of the census, with the departure of the Wesleyan Reformers from the Wesleyan Methodists. Indeed, the tables understate diversity to the extent that they do not include the figures for what the census report termed "isolated congregations," very small denominations or places of worship with a mixed or unspecified denominational allegiance. These amounted to 372 places of worship and 98,267 attendances in England and Wales, and 60 places of worship and 7,961 attendances in Scotland.[18] A substantial proportion of these were also evangelical.

[18] *Religious Worship, England and Wales,* p. clxxx; *Religious Worship and Education, Scotland,* p. 3.

Denominational diversity was also a feature of evangelicalism in other English-speaking societies. In British North America, exposed to the fractiousness of both Britain and the United States, the broad Baptist, Methodist and Presbyterian traditions were all extensively subdivided. A similar combination of influences were at work in the West Indies, where during the first half of the nineteenth century Congregationalism and a variety of forms of Presbyterianism established a presence alongside the earlier Baptist, Methodist and Moravian missions. The Anglican Church in the Caribbean remained predominantly High Church in ethos, but growing activity by the CMS promoted the development of an Evangelical wing.[19] In South Africa, the arrival of Moravian missionaries in 1792 and of London Missionary Society (LMS) ones in 1799 pre-dated the reestablishment of British imperial rule in 1806, when the Church of England acquired privileged status, albeit little effective pastoral machinery. A fledgling Presbyterian church was set up in 1813, and there was already a substantial Methodist presence among soldiers in the garrison before the first civilian preacher, Barnabas Shaw, began his ministry in Cape Colony in 1815. Baptists arrived in 1820.[20] In Australia, the Anglican chaplains were joined in 1798 by a contingent of missionaries from the LMS, who represented Calvinistic Methodism as well as Congregationalism and Presbyterianism. Wesleyan Methodist class meetings began in New South Wales in 1812, and the first preacher, Samuel Leigh, arrived in 1815. John Dunmore Lang, the first permanent Presbyterian minister, arrived in 1823 and quickly raised money for a church-building in Sydney. Baptist beginnings were relatively late and tentative, but Bathurst Street Baptist Chapel was constituted in 1836. In the following year New South Wales Presbyterianism showed itself a true child of its Scottish parent by undergoing its first schism.[21] European settlement in South Australia only began in

---

[19] Arthur Charles Dayfoot, *The Shaping of the West Indian Church 1492-1962* (Gainesville: University Press of Florida, 1998), pp. 167-77.

[20] Rodney Davenport, "Settlement, Conquest and Theological Controversy: The Churches of Nineteenth-Century European Immigrants," in *Christianity in South Africa: A Political, Social & Cultural History*, ed. Richard Elphick and Rodney Davenport (Cape Town: David Philip, 1997), pp. 51-54; Michael Snape, *The Redcoat and Religion: The Forgotten History of the British Solider from the Age of Marlborough to the Eve of the First World War* (London: Routledge, 2005), p. 147.

[21] Stuart Piggin, *Evangelical Christianity in Australia: Spirit, Word and World* (Melbourne: Oxford University Press, 1996), pp. 17-21; J. D. Bollen, *Australian Baptists—A Religious Minority* (London: The Baptist Historical Society, 1975), pp. 6-11; D. W. A. Baker, *Days of Wrath: A Life of John Dunmore Long* (Carlton: Melbourne University Press, 1985), pp. 143-45.

1836, but by 1844 there were already in the Adelaide area congregations of the Church of England, Church of Scotland, a Presbyterian secession, Wesleyans, breakaway "Australian Methodists," the Methodist New Connexion, Primitive Methodists, Independents and Baptists (as well as Roman Catholics, Quakers and German Lutherans) serving a total population of just over 17,000.[22]

In Ireland the minority and somewhat embattled situation of Protestants in the face of the Roman Catholic majority exercised something of a brake on evangelical fragmentation. Irish Methodism split in 1816, but a key issue was the reluctance of many to risk undermining the Church of Ireland by a decisive rupture with Anglicanism. The (Presbyterian) Synod of Ulster also split, in 1829, with the withdrawal of an Arian[23] minority to form the Remonstrant Synod. This division, however, confirmed the evangelical identity of the majority and prepared the ground for their merger in 1840 with the Secession Synod, a legacy of eighteenth-century conflicts, to form the Presbyterian Church in Ireland.[24] Other evangelical groups remained very small: even in 1861 there were still only 5,602 Congregationalists and 4,165 Baptists in the whole of Ireland.[25]

Elsewhere institutional divisions did not necessarily imply disunity. Indeed, it has been argued that the development in early nineteenth-century Britain of organizations with a genuinely interdenominational basis of support such as the LMS, the Bible Society and the Religious Tract Society are indicative of something of a golden age of evangelical unity. A similar argument can be made for the United States in the same period.[26] Even in 1835, when political tensions between the Church of England and Nonconformity were running high, it was still possible to set up the London City Mission on an interdenominational basis. Nevertheless, cooperation in such organizations could be superficial: Francis Cox, one of the two Baptist ministers who had visited the United States in 1835, observed that fulsome speeches professing brotherly love did

---

[22]Douglas Pike, *Paradise of Dissent: South Australia 1829-1857* (Carlton: Melbourne University Press, 1957), pp. 250-64, 274. Both of the first two Anglican clergy in the colony, Charles Beaumont Howard and James Farrell, were evangelicals.

[23]Arians hold unorthodox views in denying the full divinity of Christ.

[24]Hempton and Hill, *Evangelical Protestantism in Ulster Society*, pp. 69-78.

[25]*Census of Ireland for 1861*, p. 11.

[26]R. H. Martin, *Evangelicals United: Ecumenical Stirrings in Pre-Victorian Britain* (Metuchen, N.J.: Scarecrow Press, 1983), pp. 196-200; Charles I. Foster, *An Errand of Mercy: The Evangelical United Front 1790-1837* (Chapel Hill: University of North Carolina Press, 1960).

not in reality remove underlying "prejudices, jealousies and dislikes," nor were occasional shared public platforms evidence of regular day-to-day contact.[27]

In *Religion in America*, Robert Baird, having surveyed the range of evangelical denominations in the United States, was concerned to answer the charges of fragmentation and lack of harmony. He argued that such diversity was a natural consequence of religious liberty and of the diverse ethnic origins of the various settlers in the country. In reality, all evangelical denominations were united "on all doctrines necessary to salvation" and should be regarded not as competitors, but as regiments in the same army each with "its own banner, and its own part of the field to occupy."[28] There was general "mutual respect and fraternal affection," a readiness to exchange pulpits, and a preparedness by the laity to attend the services of other denominations as well as their own.[29] Baird recognized that in sparsely populated districts the multiplication of churches could dissipate Christian energy, and that a minority of tactless preachers might offend their neighbors. In general, he argued, institutional diversity was no obstacle to genuine unity of effort, and individuals benefited from having a range of local religious options open to them rather than

> being reduced to the sad alternative of either joining in forms of worship which they conscientiously disapprove, and of listening to a minister whom they find unedifying, or of abstaining from public worship altogether.[30]

Baird's portrayal of the implications of institutional disunity was too optimistic and complacent. He underestimated the negative consequences of denominational competition, which seemed to be increasing at the very time he was writing. Moreover, as an educated Presbyterian Northerner, who spent much of his working life outside the United States, he appeared ignorant of the more visceral antagonisms that developed between the two leading popular evangelical denominations in the South, the Baptists and the Methodists.[31] Nevertheless, his

---

[27]F. A. Cox, *On Christian Union* (London: John Snow, 1845), p. 7; see above, pp. 83-84.

[28]Baird, *Religion in America*, pp. 604-6.

[29]Ibid., pp. 608-9.

[30]Ibid., pp. 606-8.

[31]Richard Carwardine, "Unity, Pluralism and the Spiritual Market-Place: Interdenominational Competition in the Early American Republic," in *Unity and Diversity in the Church: Studies in Church History* 32, ed. R. N. Swanson (Oxford: Blackwell/Ecclesiastical History Society, 1996), pp. 297-335.

essential point that diversity was not inherently a "bad thing" deserves considerable weight.

The kind of practical cooperation and sympathy on the ground described by Baird in the United States was also apparent elsewhere. Although the first half-century of Australian evangelical history saw the emergence of the full range of denominational families, it was also a period in which the practical constraints of sparsely settled territories made the benefits of cooperation apparent to all. At the turn of the nineteenth century Samuel Marsden, for all his combativeness on other fronts, warmly welcomed and supported the newly arrived LMS missionaries in New South Wales, and in 1849 early Presbyterian, Congregationalist and Baptist settlers in Queensland joined forces to form a short-lived United Evangelical Church.[32] The British Religious Census of 1851 reveals not only a scattering of places of worship shared between different denominations, the most widespread combination being Congregationalists and Baptists, but also, when one reads between the lines, tacit cooperation in delineating different rather than competing social and geographical territories for evangelistic effort. It was common, especially in rural districts, for Methodists and Anglicans to avoid clashing service times, in the expectation that many people would want to attend both church and chapel.[33]

There were also explicit aspirations for unity among "true believers." In Bedfordshire in 1797 a series of interdenominational meetings adopted a "Plan of a General Union among real Christians." It was hoped that "pious persons of the Established Church," Methodists, Moravians, Independents and Baptists might "unite for purposes that do not infringe upon the sentiments, the forms, or the discipline, of their several societies."[34] In a sermon at Bedford on October 31, Samuel Greatheed, an Independent minister, urged believers to think of themselves as "brethren" bound to each other because they were united in

---

[32]Piggin, *Evangelical Christianity in Australia*, pp. 17, 36.

[33]*Religious Worship, England and Wales*, p. clxxx; for examples, see John Wolffe, ed., *Yorkshire Returns of the 1851 Census of Religious Worship, Vol. 2 West Riding (North)*, Borthwick Texts and Studies (York: University of York, 2005), pp. 17, 114, 129 (an Independent Chapel with branch preaching stations providing for those who "do not belong to any Congregation").

[34]Samuel Greatheed, *General Union Recommended to Real Christians, in a Sermon, preached at Bedford, October 31, 1797. With an Introductory Account of an Union of Christians of Various Denominations, which was then Instituted to Promote the Knowledge of the Gospel; Including a Plan for Universal Union in the Genuine Church of Christ* (London; T. Conder, 1798), pp. v, xvi.

Christ. They should seek to dwell together in unity (Psalm 133:1) while eschewing authoritarian attempts to impose uniformity, which had been a major root of division in church history. Such unity, Greatheed argued, would lead to much enhanced effectiveness in "spreading the knowledge of the Gospel."[35] While the Bedfordshire Union's claims were not matched by its achievements, it was representative of more widespread undenominational aspirations among English evangelicals at the turn of the nineteenth century.[36] Other early advocates of Christian union included Ezra Weld at Wrentham, Massachussetts, in 1794 and William Innes in Edinburgh in 1811.[37]

Such sentiments were expressed throughout the period, but became more widespread in the later 1830s and early 1840s, despite, or perhaps because of, the increasing institutional fragmentation of evangelicalism. In 1834, George Redford, a Congregational minister in Worcester, England, advocated the holding of a general convention of all the orthodox Protestant churches of Britain, Europe and America.[38] In 1837, Baptist Noel published a pamphlet titled *The Unity of the Church*, in which he sought to establish a biblical basis for identifying the true "children of God," who should respect each other's conscientious convictions on matters such as episcopacy and infant baptism on which believers disagreed.[39] Parallel stirrings in the United States were led by a Lutheran, Samuel Simon Schmucker, whose *Fraternal Appeal to the American Churches* was published in 1838. Schmucker advocated a loose confederation of churches that would retain their own organizational structures, but agree to a common creed, base ministerial education on the Bible rather than sectarian textbooks, cooperate with each other as far as possible, and practice full inter-communion.[40]

---

[35]Ibid., pp. 28, 35-48, 77.

[36]Lovegrove, *Established Church, Sectarian People*, pp. 34-37.

[37]Ezra Weld, *A Sermon on Christian Union* (Boston, 1794); William Innes, *Remarks on Christian Union* (Edinburgh, 1811).

[38]London, Dr. Williams's Library, Blackburn MSS L52/2/101, Redford to Blackburn, April 16, 1834.

[39]B. W. Noel, *The Unity of the Church* (London, 1837), pp. 3-5, 9.

[40]Samuel Schmucker, *Fraternal Appeal to the American Churches*, ed. Frederick K. Wentz (Philadelphia: Fortress, 1965), pp. 136-75; Philip D. Jordan, *The Evangelical Alliance for the United States of America, 1847-1900: Ecumenism, Identity and the Religion of the Republic* (New York: Edwin Mellen, 1982), pp. 34-35; *BDEB*, pp. 979-80.

During the early 1840s the case for evangelical unity and the means of attaining it was developed in greater depth in a variety of publications on both sides of the Atlantic. Robert Baird was an enthusiastic supporter of this movement, and his *Religion in America* should be seen in this context. Meanwhile, in Britain, a group of leading Presbyterians and Congregationalists including Thomas Chalmers and John Angell James joined together to produce *Essays on Christian Union*, published in 1845. Edward Bickersteth offered an Anglican contribution in a series of letters on union which appeared in *The Record* newspaper. A consistent theme in all these contributions was to emphasize that the objective must be unity in diversity rather than a fruitless quest for absolute agreement and uniformity. Indeed, uniformity was not only unattainable, but the antithesis of true Christian unity, associated as it was in the eyes of these writers with the perceived spiritual authoritarianism of the Roman Catholic Church.[41]

Meanwhile, organizational steps were also underway. In the United States a Christian Union Convention was held in Syracuse, New York, in August 1838, and a Society for the Promotion of Christian Union was set up in 1839 to promote Schmucker's scheme.[42] In Britain in 1842 James began actively to urge that steps be taken to promote union, and in early January 1843 such a meeting was indeed held, attended by Baptists, Congregationalists, Moravians, Presbyterians and Wesleyans. The Scottish Disruption a few months later encouraged some to perceive potential for union in a wider realignment of British Protestant denominations. Americans such as Leonard Bacon, Robert Baird and William Patton also began to canvass the idea of an international conference of evangelicals, notably in correspondence with John Angell James. The immediate chain of events leading to the formation of the Evangelical Alliance began in Britain in the spring of 1845 with the interdenominational movement of protest against Sir Robert Peel's plans to extend the endowment of Maynooth College by the British state. Thus anti-Catholicism gave a significant stimulus to the movement, but it was also driven forward by, as Edward Bickersteth's biog-

---

[41]John Wolffe, "Unity in Diversity? North Atlantic Evangelical Thought in the Mid-Nineteenth Century," in *Unity and Diversity in the Church*, Swanson, pp. 363-75.

[42]Jordan, *Evangelical Alliance for the United States*, p. 34; *A Declaration of Sentiments Reported by S. Hawley to the "Christian Union Convention" held in Syracuse, August 31st 1838* (Casenovia, 1839); Schmucker, *Fraternal Appeal*, pp. 20-21.

rapher put it, "the growing conviction in the minds of sincere Christians . . . that their real unity of heart and judgement was far greater than the outward appearance."[43] This latter impulse was very much apparent when a conference of British evangelicals was convened in Liverpool in October 1845. A further meeting in Birmingham in April 1846 issued invitations to an international conference that August. American evangelicals were thinking on similar lines, and were already making plans for their own conference in 1846, when they received invitations to the British one and accordingly in effect abandoned their own.[44]

The conference opened at Freemasons' Hall in London on August 19, 1846. Out of a total of 910 participants, seventy-four had come from the United States and a further seven from Canada, an impressive attendance in view of the rigors of transatlantic travel and the short notice given. The great majority of the remainder came from Britain and Ireland, although there were also thirty-eight from continental Europe and six—presumably missionaries on furlough—from other parts of the world.[45] Their denominational affiliations were as follows:

Presbyterian	215
Congregational	181
Anglican/Episcopalian	172
Wesleyan	159
Other Methodist	28
Baptist	80
Lutheran	13
Other	12
Not specified	50

Thus the greatest enthusiasm for the conference relative to denominational

---

[43]Birks, *Bickersteth*, 2:303.

[44]J. W. Massie, *The Evangelical Alliance; Its Origin and Development* (London: John Snow, 1847), p. 257; Jordan, *Evangelical Alliance for the United States*, p. 36; John Wolffe, "The Evangelical Alliance in the 1840s: An Attempt to Institutionalise Christian Unity," in *Voluntary Religion: Studies in Church History* 23, ed. W. J. Sheils and Diana Wood (Oxford: Blackwell, 1986), pp. 335-40.

[45]Massie, *Evangelical Alliance*, p. 286; *Evangelical Alliance: Report of the Proceedings of the Conference, held at Freemasons' Hall, London from August 19th to September 2nd Inclusive, 1846* (London: Partridge and Oakey, 1847), pp. lxxvii-xcvii.

strength was in general found among Presbyterians and Congregationalists, although members of the Church of Scotland perceived the conference as serving the interests of the Free Church and stayed away. Evangelicals in the Church of England were divided by the Alliance, with some reluctant to commit themselves from suspicion that it would be subversive of the state churches, while others, led by Edward Bickersteth, were enthusiastic supporters. Denominations with a substantial lower-class base—Baptists, American Methodists and non-Wesleyan British Methodists—were under-represented, but nevertheless had a presence at the conference. Black evangelicals, too, at least had one representative, Molliston Madison Clark of the African Methodist Episcopal Church, who was delayed when his ship was dismasted, but arrived in time to address the conference on September 2.[46]

At the opening sessions there was a sense of spiritual euphoria, best articulated by the Boston Congregationalist and revivalist Edward Norris Kirk, who confessed himself already exhausted by the intensity and warmth of the atmosphere. Kirk hailed "the death of sectarianism" and affirmed, "It seems to me as if heaven had begun on earth . . . I am on the verge of heaven—I am on the verge of the Millennium."[47] The conference did indeed appear to be a striking expression not only of the unity of evangelicals, but of their geographical, social and cultural expansion, extending to continental Europe as well as across the English-speaking world. On the first day there were speakers not only from the United States, but also from Canada, France, Germany and Switzerland. Messages of support were received from Geneva, Berlin, The Hague, Lübeck, Königsberg, Danzig, Morges (Switzerland), Cape Town, Agra, Montreal, New York, Toronto, Baltimore, Dover (New Hampshire) and Perth (Canada).[48] An Evangelical Union in Hobart (Tasmania), "though divided from them by thousands of miles," recorded its "warmest solicitude" for the gathering and its prayers that the Holy Spirit would descend upon the participants.[49] There was evidence that interdenominational gatherings of evangelicals were taking place in numerous and diverse localities. In Tasmania monthly prayer meetings had been taking place for two years and had been well attended; in Bangor, Maine,

---

[46]*Evangelical Alliance: Report of Proceedings*, pp. 485-86.
[47]Ibid., p. 26.
[48]Ibid., pp. 19-37, Appendix A, pp. iii-xxiv.
[49]*First Report of the Hobart Town Evangelical Union* (Launceston, 1846), p. 11.

the ministers of "six or seven different Denominations" had been meeting regularly every Monday morning for the previous thirteen or fourteen years "to consult on the general interests of Religion, to pray together, and to spread before each other their own difficulties, and the state of things in each of their churches."[50] In Enstone, Oxfordshire, the Anglican vicar, who had previously sacked his schoolmistress when she became a Baptist, invited all the Christians in the parish to a union meeting and shared a platform with the Baptist and Wesleyan ministers.[51]

Sadly, though, the high hopes of August 19 were to be rapidly dented. On August 21, 22 and 24, the conference considered the Evangelical Alliance's Basis of Faith, and although agreement was rapidly secured on most points, the articles concerned with the divine institution of the Christian ministry and the eternal punishment of the wicked gave rise to significant disagreements. Those who dissented from them did so, in general, not because they personally could not accept them, but because they feared that the Alliance was circumscribing the bounds of true Christianity too tightly. Although the draft was eventually adopted with minor amendments, the difficulties were a painful reminder to the delegates that the task of translating general aspirations for unity into an agreed formal institutional basis would not be an easy one.[52] In the event, however, it was not theology but the question of slavery that exposed the most serious divisions in the Alliance. On August 28, the conference began to consider a statement on "Organization" and found itself in serious difficulties on the first clause, "That the Alliance shall consist of those persons, in all parts of the World, who shall concur in the Principles and Objects adopted by the Conference." John Howard Hinton, a London Baptist minister, proposed an amendment that the words "not being Slaveholders" be inserted after "those persons."[53] An attempted compromise softened this position slightly by only excluding those who were slave-holders "by their own fault," but it still left both sides unhappy.[54] Eventually, on September 1, it was agreed in effect to differ by deferring the "final and complete

[50]Ibid., pp. 5-7; *Evangelical Alliance: Report of Proceedings*, p. 50.

[51]*Evangelical Alliance: Report of Proceedings*, p. 56.

[52]Ibid., pp. 77-169.

[53]Ibid., p. 290.

[54]Ibid., pp. 290-385.

organization of the General Alliance" and setting up separate organizations for the United Kingdom, United States, British North America and various parts of Europe.[55]

The problem for the Americans, who predominantly came from the Northern states, was not that they were slave-holders themselves, but they did not wish the Alliance to be committed to an abolitionist stance in a manner that would inevitably appear political and divisive in the United States, and would thus exclude the possibility of restoring fellowship with evangelicals in the South. They pointed out that, in the cause of Christian unity, they were ready to forbear pressing their opposition to alcoholic drink and state churches, in deference to the different views taken of these matters in Britain. They argued unsuccessfully that the British should adopt a similar attitude to slavery in America. In an address to British evangelicals in August 1851, Robert Baird evoked the bitterness of the Americans at what he described as a "deplorable failure" that was attributed to British arrogance:

> And is England immaculate? How long is it since she washed out the deep sin of slave-holding and slave-trading from her own skirts? . . . Has she no sins in relation to Ireland, India, China, and the aborigines of Van Dieman's Land yet to be washed away? . . . Let British Christians pursue their great work of getting every right in their own vast dominion, and we will do the same in our great country. . . . We shall get clear of slavery, but not at, or in consequence of your bidding or to please you.

He noted that American evangelicals visiting London were growing tired of hearing their country insulted in religious meetings: although they were continuing to travel to Europe, many of them no longer felt welcome among British evangelicals. Accordingly, he believed that "it cannot be disguised that the very attempt which we have made to bring the churches of America and of Europe, especially those of Britain, into more friendly and fraternal relations, have ended by putting them further asunder."[56]

Contacts between Britain and America continued, but in the years after 1846 evangelicals in both countries redirected their energies toward fostering

---

[55]Ibid., pp. 436-37.

[56]R. Baird, *The Progress and Prospects of Christianity in the United States of America* (London: Partridge and Oakey, 1851), pp. 41-48.

links with continental Europe rather than with each other.[57] The vision of actual global evangelical unity, which had seemed for a few fevered late summer days to be on the verge of realization, now receded. Even at a national level, the Evangelical Alliance faltered: after its inauspicious beginning the American organization survived only for a few years and was not revived until after the Civil War.[58] The British organization enjoyed a modest prosperity and developed a distinctive role in promoting religious liberty on the continent, but its appeal was limited by the mutual suspicions of the state churches and Nonconformity. It came to appear merely as one among the kaleidoscope of evangelical societies rather than as a convincing harbinger of the millennium.

The difficulties of the Evangelical Alliance were a revealing microcosm of wider evangelical ironies and paradoxes. The campaign against slavery was one of the most important ways in which evangelicals in this period influenced society and politics, but in pursuing it as purposefully as some of them did, they had both to cooperate with others and be prepared to differ from each other. The slogan of "unity in diversity" encapsulated their affirmation of individualistic spiritual autonomy, in creative but sometimes destructive tension with their vision of the spiritual affinity of all "true believers," whether in the local congregation or the worldwide church. It was a slogan that inspired cooperative action, but also minimized the gravity of schism. As they sought to make a reality of transatlantic evangelical community, awareness of difference was accentuated rather than removed, and evangelicalism revealed its potential to inspire nationalism and even sectionalism, as well as internationalism.

Nevertheless, the Evangelical Alliance should be judged by what it symbolized and represented as well as by its failures and limited actual achievements. The very convening of the London conference was testimony to ambitious aspirations; the very issue—slavery—on which it fractured reflected a consciousness of genuinely global responsibility and influence. This was a movement that had expanded and matured enormously since the initial stirrings of the Second Great Awakening in the 1790s. In their dominance, no less than in their expansion, evangelicals were to be frustrated by their lack of visible unity, but they maintained an underlying sense of shared spiritual identity. If any single mo-

---

[57] As shown in the pages of the British Evangelical Alliance's journal *Evangelical Christendom* and the annual reports of the *American and Foreign Christian Union* (New York, 1850-1859).
[58] Jordan, *Evangelical Alliance for the United States*, pp. 52-67.

ment can be held to epitomize the transition in the history of evangelicalism between the era of expansion surveyed in this volume and the era of dominance to be examined in the next book in this series, it came as the great assembly at Freemasons' Hall united on the morning of August 19, 1846, in singing the Old Hundredth:

All people that on earth do dwell,
Sing to the Lord with cheerful voice:
Him serve with fear, His praise forth tell,
Come ye before Him, and rejoice. . . .

For why? The Lord our God is good
His mercy is for ever sure:
His truth at all times firmly stood,
And shall from age to age endure.[59]

---

[59] *Evangelical Alliance: Report of Proceedings*, p. I.F.

SELECT BIBLIOGRAPHY

This bibliography lists most works used in the preparation of this book, although merely incidental references cited in the footnotes are not repeated here. The primary sources section is limited to those specifically cited in the book; the secondary sources section includes a number of other works likely to be of particular value to the student of early nineteenth-century evangelicalism.

PRIMARY SOURCES

Manuscripts
Acland of Killerton Papers, Devon County Record Office, Exeter
Beecher/Stowe Papers, Stowe-Day Library, Hartford, Connecticut
Blackburn Papers, Dr. Williams's Library, London
Chalmers Papers, New College Library, Edinburgh
Cheever Family Papers, American Antiquarian Society, Worcester, Massachusetts
Church Missionary Society Archives, University of Birmingham Library
Colquhoun Papers, Cultybraggan Estates Office, Comrie, Perthshire
Newington Free Church Kirk Session Minutes, National Archives of Scotland, Edinburgh
Wilberforce Papers, Bodleian Library, Oxford and Wilberforce House, Hull

Magazines and Newspapers
Arminian Magazine
Christian Lady's Magazine

Christian Observer
Ladies Repository
Methodist Magazine
New York Observer
Primitive Methodist Magazine
Record

Books and Pamphlets

Aglionby, F. K. *The Life of Edward Henry Bickersteth DD Bishop and Poet.* London: Longmans, 1907.

Anon. *Hints to a Clergyman's Wife; or Female Parochial Duties Practically Illustrated.* London, 1832.

————. *History of Revivals of Religion in the British Isles, Especially in Scotland.* Edinburgh: William Oliphant & Son, 1836.

————. *Narrative of Revivals of Religion in Scotland, Ireland and Wales.* Glasgow, 1839.

————. *Memoir of the Life and Ministry of the Rev William Bramwell,* by members of his family. London: Simpkin, Marshall & Co, 1848.

————. *Enumeration Abstracts of Numbers of Inhabitants in Ireland, Religious Profession.* London: House of Commons Sessional Papers, 1861 (2854).

Bacon, Leonard. *Christian Unity.* New Haven: Foreign Evangelical Society, 1845.

Baird, Robert. *Religion in the United States of America.* Glasgow and Edinburgh: Blackie and Son, 1844.

————. *The Progress and Prospects of Christianity in the United States of America.* London: Partridge and Oakey, 1851.

Bane, John. *The Marriage of Believers with Unbelievers.* Norwich, 1839.

Beecher, Catharine. *The Duty of American Women to their Country.* New York: Harper & Bros., 1845.

————. *The Evils Suffered by American Women and American Children.* New York: Harper & Bros., 1846.

————. *The True Remedy for the Wrongs of Woman.* Boston: Phillips, Sampson & Co., 1851.

Beecher, Charles, ed. *Autobiography, Correspondence &c of Lyman Beecher, DD.* 2 vols. London: Sampson, Low & Co., 1863.

Beecher, Henry Ward. *Lectures to Young Men in Various Important Subjects.* Salem: J. P. Jewett & Co., 1846.

Beecher, Lyman. *Six Sermons on the Nature, Occasions, Signs, Evils, and Remedy of Intemperance.* Boston: Perkins and Marvin, 1829.

———. *A Plea for the West.* Cincinnati: Truman & Smith, 1835.

———, and Asahel Nettleton. *Letters of the Rev. Dr. Beecher and Rev. Mr. Nettleton on the "New Measures" in Conducting Revivals of Religion.* New York, 1828.

Bickersteth, Edward. *A Treatise on Prayer.* London: L. B. Seeley, 1818.

———. *Family Prayers.* London: R. B. Seeley & W. Burnside, 1842.

———. *Christian Psalmody, A Collection of Above 900 Psalms, Hymns and Spiritual Songs Selected and Arranged for Public, Social, Family and Private Worship.* London: Dean & Son, 1850.

Birks, Thomas Rawson. *Memoir of the Rev. Edward Bickersteth.* 2 vols. London: Seeleys, 1852.

Bourne, Hugh. *A General Collection of Hymns and Spiritual Songs, for Camp-Meetings, Revivals, &c.* Hull, 1821.

———. *History of the Primitive Methodists Giving an Account of their Rise and Progress up to the Year 1823.* Bemersley, 1823.

Bramwell, William. *A Short Account of the Life and Death of Ann Cutler.* Sheffield: John Smith, 1796.

Brown, Thomas. *Annals of the Disruption.* Edinburgh: MacNiven and Wallace, 1892.

Bunting, Jabez. *A Great Work Described and Recommended, in a Sermon, Preached on Wednesday, May 15, 1805 . . . Before the Members of the Sunday School Union.* London: Richard Edwards, 1805.

Campbell, John. *Memoirs of David Nasmith.* London: John Snow, 1844.

Carus, Willliam. *Memorials of the Right Reverend Charles Pettit McIlvaine.* London: Elliot Stock, 1882.

Census of Great Britain 1851 (1853). *Religious Worship, England and Wales—Report and Tables.* London, House of Commons Sessional Papers, 1852-1853. Vol. 89.

———. *Religious Worship and Education, Scotland.* London, House of Commons Sessional Papers, 1854. Vol. 59.

Chambers, Talbot W. *Memoir of the Life and Character of the Late Hon. Theo. Frelinghuysen, LLD.* New York: Harper and Bros., 1863.

Chapin, E. H. *Duties of Young Men.* Boston: Abel Tompkins & B. B. Mussey, 1840.

Clarkson, Thomas. *Strictures on a Life of William Wilberforce.* London: Longman, 1838.

Coke, Thomas. *Copies of Letters from the Missionaries who are Employed in Ireland.* Leeds: E. Baines, 1801.

Colquhoun, John Campbell. *William Wilberforce: His Friends and His Times.* London: Longman, Green, Reader & Dyer, 1866.

Cotterill, Thomas. *A Selection of Psalms and Hymns for Public and Private Use, Adapted to the Services of the Church of England.* 8th ed. Sheffield, 1819.

Cox, Francis Augustus. *Suggestions Designed to Promote the Revival and Extension of Religion Founded on Observations Made During a Journey in the United States of America in the Spring and Summer of 1835.* London: Thomas Ward & Co., 1836.

———. *On Christian Union.* London: John Snow, 1845.

———, and James Hoby. *The Baptists in America: A Narrative of the Deputation from the Baptist Union in England to the United States and Canada.* London: T. Ward, 1836.

Dale, Robert William, ed. *The Life and Letters of John Angell James.* London: James Nisbet, 1861.

Dow, Lorenzo. *The Dealings of God, Man and the Devil; as Exemplified in the Life, Experience and Travels of Lorenzo Dow.* New York: Cornish Lamport & Co., 1850.

Evangelical Alliance. *Report of the Proceedings of the Conference, held at Freemasons' Hall, London from August 19th to September 2nd Inclusive, 1846.* London: Partridge and Oakey, 1847.

Fields, Annie. *Life and Letters of Harriet Beecher Stowe.* London: Sampson Low, 1897.

Freylinghuysen, Theodore. *An Inquiry into the Moral and Religious Character of the American Government.* New York, 1838.

Gisborne, Thomas. *An Enquiry into the Duties of Men in the Higher and Middle Classes of Society in Great Britain.* London, 1794.

Graham, Sylvester. *A Lecture to Young Men on Chastity.* Boston, 1837.

Greatheed, Samuel. *General Union Recommended to Real Christians, in a Sermon, preached at Bedford, October 31, 1797. With an Introductory Account of an Union of Christians of Various Denominations, which was then Instituted to Promote the Knowledge of the Gospel; Including a Plan for Universal Union in the Genuine Church of Christ.* London: T. Conder, 1798.

Guthrie, Thomas. *A Plea for Ragged Schools.* Edinburgh, 1847.

Haldane, James Alexander. *Journal of a Tour Through the Northern Counties of Scotland and the Orkney Isles in Autumn 1797.* Edinburgh: J. Ritchie, 1798.

Hanna, W., ed. *Select Works of Thomas Chalmers.* Edinburgh: Constable, 1857.

Hodder, Edwin. *The Life and Work of the Seventh Earl of Shaftesbury, K.G.* 3 vols. London: Cassell, 1886.

James, John Angell. *Youth Warned. A Sermon Preached in Carr's Lane Meeting House, on Sunday Evening, January 4th 1824, and Addressed Particularly to Young Men.* Birmingham: B. Hudson, 1824.

————. *A Pastoral Letter on the Subject of Revivals in Religion.* London: F. Westley & A. H. Davis, 1829.

Johnson, Richard. *An Address to the Inhabitants of the Colonies Established in New South Wales and Norfolk Island.* London, 1792.

Livermore, Harriet. *Scriptural Evidence in Favour of Female Testimony in Meetings for Christian Worship.* Portsmouth, N.H., 1824.

MacCosh, James. *The Wheat and the Chaff Gathered Into Bundles: A Statistical Contribution Towards the History of the Great Disruption of the Scottish Establishment.* Perth: James Dewar, 1843.

McNeile, Hugh. *Letters to a Friend who has Felt it his Duty to Secede from the Church of England and who Imagines that Miraculous Gifts of the Holy Ghost are Revived Among the Seceders.* London, 1834.

Marsh, Catherine. *The Life of the Rev. William Marsh, DD.* London: James Nisbet, Hatchard, 1867.

Massie, James William. *The Evangelical Alliance; Its Origin and Development.* London: John Snow, 1847.

More, Hannah. *The History of Hester Wilmot or the Second Part of the Sunday School; The History of Hester Wilmot; or the New Gown. Part II.* Cheap Repository, 1796.

————. *Hints Towards Forming the Character of a Young Princess.* 2 vols. London: T. Cadell & W. Davies, 1805.

————. *Practical Piety.* 2 vols. London: T. Cadell & W. Davies, 1811.

————. *An Essay on the Character and Practical Writings of St Paul.* 2 vols. London: T. Cadell & W. Davies, 1815.

Nettleton, Asahel. *Village Hymns for Social Worship.* New York, 1831. First published 1824.

Newton, John. *Thoughts Upon the African Slave Trade.* London: J. Buckland, J. Johnson, 1788.

Noel, Baptist Wriothesley. *The Unity of the Church.* London, 1837.

————. *Protestant Thoughts in Rhyme.* London, 1844.

Oliphant, Margaret. *The Life of Edward Irving.* London: Hurst and Blackett, 1862.

Reed, Andrew, and James Matheson. *A Narrative of the Visit to the American Churches by the Deputation from the Congregational Union of England and Wales.* London: Jackson and Walford, 1835.

Rees, Thomas. *History of Protestant Nonconformity in Wales.* London: J. Snow, 1861.

Richmond, Legh. *The Dairyman's Daughter; an authentic narrative,* by a clergyman of the Church of England, London: W. Kent, 1810.

Ripley, Dorothy. *The Bank of Faith and Works United.* Whitby, 1822.

Sherwood, Mary. *The Little Woodman and His Dog Caesar.* Wellington, F. Houlston and Son, 1828.

Sprague, William Buell. *Letters from Europe in 1828.* New York, 1828.

———. *Life of Timothy Dwight.* The Library of American Biography Vol. XIV. Boston, 1845.

———. *Annals of the American Methodist Pulpit.* New York, 1861.

Stephen, James (father). *The Dangers of the Country.* London: J. Butterworth, J. Hatchard, 1807.

Stephen, James (son). "The Clapham Sect." *The Edinburgh Review* 80 (1844).

Stewart, Alexander. *Account of a Late Revival of Religion in a Part of the Highlands of Scotland.* Aberdeen: G. Moir, 1801.

Stewart, James Haldane. *Thoughts on the Importance of Special Prayer for the General Outpouring of the Holy Spirit.* London: Religious Tract Society, 1822.

Taft, Zachariah. *Biographical Sketches of Lives and Public Ministry of Various Holy Women.* 1825. A facsimile reprint. Peterborough: Methodist Publishing House, 1992.

Tonna, Charlotte Elizabeth. *The Wrongs of Woman.* 4 parts. London: W. H. Dalton, 1843.

———. *Personal Recollections . . . Third edition, continued to the close of her life.* London: Seeley, Burnside & Seeley, 1847.

———. *Works of Charlotte Elizabeth with an Introduction by Mrs H. B. Stowe.* 2 vols. 8th ed. New York: M. W. Dodd, 1850.

———. *Short Stories for Children.* Edinburgh: Gall & Inglis, 1861.

Walford, John. *Memoirs of the Life and Labours of the Late Venerable Hugh Bourne.* London, 1855.

Watson, William Henry. *The History of the Sunday School Union.* London, 1853.

Wilberforce, Robert and Samuel. *The Life of William Wilberforce.* 5 vols. London: John Murray, 1838.

Wilberforce, William. *A Practical View of the Prevailing Religious System of Professed Christians in the Higher and Middle Classes of this Country Contrasted with Real Christianity.* London: T. Cadell & W. Davies, 1797.

Later Editions of Primary Sources

Asbury, Francis. *The Letters and Journals of Francis Asbury.* Edited by J. Manning Potts, Elmer T. Clark and Jacob S. Payton. 3 vols. London: Epworth Press, 1958.

Bushnell, Horace. *Christian Nurture.* New Haven, Conn.: Yale University Press, 1947.

Elaw, Zilpha. "Memoirs of the Life, Religious Experience, Ministerial Travels and Labors of Mrs Zilpha Elaw." In *Sisters of the Spirit: Three Black Women's Autobiographies of the Nineteenth Century.* Edited by William L. Andrews. Bloomington: Indiana University Press, 1986.

Eliot, George. *Adam Bede.* Edited by Stephen Gill. London: Penguin, 1985.

———. *Scenes of Clerical Life.* Edited by Jennifer Gribble. London: Penguin, 1998.

Finney, Charles. *Lectures on Revivals of Religion.* Edited by William G. McLoughlin. Cambridge, Mass.: Belknap Press, 1960.

———. *The Memoirs of Charles Grandison Finney.* Edited by Garth M. Rosell and Richard A. G. Dupuis. Grand Rapids: Zondervan, 1989.

Griffiths, Ann. *Hymns and Letters.* Translated by Alan Gaunt and Alan Lu. London: Stainer and Bell, 1999.

Johnson, Richard. *Some Letters of Rev. Richard Johnson, BA, First Chaplain of New South Wales.* Edited by George Mackarness. Sydney: D. S. Ford, 1954.

McCheyne, Robert. *The Life of Robert Murray McCheyne.* Andrew Bonar. Banner of Truth, 1960.

Marsden, Samuel. *The Letters and Journals of Samuel Marsden.* Edited by John R. Elder. Dunedin: Otago University Council, 1932.

———. *Some Private Correspondence of the Rev. Samuel Marsden and Family 1794-1824.* Edited by George Mackarness. Sydney: D. S. Ford, 1942.

More, Hannah. *Coelebs in Search of a Wife.* Edited by Mary Waldron. Bristol: Thoemmes Press, 1995.

———. *Selected Writings of Hannah More.* Edited by Robert Hole. London: William Pickering, 1996.

————. *Tales for the Common People and Other Cheap Repository Tracts.* Edited by Clare Macdonald Shaw. Nottingham: Trent Editions, 2002.

Schmucker, Samuel. *Fraternal Appeal to the American Churches.* Edited by Frederick K. Wentz. Philadelphia: Fortress, 1965.

Shaw, William. *The Journal of William Shaw.* Edited by W. D. Hammond-Tooke. Cape Town: A. A. Balkema, 1972.

Sherwood, Mary. *The History of the Fairchild Family.* Edited by Barry Westburg. New York: Garland, 1977.

Stowe, Harriet Beecher. *Uncle Tom's Cabin.* Edited by Ann Douglas. New York: Penguin, 1986.

Tocqueville, Alexis de. *Democracy in America.* Edited by Alan Ryan. 2 vols. London: Everyman's Library, 1994.

Trollope, Fanny. *Domestic Manners of the Americans.* Edited by Richard Mullen. Oxford: Oxford University Press, 1984.

Wilberforce, William. *Private Papers of William Wilberforce.* Edited by A. M. Wilberforce. London: T. F. Unwin, 1897.

SECONDARY SOURCES

Reference Works

Cameron, Nigel M. de S., et al., eds. *Dictionary of Scottish Church History and Theology.* Edinburgh: T & T Clark, 1993.

Cross, F. L., and E. A. Livingstone, eds. *The Oxford Dictionary of the Christian Church.* 3rd rev. ed. Oxford: Oxford University Press, 2005.

Currie, Robert, Alan Gilbert, and Lee Horsley. *Churches and Churchgoers: Patterns of Church Growth in the British Isles since 1700.* Oxford: Oxford University Press, 1977.

Frost, Maurice, ed. *Historical Companion to Hymns Ancient & Modern.* London: William Clowes & Sons, 1962.

Gaustad, Edwin Scott, and Philip L. Barlow. *New Historical Atlas of Religion in America.* New York: Oxford University Press, 2001.

Johnson, Allen, et al., eds. *The Dictionary of American Biography.* 20 vols. New York: Oxford University Press, 1928-1936.

Julian, John, ed. *A Dictionary of Hymnology.* Rev. ed. London: Murray, 1907.

Lewis, Donald M., ed. *The Blackwell Dictionary of Evangelical Biography, 1730-1860.* Oxford: Blackwell, 1995.

Matthew, H. C. G., and Brian Harrison, eds. *The Oxford Dictionary of National Biography.* 61 vols. Oxford: Oxford University Press, 2004.

Mitchell, B. R. *Abstract of British Historical Statistics.* Cambridge: Cambridge University Press, 1962.

————. *International Historical Statistics: Africa, Asia and Oceania 1750-2000.* Basingstoke: Palgrave Macmillan, 2003.

————. *International Historical Statistics: The Americas 1750-2000.* Basingstoke: Palgrave Macmillan, 2003.

————. *International Historical Statistics: Europe 1750-2000.* Basingstoke: Palgrave Macmillan, 2003.

Other Secondary Works

When more than one chapter in a book of essays is cited in the footnotes, the work is only listed once below, under the overall editor and title.

Abzug, Robert. *Cosmos Crumbling: American Reform and the Religious Imagination.* New York: Oxford University Press, 1994.

Akenson, Donald H. *The Irish Education Experiment: The National System of Education in the Nineteenth Century.* London: Routledge & Kegan Paul, 1970.

Allchin, A. M. *Ann Griffiths: The Furnace and the Fountain.* Cardiff: University of Wales Press, 1987.

Altholz, J. L. "Alexander Haldane, the *Record* and Religious Journalism." *Victorian Periodicals Review* 20 (1987): 23-31.

Ambler, R. W. *Ranters, Revivalists and Reformers: Primitive Methodism and Rural Society: South Lincolnshire 1817-1875.* Hull: Hull University Press, 1989.

Anstey, Roger. *The Atlantic Slave Trade and British Abolition 1760-1810.* London: Macmillan, 1975.

Baker, D. W. A. *Days of Wrath: A Life of John Dunmore Lang.* Carlton: Melbourne University Press, 1985.

Balleine, G. R. *A History of the Evangelical Party in the Church of England.* London: Longmans, 1933.

Barclay, Oliver. *Thomas Fowell Buxton and the Liberation of the Slaves.* York: William Sessions, 2001.

Baxter, John. "The Great Yorkshire Revival of 1792-6: A Study of Mass Revival among the Methodists." *Sociological Yearbook of Religion in Britain* 7 (1974): 46-76.

Bebbington, David W. "The Life of Baptist Noel: Its Setting and Significance." *Baptist Quarterly* 24 (1972): 389-411.

—————. *Evangelicalism in Modern Britain: A History from the 1730s to the 1980s.* London: Unwin Hyman, 1989.

—————. *Holiness in Nineteenth-Century England.* Carlisle: Paternoster Press, 2000.

—————. *The Dominance of Evangelicalism: The Age of Spurgeon and Moody.* Leicester, U.K.: Inter-Varsity Press, 2005.

Bell, Marion L. *Crusade in the City: Revivalism in Nineteenth-Century Philadelphia.* Cranbury, N.J.: Associated University Presses, 1977.

Berkhofer, Robert F. *Salvation and the Savage: An Analysis of Protestant Missions and American Indian Response, 1787-1862.* Lexington: University of Kentucky Press, 1965.

Best, G. F. A. "The Evangelicals and the Established Church in the Early Nineteenth Century." *Journal of Theological Studies* 10 (1959): 63-78.

—————. *Shaftesbury.* London: Batsford, 1964.

Bilhartz, Terry. *Urban Religion and the Second Great Awakening: Church and Society in Early National Baltimore.* Cranbury, N.J.: Farleigh Dickinson University Press, 1986.

Billington, R. A. *The Protestant Crusade 1800-1860.* New York: Macmillan, 1938.

Blumhofer, Edith F., and Randall H. Balmer, eds. *Modern Christian Revivals.* Urbana: University of Illinois Press, 1993.

Boles, John B. *The Great Revival 1787-1805.* Lexington: University Press of Kentucky, 1972.

—————, ed. *Masters & Slaves in the House of the Lord: Race and Religion in the American South, 1740-1870.* Lexington: University Press of Kentucky, 1988.

Bollen, J. D. *Australian Baptists—A Religious Minority.* London: The Baptist Historical Society, 1975.

—————. "English Missionary Societies and the Australian Aborigine." *Journal of Religious History* 9 (1977): 263-291.

Bossy, John. *The English Catholic Community 1570-1850.* London: Darton, Longman & Todd, 1975.

Bowen, Desmond. *The Protestant Crusade in Ireland, 1800-70.* Dublin: Gill and Macmillan, 1978.

Boylan, Anne M. *Sunday School: The Formation of an American Institution.* New Haven, Conn.: Yale University Press, 1988.

————. *The Origins of Women's Activism: New York and Boston, 1797-1840.* Chapel Hill: University of North Carolina Press, 2002.

Bradley, Ian. "The Politics of Godliness: Evangelicals in Parliament 1784-1832." Unpublished University of Oxford D.Phil. thesis, 1974.

————. *The Call to Seriousness: The Evangelical Impact on the Victorians.* London: Jonathan Cape, 1976.

Bratt, James D. "From Revivalism to Anti-Revivalism to Whig Politics: The Strange Career of Calvin Colton." *Journal of Ecclesiastical History* 52 (2001): 63-82.

Brekus, Catherine A. *Strangers and Pilgrims: Female Preaching in America, 1740-1845.* Chapel Hill: University of North Carolina Press, 1998.

Brown, Callum G. *Religion and Society in Scotland since 1707.* Edinburgh: Edinburgh University Press, 1997.

Brown, Ford K. *Fathers of the Victorians.* Cambridge: Cambridge University Press, 1961.

Brown, Stewart J. *Thomas Chalmers and the Godly Commonwealth in Scotland.* Oxford: Oxford University Press, 1982.

————. *The National Churches of England, Ireland and Scotland 1801-46.* Oxford: Oxford University Press, 2001.

Bruce, Dickson D. *And They All Sang Hallelujah: Plain-Folk Camp-Meeting Religion 1800-1845.* Knoxville: University of Tennessee Press, 1974.

Butler, Diana H. *Standing Against the Whirlwind: Evangelical Episcopalians in Nineteenth-Century America.* New York: Oxford University Press, 1995.

Campbell, James T. *Songs of Zion: The African Methodist Episcopal Church in the United States and South Africa.* New York: Oxford University Press, 1995.

Carter, Grayson. *Anglican Evangelicals: Protestant Secessions from the Via Media c. 1800-1850.* Oxford: Oxford University Press, 2001.

Carwardine, Richard. *Transatlantic Revivalism: Popular Evangelicalism in Britain and America 1790-1865.* Westport, Conn.: Greenwood Press, 1978.

————. "The Welsh Evangelical Community and 'Finney's Revival.'" *Journal of Ecclesiastical History* 29 (1978): 463-80.

————. *Evangelicals and Politics in Antebellum America.* New Haven, Conn.: Yale University Press, 1993.

Caskey, Marie. *Chariot of Fire: Religion and the Beecher Family.* New Haven, Conn.: Yale University Press, 1978.

Chadwick, W. Owen. *The Victorian Church Part 1 1829-1859.* London: SCM, 1987. First published 1966.

Chapman, S. D. "The Evangelical Revival and Education in Nottingham." *Transactions of the Thoroton Society of Nottinghamshire* 66 (1962): 35-66.

Checkland, Olive. *Philanthropy in Victorian Scotland.* Edinburgh: John Donald, 1980.

Chorley, E. Clowes. *Men and Movements in the American Episcopal Church.* Hamden, Conn.: Archon Books, 1961.

Christie, Ian R. *Wars and Revolutions; Britain 1760-1815.* London: Edward Arnold, 1982.

Christie, Nancy F., ed. *Households of Faith: Family, Gender, and Community in Canada, 1760-1969.* Montreal and Kingston: McGill-Queen's University Press, 2002.

Christ-Janer, Albert, Charles W. Hughes, and Carleton Sprague Smith. *American Hymns Old and New.* New York: Columbia University Press, 1980.

Clark, G. Kitson. *The Making of Victorian England.* London: Methuen, 1965.

Clark, S. D. *Church and Sect in Canada.* Toronto: University of Toronto Press, 1948.

Cleveland, Catharine C. *The Great Revival in the West 1797-1805.* Chicago: University of Chicago Press, 1916.

Cliff, Philip B. *The Rise and Development of the Sunday School Movement in England 1780-1980.* Redhill: National Christian Education Council, 1986.

Colley, Linda. *Britons: Forging the Nation 1707-1837.* London: Pimlico, 1994.

Connolly, Sean. *Religion and Society in Nineteenth-Century Ireland.* Dundalk: Dundalgan Press, 1985.

Cornelius, Janet Duitsman. *Slave Missions and the Black Church in the Antebellum South.* Columbia: University of South Carolina Press, 1999.

Cott, Nancy F. *The Bonds of Womanhood: "Women's Sphere" in New England 1780-1835.* New Haven, Conn.: Yale University Press, 1977. 2nd ed. 1997.

Cowie, Leonard W. "Exeter Hall." *History Today* 18:6 (1968): 390-97.

Cremin, Lawrence A. *American Education: The National Experience 1783-1876.* New York: Harper Row, 1980.

Cross, Whitney R. *The Burned-over District: The Social and Intellectual History of Enthusiastic Religion in Western New York, 1800-1850.* Ithaca, N.Y.: Cornell University Press, 1950.

Cutt, M. Nancy. *Mrs Sherwood and her Books for Children.* London: Oxford University Press, 1974.

Daly, John Patrick. *When Slavery was Called Freedom: Evangelicalism, Proslavery, and the Causes of the Civil War.* Lexington: University Press of Kentucky, 2002.

Davenport, Rodney. "Settlement, Conquest and Theological Controversy: The Churches of Nineteenth-Century European Immigrants." In *Christianity in South Africa: A Political, Social & Cultural History.* Edited by Richard Elphick and Rodney Davenport. Cape Town: David Philip, 1997.

Davidoff, Leonore, and Catherine Hall. *Family Fortunes: Men and Women of the English Middle Class 1780-1850.* London: Hutchinson, 1987. 2nd ed. 2002

Davies, E. T. *Religion in the Industrial Revolution in South Wales.* Cardiff: University of Wales Press, 1965.

Davies, Horton. *Worship and Theology in England III: From Watts and Wesley to Maurice, 1690-1850.* Grand Rapids: Eerdmans, 1996. First published 1961.

Davies, Rupert, A. Raymond George and Gordon Rupp, eds. *A History of the Methodist Church in Great Britain.* 4 vols. London: Epworth Press, 1965-1988.

Davis, David Brion. *Slavery and Human Progress.* New York: Oxford University Press, 1984.

——. *The Problem of Slavery in the Age of Revolution 1780-1823.* New York: Oxford University Press, 1999.

Dayfoot, Arthur Charles. *The Shaping of the West Indian Church 1492-1962.* Gainesville: University Press of Florida, 1998.

Dolan, Jay P. *The American Catholic Experience: A History from Colonial Times to the Present.* Notre Dame, Ind.: University of Notre Dame Press, 1992.

Drescher, Seymour. *Econocide: British Slavery in the Era of Abolition.* Pittsburgh: University of Pittsburgh Press, 1977.

——. "Whose Abolition? Popular Pressure and the Ending of the British Slave Trade." *Past and Present* 143 (1994): 136-66.

Dresser, Madge. *Slavery Obscured: The Social History of the Slave Trade in an English Provincial Port.* London: Continuum, 2001.

Epstein, Barbara Leslie. *The Politics of Domesticity: Women, Evangelism and Temperance in Nineteenth Century America.* Middletown, Conn.: Wesleyan University Press, 1981.

Eslinger, Ellen. *Citizens of Zion: The Social Origins of Camp Meeting Revivalism.* Knoxville: University of Tennessee Press, 1999.

Essig, James. *The Bonds of Wickedness: American Evangelicals Against Slavery, 1770-1808.*

Philadelphia: Temple University Press, 1982.

Field, Clive D. "Adam and Eve: Gender in the English Free Church Constituency." *Journal of Ecclesiastical History* 44 (1993): 63-79.

———. "The 1851 Census of Religious Worship: A Bibliographical Guide for Local and Regional Historians." *The Local Historian* 27 (1997): 194-217.

Finlayson, Geoffrey B. A. M. *The Seventh Earl of Shaftesbury.* London: Eyre Methuen, 1981.

Flegg, Columba Graham. *"Gathered under Apostles": A Study of the Catholic Apostolic Church.* Oxford: Oxford University Press, 1992.

Follett, Richard R. *Evangelicalism, Penal Theory and the Politics of Criminal Law Reform in England, 1808-30.* Basingstoke: Palgrave, 2001.

Foote, Henry Wilder. *Three Centuries of American Hymnody.* Cambridge, Mass.: Harvard University Press, 1940.

Forster, E. M. *Marianne Thornton. A Domestic Biography.* London: Edward Arnold, 1956.

Foster, Charles I. *An Errand of Mercy: The Evangelical United Front 1790-1837.* Chapel Hill: University of North Carolina Press, 1960.

French, Goldwin. *Parsons and Politics: The role of the Wesleyan Methodists in Upper Canada and the Maritimes from 1780 to 1855.* Toronto: Ryerson Press, 1962.

Frey, Sylvia R., and Betty Wood. *Come Shouting to Zion: African American Protestantism in the American South and British Caribbean to 1830.* Chapel Hill: University of North Carolina Press, 1998.

Garnett, Jane, and Colin Matthew, eds. *Revival and Religion since 1700: Essays for John Walsh.* London: The Hambledon Press, 1993.

Gash, Norman. *Aristocracy and People: Britain 1815-1865.* London: Edward Arnold, 1979.

Gauvreau, Michael. "Protestantism Transformed: Personal Piety and the Evangelical Social Vision." In *The Canadian Protestant Experience 1760-1990,* edited by George A. Rawlyk. Kingston and Montreal: McGill-Queen's University Press, 1990.

———. "Reluctant Voluntaries: Peter and George Brown; The Scottish Disruption and the Politics of Church and State in Canada." *Journal of Religious History* 25 (2001): 134-57.

Gilbert, A. D. *Religion and Society in Industrial England: Church, Chapel and Social Change, 1740-1914.* London: Longman, 1976.

Gilley, Sheridan. *Newman and His Age.* London: Darton, Longman & Todd, 1990.

Gordon, James M. *Evangelical Spirituality from the Wesleys to John Stott.* London: SPCK, 1991.

Grant, John Webster. *A Profusion of Spires: Religion in Nineteenth-Century Ontario.* Toronto: University of Toronto Press, 1988.

Gregory, Jeremy, and Jeffrey Chamberlain, eds. *The National Church in Local Perspective.* Woodbridge: The Boydell Press, 2003.

Griffin, Clifford S. *Their Brothers' Keepers: Moral Stewardship in the United States, 1800-1865.* New Brunswick, N.J.: Rutgers University Press, 1960.

Grocott, Allan M. *Convicts, Clergymen and Churches: Attitudes of Convicts and Ex-Convicts towards the Churches and Clergy in New South Wales from 1788-1851.* Sydney: Sydney University Press, 1980.

Handy, Robert T. *A History of the Churches in the United States and Canada.* Oxford: Clarendon Press, 1976.

Hardesty, Nancy A. *Your Daughters Shall Prophesy: Revivalism and Feminism in the Age of Finney.* Brooklyn: Carlson, 1991.

Hardman, Keith J. *Charles Grandison Finney 1792-1875: Revivalist and Reformer.* Grand Rapids: Baker, 1987.

Harrison, Brian. *Drink and the Victorians: The Temperance Question in England 1815-1872.* Keele: Keele University Press, 1994.

Hatch, Nathan O. *The Democratization of American Christianity.* New Haven, Conn.: Yale University Press, 1989.

Heasman, Kathleen. *Evangelicals in Action: An Appraisal of their Social Work in the Victorian Era.* London: Geoffrey Bles, 1962.

Hempton, David. *Methodism and Politics in British Society 1750-1850.* London: Hutchinson, 1984.

————. *The Religion of the People: Methodism and Popular Religion, c. 1750-1900.* London: Routledge, 1996.

————. *Methodism: Empire of the Spirit.* New Haven, Conn.: Yale University Press, 2005.

————, and Myrtle Hill. *Evangelical Protestantism in Ulster Society 1740-1890.* London: Routledge, 1992.

Heyrman, Christine Leigh. *Southern Cross: The Beginnings of the Bible Belt.* New York: Alfred A. Knopf, 1997.

Hilton, Boyd. *The Age of Atonement: The Influence of Evangelicalism on Social and Economic Thought 1785-1865.* Oxford: Clarendon Press, 1988.

Hindmarsh, Bruce. *John Newton and the English Evangelical Tradition.* Oxford: Clarendon Press, 1996.

Howe, Daniel Walker. *The Political Culture of the American Whigs.* Chicago: University of Chicago Press, 1979.

Howsam, Leslie. *Cheap Bibles: Nineteenth-Century Publishing and the British and Foreign Bible Society.* Cambridge: Cambridge University Press, 1991.

Howse, Ernest Marshall. *Saints in Politics: The "Clapham Sect" and the Growth of Freedom.* London: Allen and Unwin, 1971.

Hurwitz, Edith F. *Politics and the Public Conscience: Slave Emancipation and the Abolitionist Movement in Britain.* London: Allen and Unwin, 1973.

Hutchison, I. G. C. *A Political History of Scotland 1832-1924: Parties, Elections and Issues.* Edinburgh: John Donald, 1986.

Isaac, Peter. *A History of Evangelical Christianity in Cornwall.* Gerrards Cross: WEC Press, n.d.

Jackson, George Pullen. *White and Negro Spirituals: Their Life Span and Kinship.* New York: J. J. Augustin, 1943.

Jay, Elisabeth. *The Religion of the Heart: Anglican Evangelicalism and the Nineteenth-Century Novel.* Oxford: Clarendon Press, 1979.

Jenkins, D. E. *The Rev. Thomas Charles of Bala.* 3 vols. Denbigh: Llewelyn Jenkins, 1908.

Jennings, Judith. *The Business of Abolishing the Atlantic Slave Trade 1783-1807.* London: Frank Cass, 1997.

Johnson, Curtis D. *Islands of Holiness: Rural Religion in Upstate New York 1790-1860.* Ithaca, N.Y.: Cornell University Press, 1989.

Johnson, Paul E. *A Shopkeeper's Millennium: Society and Revivals in Rochester, New York, 1815-1837.* New York: Hill and Wang, 1978.

Johnson, William Courtland. "'A Delusive Clothing': Christian Conversion in the Antebellum Slave Community." *The Journal of Negro History* 82 (1997): 295-311.

Jones, Maldwyn A. *The Limits of Liberty: American History 1607-1992.* Oxford: Oxford University Press, 1995.

Jordan, Philip D. *The Evangelical Alliance for the United States of America, 1847-1900: Ecumenism, Identity and the Religion of the Republic.* New York: Edwin Mellen Press, 1982.

Juster, Susan. " 'In a Different Voice': Male and Female Narratives of Religious Conversion in Post-Revolutionary America." *American Quarterly* 41 (1989): 34-62.

————. *Disorderly Women: Sexual Politics and Evangelicalism in Revolutionary New England.* Ithaca, N.Y.: Cornell University Press, 2004.

Karl, Frederick. *George Eliot: A Biography.* London: Harper Collins, 1995.

Keller, C. R. *The Second Great Awakening in Connecticut.* New Haven, Conn.: Yale University Press, 1942.

Kestner, Joseph. "Charlotte Elizabeth Tonna's *The Wrongs of Woman:* Female Industrial Protest." *Tulsa Studies in Women's Literature* 2 (1983): 193-214.

Kling, David W. *A Field of Divine Wonders: The New Divinity and Village Revivals in Northwestern Connecticut 1792-1822.* University Park: Pennsylvania State University Press, 1993.

Kovacevic, Ivanka, and S. Barbara Kanner. "Blue Book into Novel: the Forgotten Industrial Fiction of Charlotte Elizabeth Tonna." *Nineteenth-Century Fiction* 25 (1970): 152-73.

Kuykendall, John W. *Southern Enterprise: The Work of National Evangelical Societies in the Antebellum South.* Westport, Conn.: Greenwood Press, 1982.

Lange, Raeburn. "Indigenous Agents of Religious Change in New Zealand, 1830-1860." *Journal of Religious History* 24 (2000): 279-95.

Laqueur, Thomas Walter. *Religion and Respectability: Sunday Schools and Working Class Culture 1780-1850.* New Haven, Conn.: Yale University Press, 1976.

Lewis, Donald M. *Lighten Their Darkness: The Evangelical Mission to Working Class London, 1828-1860.* Westport, Conn.: Greenwood Press, 1986.

Lloyd, T. O. *The British Empire 1558-1995.* Oxford: Oxford University Press, 1996.

Lovegrove, Deryck W. *Established Church, Sectarian People: Itinerancy and the transformation of English Dissent, 1780-1830.* Cambridge: Cambridge University Press, 1980.

Loveland, Anne C. *Southern Evangelicals and the Social Order 1800-1860.* Baton Rouge: Louisiana State University Press, 1980.

Luker, David. "Revivalism in Theory and Practice: The Case of Cornish Methodism." *Journal of Ecclesiastical History* 37 (1986): 603-19.

MacInnes, John. *The Evangelical Movement in the Highlands of Scotland 1688-1800.* Aberdeen: Aberdeen University Press, 1951.

Macintosh, Neil K. *Richard Johnson: Chaplain to the Colony of New South Wales: His Life and Times 1755-1827.* Sydney: Library of Australian History, 1978.

Machin, G. I. T. *Politics and the Churches in Great Britain 1832 to 1868.* Oxford: Oxford University Press, 1977.

Malmgreen, Gail, ed. *Religion in the Lives of English Women, 1760-1830.* London: Croom Helm, 1986.

Marini, Stephen. "Hymnody as History: Early American Hymns and the Recovery of American Popular Religion." *Church History* 71 (2002): 273-306.

Marks, Lynne. "No Double Standard?: Leisure, Sex and Sin in Upper Canadian Church Discipline Records, 1800-1860." In *Gendered Pasts: Historical Essays in Femininity and Masculinity in Canada.* Edited by Kathryn McPherson, Cecilia Morgan and Nancy M. Forestell. Toronto: University of Toronto Press, 2003.

Marshall, P. J., ed. *The Oxford History of the British Empire: Volume II The Eighteenth Century.* Oxford: Oxford University Press, 1998.

Martin, Mary Clare. "Children and Religion in Walthamstow and Leyton, c 1740-c 1870." Ph.D. thesis, University of London, 2000.

Martin, R. H. *Evangelicals United: Ecumenical Stirrings in Pre-Victorian Britain.* Metuchen, N.J.: Scarecrow Press, 1983.

Mason, J. C. S. *The Moravian Church and the Missionary Awakening in England 1760-1800.* Woodbridge: Royal Historical Society/Boydell Press, 2001.

Mathias, Peter. *The First Industrial Nation: An Economic History of Britain 1700-1914.* London: Methuen, 1969.

McCloughlin, William G. *Revivals, Awakenings and Reform: An Essay on Religion and Social Change in America.* Chicago: University of Chicago Press, 1978.

McClymond, Michael J., ed. *Embodying the Spirit: New Perspectives on North American Revivalism.* Baltimore: Johns Hopkins University Press, 2004.

McKivigan, John R. *The War Against Proslavery Religion: Abolitionism and the Northern Churches.* Ithaca, N.Y.: Cornell University Press, 1984.

Mears, G. *Barnabas Shaw: Founder of South African Methodism.* Rondebosch: Methodist Missionary Department, 1957.

Mechie, Stewart. *The Church and Scottish Social Development 1780-1870.* London: Oxford University Press, 1960.

Melton, Julius. *Presbyterian Worship in America: Changing Patterns since 1787.* Richmond, Va.: John Knox Press, 1967.

Midgley, Claire. *Women Against Slavery: The British Campaigns 1780-1870.* London: Routledge, 1992.

Minkema, Kenneth P., and Harry S. Stout. "The Edwardsean Traditon and the Antislavery Debate, 1740-1865." *Journal of American History* 92 (2005): 47-74.

Mintz, Steven. *Moralists and Modernizers: America's Pre-Civil War Reformers.* Baltimore: Johns Hopkins University Press, 1995.

Moir, John S. *Enduring Witness: A History of the Presbyterian Church in Canada.* Toronto: Presbyterian Church in Canada, 1987.

Morgan, D. D. J. "The Development of the Baptist Movement in Wales between 1714 and 1815 with particular reference to the Evangelical Revival." Unpublished Oxford D.Phil. thesis, 1986.

Morris, R. J. *Cholera 1832: The Social Response to an Epidemic.* London: Croom Helm, 1976.

Muir, Elizabeth Gillan, and Marilyn Fardig Whiteley, eds. *Changing Roles of Women within the Christian Church in Canada.* Toronto: University of Toronto Press, 1995.

Munden, A. F. *A Cheltenham Gemaliel: Dean Close of Cheltenham.* Cheltenham: Dean Close School, 1997.

Murphy, James. *The Religious Problem in English Education: The Crucial Experiment.* Liverpool: Liverpool University Press, 1959.

Murphy, Terrence, and Roberto Perin, eds. *A Concise History of Christianity in Canada.* Toronto: Oxford University Press, 1996.

Newsome, David. *The Parting of Friends: A Study of the Wilberforces and Henry Manning.* London: John Murray, 1966.

Noll, Mark A. *A History of Christianity in the United States and Canada.* Grand Rapids: Eerdmans, 1992.

———. "Thomas Chalmers (1780-1847) in North America (ca. 1830-1917)." *Church History* 66 (1997): 762-77.

———. *America's God From Jonathan Edwards to Abraham Lincoln.* New York: Oxford University Press, 2002.

———. *The Rise of Evangelicalism: The Age of Edwards, Whitefield and the Wesleys.* Leicester, U.K.: Inter-Varsity Press, 2004.

———, ed. *Religion and American Politics from the Colonial Period to the 1980s.* New York: Oxford University Press, 1990.

————, David W. Bebbington and George A. Rawlyk, eds. *Evangelicalism: Comparative Studies of Popular Protestantism in North America, the British Isles and Beyond, 1700-1990*. New York: Oxford University Press, 1994.

Obelkevich, J. *Religion and Rural Society: South Lindsey 1825-1875*. Oxford: Clarendon Press, 1976.

————, Lyndal Roper and Raphael Samuel, eds. *Disciplines of Faith: Studies in Religion, Politics and Patriarchy*. London: Routledge & Kegan Paul, 1987.

O'Brien, Anne. *God's Willing Workers: Women and Religion in Australia*. Sydney: UNSW Press, 2005.

Oldfield, J. R. *Popular Politics and British Anti-Slavery: The mobilisation of public opinion against the slave trade 1787-1807*. Manchester: Manchester University Press, 1995.

Pedersen, Susan. "Hannah More Meets Simple Simon: Tracts, Chapbooks and Popular Culture in Late Eighteenth-Century England." *Journal of British Studies* 25 (1986): 1986.

Pegram, Thomas R. *Battling Demon Rum: The Struggle for a Dry America, 1800-1933*. Chicago: Ivan R. Dee, 1998.

Perciacannte, Marianne. *Calling Down Fire: Charles Grandison Finney and Revivalism in Jefferson County, New York, 1800-1840*. Albany: State University of New York Press, 2003.

Piggin, Stuart. *Evangelical Christianity in Australia: Spirit, Word and World*. Melbourne: Oxford University Press, 1996.

Pike, Douglas. *Paradise of Dissent: South Australia 1829-1857*. Carlton: Melbourne University Press, 1957.

Pollock, John. *Wilberforce*. London: Constable, 1977.

Porter, Andrew. *Religion versus empire? British Protestant missionaries and overseas expansion, 1700-1914*. Manchester: Manchester University Press, 2004.

————, ed. *The Oxford History of the British Empire: Volume III: The Nineteenth Century*. Oxford: Oxford University Press, 1999.

Prior, Karen Swallow. *Hannah More's "Coelebs in Search of A Wife"—A Review of Criticism and New Analysis*. Lewiston: Edwin Mellon Press, 2003.

Raboteau, Albert J. *Slave Religion: The Invisible Institution in the Antebellum South*. New York: Oxford University Press, 1978.

Rawlyk, G. A. *The Canada Fire: Radical Evangelicalism in British North America, 1775-1812*. Montreal and Kingston: McGill-Queen's University Press, 1994.

Reinier, Jacqueline S. *From Virtue to Character: American Childhood, 1775-1850.* New York: Twayne, 1996.

Rennie, I. S. "Evangelicalism and English Public Life." Ph.D. thesis, University of Toronto, 1962.

Richey, Russell E., and Kenneth E. Rowe, eds. *Rethinking Methodist History.* Nashville: Kingswood Books, 1985.

Robertson, Allen B. " 'Give All You Can' Methodists and Charitable Causes in Nineteenth-Century Nova Scotia." In *The Contribution of Methodism to Atlantic Canada.* Edited by Charles H. H. Scobie and John Webster Grant. Montreal and Kingston: McGill-Queen's University Press, 1992.

Rosenberg, Carroll Smith. *Religion and the Rise of the American City: The New York City Mission Movement 1812-1870.* Ithaca, N.Y.: Cornell University Press, 1971.

Rosman, Doreen. *Evangelicals and Culture.* London: Croom Helm, 1984.

Roth, Randolph A. *The Democratic Dilemma: Religion, Reform and the Social Order in the Connecticut River Valley of Vermont, 1791-1850.* Cambridge: Cambridge University Press, 1987.

Rotundo, E. Anthony. *American Manhood: Transformations in Masculinity from the Revolution to the Modern Era.* New York: Basic Books, 1993.

Rowdon, H. H. *The Origins of the Brethren 1825-1850.* London: Pickering and Inglis, 1967.

Roxborogh, John. *Thomas Chalmers: Enthusiast for Mission.* Carlisle: Paternoster, 1999.

Ryan, Mary P. *Cradle of the Middle Class: The Family in Oneida County, New York, 1790-1865.* Cambridge: Cambridge University Press, 1981.

Saillant, John. *Black Puritan, Black Republican: The Life and Thought of Lemuel Haynes 1753-1833.* New York: Oxford University Press, 2003.

Sangster, Paul. *Pity my Simplicity: The Evangelical Revival and the Religious Education of Children 1738-1800.* London: Epworth Press, 1963.

Sassi, Jonathan D. *A Republic of Righteousness: The Public Christianity of the Post-Revolutionary New England Clergy.* New York: Oxford University Press, 2001.

Schlossberg, Herbert. *The Silent Revolution and the Making of Victorian England.* Columbus: Ohio State University Press, 2000.

Schmidt, Leigh Eric. *Holy Fairs: Scottish Communions and American Revivals in the Early Modern Period.* Princeton, N.J.: Princeton University Press, 1989.

Schneider, A. Gregory. "The Ritual of Happy Dying Among Early American

Methodists." *Church History* 56 (1987): 348-63.

———. *The Way of the Cross Leads Home: The Domestication of American Methodism.* Bloomington: Indiana University Press, 1993.

Sernett, Milton C. *Black Religion and American Evangelicalism: White Protestants, Plantation Missions and the Flowering of Negro Christianity, 1787-1865.* Metuchen, N.J.: Scarecrow Press, 1975.

Seymour, Claire. *Ragged Schools, Ragged Children.* London: Ragged School Museum Trust, 1995.

Shaw, Thomas. *A History of Cornish Methodism.* Truro: D. Bradford Barton, 1967.

Sheils, Richard D. "The Feminization of American Congregationalism, 1770-1835." In *Religion*, vol. 13, History of Women in the United States. Edited by Nancy F. Cott. Munich: K. G. Saur, 1993.

Sissons, C. B. *Egerton Ryerson: His Life and Letters.* 2 vols. Toronto: Clark, Irwin & Co., 1937, 1947.

Sklar, Kathryn Kish. *Catharine Beecher: A Study in American Domesticity.* New Haven, Conn.: Yale University Press, 1973.

Smellie, Alexander. *Biography of R. M. McCheyne: A Shining Light.* Fearn: Christian Focus, 1995. Originally published 1919.

Smith, Mark. *Religion and Industrial Society: Oldham and Saddleworth 1740-1865.* Oxford: Clarendon Press, 1994.

Snape, Michael. *The Redcoat and Religion: The Forgotten History of the British Soldier from the Age of Marlborough to the Eve of the First World War.* London: Routledge, 2005.

Snell, K. D. M., and Paul Ell. *Rival Jerusalems: The Geography of Victorian Religion.* Cambridge: Cambridge University Press, 2000.

Southern, Eileen. *The Music of Black Americans: A History.* New York: W. W. Norton, 1997.

Spinney, G. H. "Cheap Repository Tracts: Hazard and Marshall Edition." *The Library*, 4th series (1939): 295-340.

Stott, Anne. *Hannah More: The First Victorian.* Oxford: Oxford University Press, 2003.

Stunt, Timothy C. F. *From Awakening to Secession: Radical Evangelicals in Switzerland and Britain.* Edinburgh: T & T Clark, 2000.

Sutherland, Kathryn. "Hannah More's Counter-Revolutionary Femimism." In *Revolution in Writing: British Literary Responses to the French Revolution.* Edited by Kelvin Everest. Milton Keynes: Open University Press, 1991.

Swanson, R. N., ed. *Unity and Diversity in the Church.* Studies in Church History 32. Oxford: Blackwell/Ecclesiastical History Society, 1996.

Sweet, Leonard I. *The Minister's Wife: Her Role in Nineteenth-Century American Evangelicalism.* Philadelphia: Temple University Press, 1983.

Thomas, A. D. "Reasonable Revivalism: Presbyterian Evangelization of Educated Virginians 1787-1837." *Journal of Presbyterian History* 61 (1983): 316-34.

Thompson, E. P. *The Making of the English Working Class.* Harmondsworth, U.K.: Penguin, 1968. First published 1963.

Tolley, Christopher. *Domestic Biography: The Legacy of Evangelicalism in Four Nineteenth-Century Families.* Oxford: Oxford University Press, 1997.

Tosh, John. *A Man's Place: Masculinity and the Middle Class Home in Victorian England.* New Haven, Conn.: Yale University Press, 1999.

Tucker, Karen B. Westerfield. *American Methodist Worship.* New York: Oxford University Press, 2001.

Turner, Mary. *Slaves and Missionaries: The Disintegration of Jamaican Slave Society 1787-1834.* Urbana: University of Illinois Press, 1982.

Turner, Steve. *Amazing Grace: John Newton, Slavery and the world's most enduring song.* Oxford: Lion, 2005.

Tyrrell, Ian R. *Sobering Up: From Temperance to Prohibition in America.* Westport, Conn.: Greenwood Press, 1979.

Valenze, Deborah M. *Prophetic Sons and Daughters: Female Preaching and Popular Religion in Industrial England.* Princeton, N.J.: Princeton University Press, 1985.

Vickery, Amanda. *The Gentleman's Daughter: Women's Lives in Georgian England.* New Haven, Conn.: Yale University Press, 1998.

Walsh, John, Colin Haydon and Stephen Taylor, eds. *The Church of England c. 1689-c. 1833 From Toleration to Tractarianism.* Cambridge: Cambridge University Press, 1993.

Ward, W. R. *Religion and Society in England 1790-1850.* London: B. T. Batsford, 1972.

Watts, Michael R. *The Dissenters, Volume II: The Expansion of Evangelical Nonconformity.* Oxford: Oxford University Press, 1995.

Weiss, Harry B. *Hannah More's Cheap Repository Tracts in America.* New York: New York Public Library, 1946.

Werner, Julia S. *The Primitive Methodist Connexion: Its Background and Early History.* Madison: University of Wisconsin Press, 1984.

Westfall, William. *Two Worlds: The Protestant Culture of Nineteenth-Century Ontario.* Kingston and Montreal: McGill-Queen's University Press, 1989.

Westerkampf, Marilyn J. *Women and Religion in Early America 1600-1850: The Puritan and Evangelical Traditions.* London and New York: Routledge, 1999.

Wigger, John H. "Taking Heaven by Storm: Enthusiasm and Early American Methodism, 1770-1820s." *Journal of the Early Republic* 14 (1994): 167-94.

—————. *Taking Heaven by Storm: Methodism and the Rise of Popular Christianity in America.* New York: Oxford University Press, 1998.

Wigley, John. *The Rise and Fall of the Victorian Sunday.* Manchester: Manchester University Press, 1980.

Williams, William Henry. *The Garden of American Methodism: The Delmarva Peninsula 1769-1820.* Dover, Del.: United Methodist Church Peninsula Conference, 1984.

Wilson, Linda. *Constrained by Zeal: Female Spirituality Among Nonconformists 1825-1875.* Carlisle: Paternoster, 2000.

Wolffe, John. "The Evangelical Alliance in the 1840s: An Attempt to Institutionalise Christisn Unity," pp. 335-40. In *Voluntary Religion.* Studies in Church History 23. Edited by W. J. Sheils and Diana Wood. Oxford: Blackwell, 1986.

—————. *The Protestant Crusade in Great Britain 1829-1860.* Oxford: Clarendon Press, 1991.

—————. " 'Praise to the Holiest in the Height': Hymns and Church Music," pp. 59-99. In *Religion in Victorian Britain v: Culture and Empire.* Edited by John Wolffe. Manchester: Open University/Manchester University Press, 1997.

—————. *The Religious Census of 1851 in Yorkshire,* Borthwick Paper 108. York: University of York, 2005.

—————, ed. *Evangelical Faith and Public Zeal: Evangelicals and Society in Britain 1780-1980.* London: SPCK, 1995.

Wyatt-Brown, Bertram. *Lewis Tappan and the Evangelical War Against Slavery.* Cleveland: Press of Case Western University, 1969.

—————. "The Antimission Movement in the Jacksonian South: A Study in Regional Folk Culture." *The Journal of Southern History* 36 (1970): 501-29.

Yarwood, A. T. *Samuel Marsden: The Great Survivor.* Carlton: Melbourne University Press, 1977.

York, Robert M. *George B. Cheever: Religious and Social Reformer 1807-1890.* Orono: University of Maine Press, 1955.

Young, G. M. *Victorian England: Portrait of an Age.* London: Oxford University Press, 1936.

Young, Stephen. "William Dodsworth and the Origins of Tractarianism in London." Ph.D. thesis, Open University, 2004.

Zilversmit, Arthur. *The First Emancipation: The Abolition of Slavery in the North.* Chicago: University of Chicago Press, 1967.

Index